Constructive Illusions

Constructive Illusions

*Misperceiving the Origins
of International Cooperation*

Eric Grynaviski

Cornell University Press

Ithaca and London

Cornell University Press gratefully acknowledges receipt of a subvention
from the George Washington University, which aided in the publication
of this book.

First published 2014 by Cornell University Press
Printed in the United States of America

Library of Congress Cataloging-in-Publication Data

Grynaviski, Eric, 1977– author.
  Constructive illusions : misperceiving the origins of international
cooperation / Eric Grynaviski.
      pages cm
  Includes bibliographical references and index.
  ISBN 978-0-8014-5206-2 (cloth : alk. paper)
  1. International relations—Philosophy. 2. International cooperation.
3. Miscommunication—Political aspects. 4. Detente. 5. United States—
Foreign relations—1969–1974. I. Title.
  JZ1318.G799   2014
  327.1'1—dc23   2014003190

Cornell University Press strives to use environmentally responsible suppliers
and materials to the fullest extent possible in the publishing of its books. Such
materials include vegetable-based, low-VOC inks and acid-free papers that are
recycled, totally chlorine-free, or partly composed of nonwood fibers. For further
information, visit our website at www.cornellpress.cornell.edu.

Cloth printing   10 9 8 7 6 5 4 3 2 1

Contents

For Mara and Ethan

ACKNOWLEDGMENTS

Like most first books, this one is a collective more than an individual effort. It began with the idea that many in International Relations draw too much on the idea that international politics takes place in an information-rich or thick social environment, and that even scholars interested in incomplete information or uncertainty implicitly posit more information or more shared ideas than is usually realized. Converting that idea into a book-length project, however, required a lot of assistance.

Countless friends and mentors have helped me on this project. In particular, I have benefited from comments, discussions, and suggestions from Robert Adcock, Bentley Allan, Michael Barnett, Austin Carson, Ingrid Creppell, Matthew Evangelista, Henry Farrell, Martha Finnemore, Charlie Glaser, Danny Hayes, Ted Hopf, Josh Kertzer, Tim Leucke, Eric MacGilvray, Jennifer Mitzen, Michael Neblo, Daniel Nexon, John Oates, Elizabeth Saunders, Susan Sell, Duncan Snidal, Daniel Verdier, and Clement Wyploscz. A deep debt goes to Randy Schweller and Alexander Thompson, who devoted time and patience seeing this project through to fruition, and especially to Alexander Wendt who served as a mentor, sounding board, and tough critic. He made sure I had the intellectual space to work on a project that, to the end, he disagreed with. He was unusually patient and generous, intellectually and personally. George Washington University also aided me through the University Facilitating Fund. Susan Sell and the Institution for Globalization and International Studies generously organized and hosted a book workshop. I am also indebted to the team at Cornell University Press, especially Roger Haydon, for walking me through the publication process with patience and good humor.

My biggest debt goes to my family. My wife has been supportive of me from the first day of the project, wearing a lot of hats as proofreader, interlocutor, and best friend. She will be glad that, if in finishing this project, she does not have to hear any more about Khrushchev, Brezhnev, Nixon, and Kissinger. This book (and especially the mistakes) is as much her product as it is my own. Our son Ethan was born as the first drafts were being completed and is amazingly now four years old. Watching him grow is the best mark of time passed in working on this book. He will be glad if he does not have to wear his Nixon shirt anymore to put me in the mood to write.

One fortunate aspect of research on the Nixon administration is the growing availability of high-quality books that document the Nixon administration's foreign policy. When I began this book, I spent substantial time working in the archives. By the end of the project, every find I had discovered was available through the Digital National Security Archives or published by the State Department through the *Foreign Relations of the United States* series. The Miller Center also produced easily accessible audio recordings. I include full citations to these documents, although most of them are now available electronically.

INTRODUCTION

> To be sure, the international order had been founded on
> a misunderstanding and a misconception.
>
> HENRY KISSINGER, *A World Restored*

When Captain Cook "discovered" Hawaii at the end of the eighteenth century, a remarkable case of cooperation began, perhaps one of the most remarkable in world history. As Marshall Sahlins controversially recounts the story of Cook's first contact with the Hawaiians, a series of coincidences led the Hawaiians to mistake Cook for Lono, the god of peace, music, and fertility.[1] When the *Discovery* and the *Resolution* approached the island of Hawaii, they chanced to circumnavigate it in a clockwise direction that mirrored the mythical process made on land by Lono. Cook's progression around the island occurred in the same direction and on the same days as predicted by the myth. By this accident, the "islanders knew Captain Cook as 'Lono' before they set eyes on him."[2] When Cook landed at Kealakekua, the Hawaiians dressed him as Lono, wrapping him in a red tapa cloth. Then they offered him a small pig as a sacrifice before ushering him into a temple for a lengthy ritual that culminated in a ceremonial "feeding." The belief that Cook was Lono was so engrained that more than one hundred years later his bones were carried in the annual religious procession that honored him as a god.

When Cook first landed, the European explorers and Hawaiians cooperated to the benefit of both. For the Hawaiians, the belief that Cook was Lono fulfilled their religious needs, and Cook's willingness to engage in the ritual ceremonies enabled the religious views of the islanders to go unchallenged. The sailors, especially Cook, acted the required role, wore the right clothing, engaged in the right rituals, and generally avoided mistakes. For the British, the story is more complicated. Before they reached the island of Hawaii, a man on Kauai was killed by a member of Cook's expedition. On reaching Hawaii, Cook's men were ready for a fight. However, as they approached, they noticed white flags on the beaches. Cook's sailors took these to be flags of truce and expected to be welcomed. They did not know that the flags were ceremonial and indicated a taboo against going to sea during the period. Furthermore, when the Hawaiians provisioned Cook's men with supplies, it was often done at elaborate feasts. The Europeans were unaware that the number and timing of the feasts, as well as the kinds of food served, was dictated by Hawaiian religious beliefs. This series of accidents was crucial for successful cooperation. If Cook had not landed at the proper time, if the Hawaiians had not flown the white flag, or if the Hawaiian religious system did not call for feeding the sailors, then one can imagine that the situation would have been much less amicable. The first encounter may have led to a lasting legacy of violence, rather than a peaceful encounter explained by the rites of Lono. Cook's first departure was also successful because he left the island on the schedule set for Lono. However, his ship's mast broke soon after, which forced Cook to return to the island where he met his end.[3] Had that mast not broken, cooperation would have been a complete success, enabling the explorers to obtain food and water and the Hawaiians to avoid challenges to their religious beliefs.

If there are Cooks and Hawaiians in international politics—actors whose decisions to cooperate are "founded on a misunderstanding"—then it becomes a puzzle for much of International Relations (IR) theory. We usually think of misconceptions and misunderstandings as a source of discord: if only we understood one another better, it would be a more peaceful world. This episode, and others explored in this book, suggest otherwise: incomplete information, misperceptions, or sheer ignorance may generate cooperation in cases where complete information or shared ideas might lead to violence. Actors may cooperate precisely *because* they lack mutual understanding.

Most IR scholars broadly agree that misperception tends to be a road-block to peace and that common knowledge, mutual understanding, or intersubjectivity create the conditions under which peace and cooperation bloom.[4] All of the major schools of IR theory agree that a world of Cooks and islanders—where actors fundamentally misperceive others—would be a violent world with little to no cooperation. Liberal institutionalists expect a lack of information to impede cooperation. Realists describe the routes through which misperceptions cause wars or costly arms races.[5] And many constructivists argue that shared norms or identities are critical to the creation of peace and cooperation, which suggests that misunderstandings may cause conflict.[6] Scholars of all stripes tend to agree on the importance of improving communication, engaging in deliberation, and reducing misperceptions to solve conflicts and manage common problems.

Yet this agreement might be premature: Cooks and islanders do cooperate. There are many cases in international politics in which cooperation proceeds because of misperception, not shared ideas. During the Second World War, the US relationship with several allies suffered from serious delusions. As discussed in the next chapter, during the war the American public supported the Russian war-fighting effort and the lend-lease program that provided Russia with material support, in part, because of the odd belief that the Soviet Union was a burgeoning democracy with which it shared fundamental values. During the same war, most Europeans were shot on sight in Vietnam, but the United States and the Viet Minh engaged in extensive intelligence cooperation. While Europeans in general, and the French in particular, were viewed as imperialist enemies of Vietnamese nationalism, the US legacy as a former colony and Roosevelt's anti-imperialism convinced the Viet Minh leadership that America was a dependable ally. As Captain Herbert Bluechel, an American officer serving in Vietnam during the war, reported in 1945, "the Viet Minh leaders expressed the hope that Americans would view favorably their bid for independence, since we ourselves fought for and gained our independence under a situation considered to be similar to that as exists in Indo China today."[7] Ho Chi Minh cooperated with the United States because of a mistaken belief that his impression of their friendly attitude was reciprocated. Roosevelt did not share this impression of their relationship during the war, did not intend to support the Viet Minh against the French, and there is no evidence that he was aware of Ho's beliefs.[8]

After the advent of the Cold War, misperceptions continued to create important alliances. For example, the United States continued its relationship with Chiang Kai-shek in part because the China lobby in Washington viewed Chinese nationalists as liberators of an oppressed people longing to become Christians. As David Halberstam explains, "the China that existed in the minds of millions of Americans was the most illusory of countries, filled as it was with the dutiful, obedient peasants who liked America and loved Americans, who longed for nothing so much as to be like them. It was a country where ordinary peasants allegedly hoped to be more Christian and were eager, despite the considerable obstacles in their way, to rise out of what Americans considered a heathen past."[9] The origins of US involvement in Taiwan, which has led to an unlikely and prolonged episode of international cooperation, was in part premised on a mistaken judgment of China and its people by "Asia first" Republicans in the 1950s.

Many cases of cooperation among European powers are also, in part, the result of misperceptions. Before the First World War, for example, Great Britain and Germany entered a détente in 1911 that resulted in successful crisis management, an understanding concerning the division of Portuguese colonies in the event of the collapse of the Portuguese empire, an agreement on the Baghdad Railway, and an implicit deal on naval arms. Sean Lynn-Jones argues persuasively that the Anglo-German détente was based on "mutual misperceptions." Germany thought cooperation meant British neutrality in the event of a Continental war, whereas Britain believed that détente meant a limitation on German military ambitions through cooperation.[10] In each case, cooperation was made possible because of a failure to communicate.

This book has two primary arguments. The first, outlined in the next section, is that under certain conditions there are illusions that are necessary for international cooperation, which undermines the familiar narrative of the importance of communication and mutual understanding for peace. The second, outlined at the end of this chapter, explains why this matters for IR theory in its broadest dimensions. One of the primary reasons we posit the prevalence of common knowledge, shared ideas, and norms is that there are high levels of cooperation in the international system. Many IR scholars, influenced by sociological or economic theories, argue that the existence of cooperation is prima facie evidence for the existence of shared ideas. This argument takes direct aim at the prevalence of common knowledge or shared ideas. If cooperation occurs without shared ideas in important cases—if there are constructive illusions—then we should rethink the ways in which we describe the international system.

Misperception and Cooperation

Misperception does not always lead to conflict. In certain cases, the illusions that we hold about others help secure cooperation. This corroborates what Robert Jervis, a prominent observer of the role of misperceptions in conflict, postulates when he says that a "difficulty is that historians and political scientists are drawn to the study of conflict more often than to the analysis of peaceful interactions. As a result, we know little about the degree to which harmonious relationships are characterized by accurate perceptions."[11]

Can misperceptions enhance rather than diminish the chances for cooperation? In brief, I argue, yes, it is possible to form what the former French president Valéry Giscard d'Estaing called "a superb agreement based on complete misunderstanding."[12] In many cases, cooperation is enhanced when actors believe that intersubjectivity—common knowledge, common norms, or common identities—exists, even when they are wrong. The central argument of this book is that false intersubjective beliefs (FIBs)—wrongly held beliefs that something is intersubjective or common knowledge—accounts for many of the most important cases of cooperation in international politics. FIBs make us think that a belief is shared, tricking us into cooperating when we otherwise would not.

The intuition of this argument is that cooperation is more likely when beliefs are inaccurate. Our experiences in cooperating with others bear this out in everyday life. Imagine two friends meeting for dinner. One believes it is a first date while the other believes it is a friendly dinner. The evening goes well, as neither behaves in a manner that contradicts the other's understanding. The evening would likely not be satisfying if the misunderstanding was revealed (by leaning in for a kiss). Or imagine two children playing a game, not realizing that each has an idiosyncratic understanding of the rules of the game, and the differences are not revealed during play. If the children argued about the rules, rather than playing the game, they might never become friends. Or imagine playing a game of basketball against a friend. One person believes there is a shared competitive spirit and that playing is about winning. For the other, the game is about doing something together. If either one found out the other's principle reason for playing, he or she might not want to play in the future. But, so long as they happily do not know, the game continues.

Outside of politics, studies of marital relationships and human happiness show that misunderstanding others promotes our most intimate forms of cooperation. Psychological studies show that we are often happiest with our life mates when we do not have realistic expectations of them.[13] Especially in the beginning of relationships, there are facts about all of us that might disrupt them; something that might be revealed about us that the other may just not be able to stomach. Sometimes we intentionally hide facts—that wart, religious or political opinion, or future desires—because we suspect it would disrupt cooperation. Many of these potentially disruptive facts, however, we do not hide because we do not know they might be disruptive. Some conversations—about how to manage triplets, an opinion about the Baha'i faith, or a preference for granite countertops—simply do not come up early in our relationships. If they did, any one of these opinions might tear a budding romance apart. We cooperate with our life partners, especially in the early stages of a relationship, because we do not understand them. These findings have been extended to society at large. Many people wrongly believe that social consensus exists, imagining that others share their fundamental values and beliefs.[14] The consequences for cooperation in society may be tremendous. Holders of minority opinions, who perhaps should fear being ignored or marginalized by majorities, often perceive that their minority opinions are in fact majority opinions.

Substantive differences in the ways that actors understand one another may also promote cooperation in international politics. When there are intractable conflicts of interest or principled differences that make cooperation seem unsavory, cooperation may only be possible because of misunderstandings. Chapter 2 outlines the conditions under which different kinds of false intersubjective beliefs lead to cooperation. In general, there are two pathways through which FIBs promote cooperation. First, FIBs can lead us to overlook principled differences. A couple, for example, might have a long-lasting happy marriage only because they believe that their partner shares some principled view, say about partisan politics, religion, or charity, when in fact they don't. If those differences are discovered, the happy marriage may end in divorce. In the same way, principled differences in international politics—differences in beliefs about a shared political future of states, differences in understandings of human rights or civil liberties, or subtle ideological differences about economic systems—might undermine practical cooperation if they are revealed. FIBs can also promote cooperation by providing a false confidence that we know what behavior to expect from others in the future. Often, actors can cooperate today only because they have certain expectations for the kinds of conduct they expect in the future.

The emergence of détente between the United States and the Soviet Union affords an excellent opportunity to see if more information or less information is important for cooperation. Chapters 3 and 4 show that both types of FIBs—false perceptions about both principles and expected behavior—contributed to superpower cooperation.

Why emphasize détente? There are two reasons that détente is the most appropriate case to use to analyze the role of misperceptions in cooperation. The first is that it is a paradigmatic case of international cooperation. The arms control agreements reached during the period are often taken to be an exemplar of how sharing information and reducing misperceptions is critical to international cooperation.[15] Showing that early arms control agreements are the result of misperceptions rather than shared information undermines the conclusions reached by historians and political scientists in this paradigmatic case.

The second reason to focus on détente is that the growth of cooperation during the period is simply stunning. During the early 1970s, the United States and Soviet Union engaged in a remarkable process of cooperation on issues ranging from trade to conflict management to arms control. As part of that process, the parties agreed to establish standing committees to discuss the terms of cooperation, created back channels to ensure that signals were clearly understood, and Nixon and Brezhnev directly met at three summits. In addition, several agreements, including the 1972 Basic Principles of Relations between the United States and the Union of the Soviet Socialist Republics (the Basics Principles agreement, or BPA) and the 1973 Agreement between the United States of America and the Union of Soviet Socialist Republics on the Prevention of Nuclear War were explicit attempts to cooperate on the ground rules of the Cold War, that is, to enshrine the meaning of détente in international law. For the Soviet Union, détente fundamentally restructured the superpower relationship, and many in the United States believed it signaled the end of the Cold War. Few rivalries as severe as those between the superpowers in the Cold War have seen similarly ambitious attempts at rewriting the rules of the game, improving mutual understanding, and generating cooperation.

Broader Implications

The claim that incomplete information and beliefs that differ might be useful in securing cooperation runs contrary to many discussions of cooperation in economics, sociology, political philosophy, and political science. Not only is mutual understanding difficult to achieve but expecting that mutual understanding will promote cooperation may be dangerous. There are two sets of broad implications: a need to rethink the origins of cooperation and to rethink our description of the international system. The conventional wisdom is that mutual understanding is necessary for cooperation and peace. If, as I argue, this conventional wisdom is wrong, then this substantially should affect the way in which we think about conflict resolution processes.

Cooperation founded on misperceptions can be as long lasting and durable as cooperation founded on accurate information. There are four pathways through which false intersubjective beliefs might contribute to long-lasting cooperation. All of these pathways are in evidence in different areas of cooperation during the Soviet and American détente. The first pathway comes from theories of cooperation. One of the central difficulties in getting actors to cooperate is convincing one actor to make the first round of concessions.[16] First moves toward cooperation are tough: actors do not trust each other, worrying that if they make concessions reciprocity may not be forthcoming.[17] A FIB might enhance the prospects for cooperation in these cases. If one actor wrongly believes the other is making a concession, they might reciprocate by making a concession too. Even if the initial concession is later revealed to have been a misperception, a cycle of cooperation may have begun and trust established.[18] The history of the Anti-Ballistic Missile or ABM Treaty negotiations—especially the May 1971 agreement discussed in chapter 3—suggests this route to cooperation.

The second pathway relates to domestic politics. Political leaders often worry that if they have publicly committed to an international agreement, reneging risks a substantial political cost.[19] When actors publicly commit to an agreement, then even if that commitment was caused by a misperception of another's position, it may be difficult to back away later on, in part because it means owning up to the mistake. In the case of the ABM Treaty, Nixon and Kissinger made several moves toward enacting an ABM treaty that they quickly realized were mistakes, nevertheless, worries about Soviet disclosure of these mistakes and of a backlash in the Senate over the ABM program kept them moving ahead. Similarly, after Brezhnev publicly committed himself to détente, making it a central element of his peace program, he worried that a turn from cooperation to confrontation would undermine his authority in the politburo.

The third pathway that makes cooperation long lasting occurs when the FIB is never revealed. A misperception about what another will do in an unlikely event may contribute to cooperation over likely events if that unlikely event never occurs (or takes a long time to occur). Most successful marriages, I suspect, are underwritten by this type of mutual misperception. My wife and I likely both have expectations about what the other will do in reaction to events that will probably never occur. Having the expectation that the other will perform the roles we expect of them during these low-probability events, such as having triplets or if lightning strikes the house, may be important for cooperation over high-probability events. That is, if my wife knew that I would simply be overwhelmed by triplets or would want to move if lightning struck the house, she might not choose to stay with me now. In the same way, if France and Germany knew about US defense plans in the case of a Soviet attack on Europe—US withdrawal and later reintroduction using France and Germany as battlefields—then cooperation with US policy might have been more difficult to achieve because of disagreements about what to do in the low-probability event of a Soviet assault. The misperception is maintained, and thereby cooperation is assured, simply because it never becomes an issue.

The fourth pathway relates to changing interests. When agents commit to cooperate with each other, they often develop an interest in working together that transcends parochial interests. The sense of common commitment, being in it together or planning together, can sometimes create a sense of "we-ness" on which future cooperation can be built. This sense of common commitment that pervades some cases of collective action may exercise an independent influence on agents that makes working together seem normal and defection appear to be treachery. Therefore, misperceptions that lead to a sense of we-ness might create long-lasting cooperation by producing collective agents that survive the revelation of misperceptions.[20]

Understanding the role of misperceptions in cooperation is important in that it may lead us to develop a different, and potentially deeper, reading of the social dynamics underlying the international system. Many constructivist theorists and English school scholars conclude that the international system is dominated by shared ideas that enable cooperation, socialization, and the formation of international society.[21] These scholars draw on theories of society cast at the domestic level to articulate social theories of international politics. That is, they draw on theories traditionally used to explain local cultures, small societies, or the internal politics of a state in order to explain global cultures and international societies and to draw conclusions about the prospects for world state or nonstate futures. In general, these theories highlight the importance of intersubjectivity, common norms, and common cultures in the creation of predictable and dependable patterns of behavior in the international system.[22]

By contrast, there is a good argument against "rummaging in the 'graveyard' of sociological studies."[23] As a field, rather than borrowing the notion of shared ideas and norms from sociology and anthropology and arguments about language from philosophy, we should start from scratch. That is, we need to shift from a "social theory of international politics" that draws on the assumptions of sociological literature designed to explain small communities to an *international social theory* that begins from assumptions likely to be true of international politics that are untrue at the level of local cultures. This means that we should not draw on theories that emphasize dense societies, shared socialization practices, face-to-face contact, religious and linguistic homogeneity, a common political culture, and common scientific and moral beliefs. Instead, we should develop theoretical arguments that begin from the premise that the domestic analogue does not apply; we should assume these conditions are weak or do not exist in the international context. In IR, cooperation is not necessarily related to shared ideas but may form as the result of two or more actors engaging in an encounter with different definitions of the environment, different understandings of the interests of others, different understandings of the set of strategies each might play, and so on. We should replace the image of a homogeneous international system with an image of a pluralistic one.[24]

The bias toward treating common knowledge or intersubjectivity as common in international politics comes from two features of the way we think about IR theory. On the one hand, a significant number of IR scholars reason from domestic analogies. International socialization is usually treated as akin to socialization within the state or even local communities or families.[25] Economics research, emphasizing rudimentary applications such as coin flips, price indices, or simple experimental applications, are imported into IR research without thinking through likely differences in context. Theoretically, there are important disanalogies between the international system and local systems that should make importing local theories into IR suspect. The international system, by definition, is the least dense social system on the planet; agents speak different languages and gain their primary socialization experiences from difference cultures; and members interact much more sparingly with one another than they do with those from their own societies. The result, I suggest, is that ideas are likely to be colored differently, if not often understood in entirely different ways.

More important, the empirical evidence for intersubjectivity or common knowledge is often dodgy. Most IR scholars are more interested in showing that ideas have an influence on foreign policy, and, although they discuss ideas with the language of intersubjectivity, they do not empirically show that states share beliefs.[26] No study of sovereignty to date, for example, has shown that the Chinese understanding of the meaning of sovereignty—the rules of nonintervention—are similar to the US understanding.[27] Moreover, decades of research on international negotiations, cross-cultural psychology, anthropology, and sociology has highlighted the ways that members of different cultures (and even those within the same culture) often think very differently about things. There has been little effort to square the volumes of evidence that there are incredibly large differences in the international system (and even in local systems) with the argument for intersubjectivity.

In this book I target an indirect argument that IR theorists marshal to show that common knowledge or intersubjectivity is frequently encountered. The argument from abduction (or inference to the best explanation) may be one of the oldest arguments in social theory.[28] Durkheim, in *The*

Division of Labor, makes the argument in its clearest form. If we see a social system in which there is cooperation, there must be shared ideas because how else would cooperation arise? If shared ideas are the best explanation for cooperation, then we do not need *direct* evidence: the existence of cooperation is sufficient to indirectly infer the existence of shared ideas. In Durkheim's example, social systems characterized by a division of labor require extensive levels of cooperation. If shared ideas did not exist, "at every moment there would be renewed conflicts and quarrels" because in every interaction, every right, duty, and enforcement concern would be an issue for discussion, preventing the conclusion of agreements.[29] Therefore, if agents cooperate, there must be shared ideas to support cooperation. This is an argument from abduction, or inference to the best explanation, because it indirectly infers the cause (shared ideas) from the effect (cooperation); it never shows that shared ideas exist or traces the process through which they promote cooperation.

The argument from abduction has recently made an appearance in IR theory. Alexander Wendt, in defending his argument that the international system is ordered by shared ideas, writes that "far from facing profound uncertainty, states are confident about each other's intentions almost all the time." He reasons that without "a deep reservoir of common knowledge . . . the international system today would be far more chaotic and conflictual than it is—indeed there would not be an 'international system' at all."[30] Wendt's argument is similar to Durkheim's. If shared ideas enable us to predict others' behavior, then if others are predictable, shared ideas must exist. Wendt relies on the importance of shared ideas for cooperation as indirect evidence that shared ideas exist. I suspect that this view is common. Rarely are the ways in which common knowledge or intersubjectivity promote cooperation directly studied, demonstrating how actors rely on specific pieces of common knowledge in negotiation processes. It seems reasonable to assume shared ideas are prevalent only because we see their supposed effects, that is, cooperation.

My primary aim in this book is to demonstrate that misperceptions, especially FIBs, promote cooperation. Important cases of international cooperation might have failed if actors actually understood others' situations, values, interests, understanding of norms, and expectations for future behavior. I undermine the argument from abduction: international life is possible without shared definitions of situations because there are routes to cooperation that do not require deep mutual understanding. My chief argument, that FIBs can effectively create the conditions under which cooperation occurs, can then be regarded as a ground-clearing exercise, pointing to new and better ways of thinking about information and meaning in the international system.

The study of détente shows how and why actors can cooperate without shared ideas. The superpowers were largely predictable in the early 1970s. Brezhnev, Nixon, Kissinger, and others believed they knew the score, understood how the international climate of the 1970s affected the other side's situation, and expected that their understanding of the international situation was shared. On most counts, the superpowers were simply wrong; they did not understand each other as well as they thought. The study of détente reveals that being wrong about what to expect from others may be useful in securing cooperation because it enables agents to cooperate despite ideational and interest-based conflicts that might derail cooperation. These FIBs, in sum, may be powerful enough to create an intersubjective sense of order, a route to cooperation that does not rely on the argument from abduction.

Overview of the Book

In order to demonstrate how a pluralistic international system yields cooperation, I show that during the US-Soviet détente, cooperation improved because of false intersubjective beliefs.

In chapter 1, I outline the theory of FIBs and develop a research design for testing FIBs in relation to liberal institutionalist arguments about common knowledge and constructivist arguments about intersubjectivity in the context of détente between the US and the USSR during the Cold War. I argue that FIBs are an example of "public beliefs": beliefs that beliefs are shared by members of a group. They are distinguishable from intersubjectivity or common knowledge because they are inaccurate beliefs that beliefs are shared. I outline three types of FIBs and identify the scope conditions under which they are likely to enhance cooperation. During détente, one species of FIB, *imagined intersubjectivity,* developed that contributed to the growth and maintenance of cooperation. I outline a research strategy that derives hypotheses from imagined intersubjectivity, common knowledge, and intersubjectivity and assesses their relative importance.

In chapter 2, I compare the explanatory power of imagined intersubjectivity with that of intersubjectivity in the context of US and Soviet beliefs about the rise of détente in the late 1960s and 1970s. Wendt argues that shifts from conflict to cooperation occur when a noncooperative culture of anarchy (enmity) gives way to a culture of cooperation (rivalry). I show that US-USSR détente provides a good case for inspecting this shift. I find that Wendt's theory is partly correct in this case. The leadership in both states understood their relationship as a rivalry. But they understood the aims and rules of the rivalry differently, and they believed that their views of the relationship were shared. I trace the effects of this FIB during the negotiation of the 1972 Basic Principles agreement and the ceasefire resolutions during the 1973 Arab-Israeli War (also known as the Yom Kippur War or October War).

In chapter 3, I examine microlevel issues, comparing imagined intersubjectivity to common knowledge in the negotiation of the Anti-Ballistic Missile (ABM) Treaty. I argue that at three crucial moments during the negotiation process, imagined intersubjectivity pushed the parties toward cooperation. Through counterfactual analysis, I show that if common knowledge had existed at these three moments, cooperation likely would have been shallow or would not have occurred at all.

In chapter 4, I use the arguments developed in chapters 2 and 3 to examine two pieces of conventional wisdom about the period. On the one hand, some realist, liberal, and institutionalist scholars who have addressed détente posit that changes in material conditions—especially the balance of power and expectations for international trade—were sufficient for détente to come about. If material or institutional changes in the international system were sufficient, then FIBs cannot be a necessary condition for cooperation. At the same time, many diplomatic historians suggest that the misperceptions existing during the formation of détente contributed to its decline. If this conventional wisdom is right, then FIBs may be more of a threat to cooperation than otherwise. I evaluate these arguments by looking at the decline of détente.

While this book only deeply explores misperceptions during détente, there are reasons to suggest that FIBs are deeply rooted in the international system. Unlike the kinds of systems in which shared meanings are the most robust—where children learn from their parents, go through decades of school together, speak the same language, and interact with one another constantly in dense local systems—the international system likely does not contain the same degree of intersubjectivity because there are fewer and weaker ideational transmission mechanisms. The international system, in short, is less homogenous. When we think about how to design international institutions, the role of mutual understanding in conflict resolution, or the chances for reaching some deep level of global integration, we need to think through whether this might occasion more conflict than cooperation. A world of Cooks and islanders might not be as likely to lead to war as we suppose, and the effort to establish shared meanings may be so dangerous that it is not worthwhile.

1

When Common Knowledge Is Wrong

The best friendships are founded on misunderstandings.

Joseph Stalin, quoted in S. M. Plokhy, *Yalta*

Do shared ideas promote cooperation? Many of the most interesting and widely used theories of international cooperation suggest that shared ideas are crucial for ameliorating conflict. Realists suggest that misperceptions and uncertainty are drivers of conflict; liberal institutionalists highlight the importance of information for cooperation; and constructivists emphasize how shared cultures and norms promote peace. By contrast, I argue that Stalin was right: sometimes the best friendships are founded on misunderstandings. Misunderstandings can promote cooperation, and mutual understanding can promote conflict. False intersubjective beliefs—inaccurate beliefs that a piece of knowledge is held in common—may enable cooperation when shared ideas may lead to confrontation because they allow actors to cooperate when there are principled differences and conflicts of interest that may undermine cooperation.

In this chapter I explain how misperceptions enable cooperation. The first section outlines the prevalent view that common knowledge or intersubjectivity is a necessary condition for cooperation. As this discussion is usually implicit, I discuss these claims in detail. Then, I present an alternative theory of cooperation, emphasizing FIBs. In the following chapters

I test whether FIBs are able to explain cooperation in a hard case, the agreements reached between the United States and Soviet Union during détente.

Intersubjective Beliefs

Many IR scholars focus on how misperceptions or incomplete information contribute to conflict. The flipside, however, is more sparingly discussed. Does mutual understanding make cooperation more likely? IR scholars interested in this question often use the term "intersubjectivity" to point to the role of shared ideas. What do IR scholars mean by intersubjectivity? And why is there a consensus that intersubjectivity is so important for cooperation? There are two approaches to answering these questions: a rationalist approach, influenced by economics, that focuses on the role of common knowledge and a constructivist approach, influenced by sociology and the philosophy of language, that emphasizes the role of shared meanings or intersubjectivity. These are discussed in turn.

Common Knowledge

Common knowledge is often, if not always, treated as a necessary condition for cooperation to occur in accounts of international politics that rely on rational choice theory. What is common knowledge for rationalists and how does it lead to cooperation?[1]

Many rationalist IR scholars focus on how private information contributes to conflict. James Fearon influentially argued that if states knew other states' capabilities and resolve, then wars would not occur because they would know the outcome before the war began. If capabilities are common knowledge, then peace is more likely because the losing side in a prospective war would prefer to not pay the cost for a war that they know they will lose.[2] Similarly, James Morrow focuses on the laws of war, showing that international law can provide common conjectures (predictions) about expected behavior during war, enabling cooperation.[3] While Fearon's and Morrow's findings are important, the focus on information about capabilities or common conjectures rooted in international law elides the broader, more foundational ways that common knowledge is theoretically important for cooperation.

Underlying most rationalist accounts of cooperation is a broad account of the role of common knowledge. To choose to cooperate, agents need to believe that cooperating is the best alternative given what they expect others to do. In other words, I choose what I will do based on what I think you will do. I make decisions only after trying to walk in your shoes for a little bit, thinking through what you will do based on the information you have. The general assumption is that we are capable of thinking through situations as they confront others reasonably well. Rationalists, especially sophisticated formal modelers, often incorporate specific elements of private or incomplete information. On balance, however, rationalist theories, including those drawn from findings in noncooperative game theory, generally presume that enough common knowledge exists to make the successful imagining of others' reactions to our strategies possible.

The vehicle that makes this assumption work is common knowledge. If we agree on many of the most important elements of a situation that we jointly face, such as who the relevant players are and what those players want, and if we have an agreed on scheme to interpret what the other is doing, such as a common language, then we have the needed means to interact. Common knowledge is usually defined as "any information that all players know, that all players know that all players know, and so on."[4] This definition distinguishes common knowledge from other types of knowledge. It is different than "private knowledge" because all actors know the truth of a proposition.[5] It is also distinguishable from "mutual knowledge" in which two actors know the truth of a proposition but do not know whether others know.[6]

Rationalist theories of cooperation usually treat common knowledge as a necessary condition for cooperation in more explicit ways. David Hume reasoned that humans require common knowledge—conventions—because it provides them with dependable expectations for others' behavior. In explaining the origins of property rights, he wrote, "I observe, that it will be for my interest to leave another in the possession of his goods, *provided* he will act in the same manner with regard to me. He is sensible in a like interest in the regulation of his conduct. When this common sense of interest is mutually express'd, and is known to both, it produces a suitable resolution and behavior." He compared conventions to "two men who pull the oars of a boat, do it by agreement or convention, tho' they have never given promises to one another." Common knowledge enables people engaging in an activity that requires the coordination of individual plans of action to orient their activities toward one another because they believe that the other or others will engage in similar behavior.[7]

Rationalists have dramatically expanded Humean conventions to include a number of species of common knowledge, showing how these different types of common knowledge are important ingredients for international cooperation (summarized in table 1.1). *Strategic common knowledge* relates to the mathematical structure of the game. *Linguistic* and *situation specific common knowledge* relate to different ways that structure is labeled. Each of these species of common knowledge enables actors to effectively coordinate their actions with others.

Strategic common knowledge is rarely discussed, but is the foundational form for most theories of cooperation. The term *strategic* relates to the strategic form of a game, introduced in 1944 by John von Neumann and Oskar Morgenstern. Strategic common knowledge is common knowledge of crucial parts of games that are represented in mathematical form: who the players are, their preference orderings, their rationality (or mathematically described deviations), the number of strategies available to each player, and so on.[8] To cooperate with others requires them to be predictable, and to have an accurate estimate of what others will do, we need to know who matters, and usually also some idea about what others want and what strategies others might employ to get what they want. In most accounts of cooperation, IR scholars usually implicitly assume that these elements of cooperation are common knowledge.[9]

TABLE 1.1. Common Knowledge in International Cooperation

Forms of common knowledge	Uses of forms
Strategic	Number of players Preference relations Rationality of players Possible actions
Linguistic	Language (syntax and semantics) Meaning of signals and indices
Situation specific	Assorted, but in many applications includes: Focal points Precedents Cause-and-effect beliefs Institutional rules Previous game play

Linguistic common knowledge is also important for international cooperation because agents need some mechanism to communicate.[10] Put simply, in many situations agents are not able to coordinate if they are unsure
whether their signals are understood by others. If two drivers from different countries are trying to coordinate which side of the road to drive on, for
example, they need some mechanism—some verbal or other language—to
communicate whether they intend the right or left. Linguistic common
knowledge provides the basic set of tools, such as syntax and semantics, for
actors to understand the language used by others; words or signals must
have common meanings. Without common meanings, signals might be
misunderstood as confrontational rather than cooperative gestures, or they
might be taken for noise.[11] Models often assume that actors understand
which strategy others are playing; this capacity for discrimination relies on
actors having a shared capacity to interpret a specific behavior as a specific
strategy.

Insights from game theory as to the importance of communication
systems for cooperation are borne out historically by incidents where differences in the interpretation of even a single word or phrase have substantial implications for cooperation and conflict. The meaning of "strategic
bomber," for example, was crucially important in the SALT II discussions.
The US team believed that the Soviet Backfire bomber, which had the
capability of reaching the United States, was strategic because it had strategic potential. The Soviets disagreed. The Backfire was designed for Europe
and deployed in areas of the Soviet Union that prevented it from reaching
the United States; therefore it was not strategic.[12] President Nixon's visit to
China that opened the door to relations included similar, detailed linguistic
common knowledge. During the negotiations of the Joint Communiqué
of the United States of America and the People's Republic of China, commonly known as the Shanghai Communiqué, US and Chinese negotiators believed they understood the intricate nuances of words such as "will"
and "should" and phrases such as "all Chinese" and "the Chinese." These
nuances led to confusion throughout the trip, especially in the climactic
meetings between Kissinger and Qiao Guanhua in which they wrestled at
length over the precise formulation of the communiqué.[13] Former secretary
of state Dean Acheson relates a similar anecdote regarding negotiations
with the British: "In time it got around to a trouble Mr. Bevin and I had
stumbled into that morning by believing that we had both been speaking a

common language when, in fact, the common English word—in this case, 'executive'—had a different meaning on each side of the table."[14] For the British, "executive" connotes arbitrary action, whereas for the Americans, an "executive" body has the power to act. These three cases show that the common meanings of terms cannot be taken for granted and that the differences matter in important ways.

Situation-specific common knowledge is a basket of types of common knowledge that are required for cooperation but vary depending on the specific situation being modeled. Such terminology bears a resemblance to some used in the study of culture, but I choose not to employ the phrase "cultural common knowledge" because rationalist approaches are only interested in the elements of culture that implicate a strategic situation, such as the provision of nonmathematical focal points. The term *situation specific* refers to the elements that actors use to select equilibria or to make sense of others' strategies. As such, no list of situation-specific common knowledge can pretend to be exhaustive because different scholars focus on different elements of common knowledge. For example, Thomas Schelling relies on several pieces of common knowledge to solve bargaining problems, including focal points, precedents, prior arrangements, identifications, delegations, and mediations.[15] Situation-specific common knowledge draws on the rich details of diplomatic histories that are a continuing surprise, providing a wealth of insights for rationalists and others.[16]

The emphasis on common knowledge may seem strange to some students of IR. Many IR scholars treat uncertainty over rivals' future intentions, relative power, or capabilities and allies' resolve as a fundamental feature of international politics.[17] It may seem that emphasizing common knowledge avoids a serious consideration of uncertainty. One of the interesting features of contemporary treatments of uncertainty, however, is that the existence of a type and degree of uncertainty is generally considered to be common knowledge. In the most familiar example, every state is (or should be) uncertain of other states' future intentions, and every state can know that every other state is uncertain. Moreover, states often have a false confidence, a certainty, concerning world conditions. There is abundant psychological evidence indicating that actors are certain about many of their beliefs.[18] For example, in IR, states are often not uncertain about the intentions of other states in the international system.[19] The United States is neither uncertain about the unlikely prospects of a Canadian or British invasion nor uncertain that North Korea and al-Qaeda dislike the United States.

Each type of common knowledge enables efficient bargains to be reached. This general intuition resides deep in economic thought. F. A. Hayek's classic work in economic and political theory, especially *The Road to Serfdom* and *The Constitution of Liberty*, describe a main function of government as the promotion of common knowledge to assure economic performance. Governments should pass general laws affecting everyone instead of arbitrary laws affecting individuals, in part, because general laws provide for the kinds of common knowledge that allow markets to function efficiently. Laws that are too specific risk creating stocks of knowledge that are uncommon, as well as uncertainty about whether the legislature will disturb the market in the future, confusing the market and preventing efficient exchange. Moreover, one benefit of free markets is that they rely on impersonal forces—every agent has common knowledge of market behavior, principles, and rules—providing critical information for the success of agents' plans. Alternatives to the free market, in contrast, may rely on private knowledge that makes coordination in the marketplace more difficult.[20]

Without these fundamental forms of common knowledge, others become unpredictable, and thinking through how to cooperate is impossible. Common knowledge is a fundamental vehicle in rationalist thought, as it allows agents to consider problems from their interlocutors' perspectives.

The rationalist approach to the role that common knowledge plays in cooperation can be summarized by the following proposition:

> Proposition One: Common knowledge contributes to cooperation. Actors are able to cooperate once they identify relevant actors, determine the nature of the strategic situation including the payoffs for others, develop a common language through which to communicate, and other items of common knowledge crucial to the specific bargaining situation.

Intersubjectivity

IR theorists inspired by sociology rarely use the rationalist term *common knowledge*. Instead, they often argue that *intersubjectivity* or *shared understandings* are crucial for international cooperation. Since Friedrich

Kratochwil and John Ruggie's statement of purpose for constructivist studies, *shared meaning* has been used to understand international events as dissimilar as the nonuse of particular types of weapons, the creation and maintenance of military doctrine, the creation of science bureaucracies and the Red Cross, the promotion of human rights, and economic policies.[21] Intersubjectivity has been described as the central tenet of constructivist research, perhaps most prominently by Wendt, who writes that there are "two basic tenets of 'constructivism': (1) that the structures of human association are determined primarily by shared ideas rather than material forces, and (2) that the identities and interests of purposive actors are constructed by these shared ideas rather than given by nature."[22] Similarly, Theo Farrell describes the contribution of constructivist security studies as the introduction of intersubjective beliefs.[23] Furthermore, Christiansen and his coauthors, in an introduction to the study of ideas in European politics, argue that the study of intersubjectivity is the single most important contribution that constructivists have made.[24]

What is intersubjectivity and how does it explain cooperation? Despite the significance of intersubjectivity, the term is rarely explicitly defined. Beyond IR, there are countless definitions of intersubjectivity. For example, Habermas argues that intersubjectivity is simply the human capacity to use language; in psychoanalysis the term has been used to describe the interaction between patient and analyst; and in sociology it often refers to the mutual constitution of social reality by a community.[25] IR scholarship tends to use the latter definition, drawing on the work of early sociologists such as Durkheim and philosophers such as John Searle, who argue that social facts are created by agents and then act as constraints on them.[26] Even this latter conceptualization is vague. Is intersubjectivity the outcome of social interactions, that is, the social facts themselves? Or is intersubjectivity the process of interactions, that is, the way in which different subjective understandings of the world become aligned through discussion and practice? Or is intersubjectivity the human condition, that is, the necessity that humans interact with others, the inescapability of society? Few are careful in their use of the term, which creates conceptual confusion.

Despite these problems, in IR the term is most often used in one of two ways (fig. 1.1). The first interpretation directly equates common knowledge with intersubjectivity. Wendt, who prominently argues for the role of shared ideas in cooperation, writes that "the concept of common knowledge

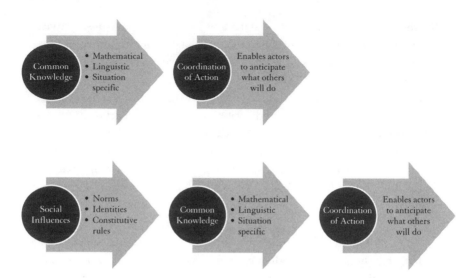

Figure 1.1. Common knowledge and social accounts of intersubjectivity

is equivalent to that of 'intersubjective understandings' favored by constructivists." Common knowledge is a set of beliefs that individuals share and realize that they share: "Knowledge of a proposition P is 'common' to a group G if the members of G all believe that P, believe that the members of G believe P, believe that the members of G believe that members of G believe P and so on."[27] This definition of common knowledge is nearly identical to the definition proposed by Robert Aumann and by David Lewis that characterizes the rationalist approach to common knowledge.[28] Similarly, Friedrich Kratochwil draws explicitly on Lewis and Schelling when he describes the nature of custom, tacit rules, and explicit rules that are the foundation of the international social system.[29] This conception of intersubjectivity includes the three forms suggested earlier—strategic, linguistic, and situation specific. The purpose of the common knowledge assumption in game theory is that common knowledge provides dependable stocks of knowledge that actors can use to make sense of a strategic situation. Intersubjectivity plays the same role: intersubjective meanings are "shared notions of the nature of social relations which tend to perpetuate habits and expectations of behavior."[30] By sharing ideas, actors have a stock of knowledge through which they know how they are to behave and how others are likely to behave. As Wendt explains, "the empirical phenomenon to which each is pointing, shared beliefs that orient action, is the same."[31]

Treating intersubjectivity as "common knowledge" is central to many empirical discussions of intersubjectivity and its role in international society. Discussions of international socialization find that as states learn from one another, knowledge is diffused throughout the international system. This implies that intersubjective ideas—shared facts or norms—are ideas held in common by "learning" states as well as their "teachers" after socialization is complete.[32] Furthermore, some of the earliest constructivist work on the development of international rules requires that these rules be common knowledge.[33] When referring to this account of intersubjectivity, I use the term "common knowledge" to distinguish it from the thicker approach discussed next.

The second account of intersubjectivity moves beyond the rationalist common knowledge tradition to emphasize the importance of common norms and common identities. The causal processes through which norms and identities affect cooperation are conceptually distinct from the roles that common knowledge often plays. Identities and norms generate the interests of actors, produce the units that interact (states), and give states' relations their social meaning.[34] Rationalists often do not probe the underlying reasons for the generation of common knowledge because they truncate the story of cooperation by only beginning the narrative after common knowledge has been generated. Constructivist accounts, in contrast, look to the origins of the ideas, interests, and identities that make cooperation possible, thereby probing the bases for the stocks of knowledge that are not treated in the rationalist account.[35]

This latter interpretation of intersubjectivity often suggests that thick ideas about interests, identities, and social norms create the stock of common knowledge on which cooperation depends.[36] In other words, the thick ideas that construct social actors only leads to cooperation through an in-between step in which common knowledge is created. Positing common knowledge as an in-between step between norms or identities and cooperation might surprise some who favor this second interpretation. This tradition emphasizes how norms and identities are directly constitutive of the types of relations that states engage in. Common knowledge, as an intervening step, does not appear to have a place in the story. For example, Martha Finnemore shows that international organizations can change the preferences that states have; Wendt argues that mutual recognition between states can drive the international system toward more cooperative and larger frameworks of governance; and Richard Price argues that states' adoption of "civilized identities" has led to a reduction in the use of chemical weapons because implicit in the identity of a civilized state is a requirement that these weapons will not be used against other civilized states.[37] The directness through which these studies equate changing norms or identities with changing relations between states may lead one to believe that common knowledge is not an element of the process through which ideational changes lead to cooperation.

However, the three forms of common knowledge always play a role in ideational change, even if the ways in which it is done are not explicit. Common norms and identities provide common knowledge of others' preferences, specifying a set of plausible strategies and establishing likely partners for cooperation. For example, Michael Barnett argues that identity politics within and between Arab states explains patterns of inter-Arab alliances after independence in the 1940s. He writes that "the history of the period exhibits numerous instances and episodes in which Arab leaders responded to the expectations that they develop . . . close strategic ties among Arab states and, at a bare minimum, that Arab states not adopt any policies that potentially might harm the security of the Arab nation. The fact of being an *Arab* state, therefore, generated certain expectations, and defying those expectations could have major consequences for an Arab leader's domestic and regional standing."[38] Barnett's argument about the role of Arab identities in security cooperation indicates the ways in which strategic common knowledge develops through identities: the relevant actors for cooperation are identified by the Arab identity. Having an Arab identity also provided common knowledge of the preferences of each actor by directing domestic pressure on every Arab leader to not engage in security arrangements that threaten the Arab security regime. Every Arab leader shared the knowledge that every other Arab leader was subject to the same pressures, and this shared knowledge enabled cooperation because leaders knew what to expect from one another due to those pressures.

Common norms also yield strategic common knowledge by providing a set of dependable strategies that states will adopt in an interaction. Within IR, "norms" are often defined as "collective expectations for the proper behavior of actors with a given identity."[39] Norms provide actors with dependable knowledge of the actions that others will undertake. For example, Finnemore argues that when actors adjusted the norms governing the use of force for debt collection, it enabled cooperative and legalistic solutions. Actors now expect states not to use gunboat diplomacy to collect debts but to cooperate through international organizations to arbitrate disputes.[40] This is a form of strategic common knowledge because it provides an equivalent to the rationalist idea of a dominant strategy: common knowledge of the expected actions of others within a situation that enables states to create cooperative responses to a problem.

Scholars who follow this second interpretation of intersubjectivity also argue that norms provide linguistic common knowledge by providing shared meanings. Kratochwil argues that all communication is norm-governed behavior. Signaling—when we "demand, warn, threaten, claim, criticize, assent, consent"—requires common linguistic norms because signals "would not make much sense if there were no underlying norms which provided the meaning for these actions."[41] Norms are critical for linguistic common knowledge because, without norms, actors would not know what terms mean—they bear no relation to a fact in the world because they are constituted by the act of speaking itself—and a norm or convention is required in order for these acts to be meaningful. Kratochwil then argues that because norms enable communication, "norms enable the parties whose goals and/or strategies conflict to sustain a 'discourse' on their grievances, to negotiate a solution, or to ask a third party for a decision on the basis of commonly accepted rules, norms, and principles."[42] For Kratochwil and others, the norms embodied in language provide linguistic common knowledge that is essential for bargains to be struck.

Norms and identities also create situation-specific common knowledge. In the case of Europe, scholars who study security communities argue that common identities make conflict between states unthinkable.[43] To stylize the argument, a common European identity has led states to feel more secure with their neighbors (cooperation) by providing common knowledge of the costs of war, the likely actions of other states (no remilitarization), and an institutional framework for resolving legitimate grievances (European Union). This common identity constitutes the interests of European states and, in so doing, provides them with common knowledge of the interests of other states.[44] These elements of common knowledge are not captured by the notion of strategic or linguistic common knowledge; they are situation specific.

The second interpretation of intersubjectivity that posits common knowledge as an in-between step between thick social ideas and cooperation is summarized by my second proposition:

> Proposition Two: Common identities and common norms contribute to cooperation. Identities and norms generate common knowledge that is the basis for cooperation.

This review of the ways in which intersubjectivity and common knowledge lead to cooperation makes explicit a claim that is normally implicit. Most accounts of cooperation rely on intersubjectivity. The thrust of these traditions is that regimes and institutions should be crafted to increase information, increase shared meaning, and enhance socialization processes. By doing so, the behavior of others becomes predictable, which enables cooperation. Conflict stems from an information or meaning deficit.

In the chapters that follow, I test whether an intersubjective understanding of the norms and identities of the superpowers existed during détente and whether it can explain the emergence of cooperation. There I focus primarily on Wendt's description of a dyadic shift from enmity to rivalry. Were the rules of the relationship understood identically by the participants? Did the United States and Soviet Union understand the meaning of being rivals in similar ways?

False Intersubjective Beliefs

Do shared ideas always promote cooperation? Most IR scholars believe that shared ideas are intrinsically tied to cooperation. In contrast, I argue that misperceptions, not shared understandings, can promote peace and cooperation in international politics. Usually, believing that shared ideas exist is enough to encourage cooperation, even if this belief is wrong.

In this section, I describe different pathways through which false intersubjective beliefs can promote cooperation. To define FIBs and show how they affect outcomes in international politics, a very brief digression is needed to show how FIBs differ from other forms of beliefs that are often discussed in political science and to classify different types of FIBs that lead to cooperation under different conditions.

Kinds of Beliefs

The central claim of this book is that false intersubjective beliefs often promote cooperation in international politics. A FIB is a specific type of misperception: an erroneous belief that a belief is shared. This subsection explains this definition and draws contrasts between FIBs and more often treated beliefs, such as common knowledge, private knowledge, and mutual knowledge, and gives the intuition concerning how FIBs lead to cooperation.

All beliefs have at least two elements: a proposition and a subject. The proposition of a belief is its content. For example, if I believe that God exists, the predicate "God exists" is the propositional content of the belief. When IR scholars investigate beliefs—whether cause-and-effect beliefs, norms, or identities—they typically focus on the effect of the propositional content.[45] For example, do actors behave differently when they adopt new beliefs?

Less attention is paid to the subject—the believer—of a belief. The subject of a belief denotes the group of actors who believe a belief is shared. For example, "We believe that God exists" includes a claim that a plural subject ("we") exists that shares a belief. If a belief invokes a plural subject, I refer to it as a *public belief*. A belief not shared among members of a public, such as "only I know the intentions of China," is a *private belief*.

Plural subjects may have effects independent of the propositional content alone because beliefs with plural subjects might lead actors to believe they are part of a public. Michael Chwe, for example, argues that royal progressions, in which a monarch travels through the countryside to assert power, depend less on the specific information communicated by the monarch (the propositional content) than on the spectacle of subjects meeting in large crowds (the plural subject). Individuals see themselves as part of a public because they see everyone, and see everyone seeing them, and so on. The spectacle of a group mutually witnessing sovereign power is different in kind from an individual in isolation seeing the monarch's procession because one realizes that the power awes the group instead of the individual in isolation.[46] The "we" seeing, in other words, is more important than the "what" seen. Similarly, in their novel *Fail-Safe*, Eugene Burdick and Harvey Wheeler imagine the effects of public beliefs on individuals who work in missile silos:

> There was also another element in the subterranean life which was pervasive, perfectly known, understood, and never discussed. There was the knowledge that the enemy was doing precisely what they were doing. Somewhere half way around the world there was another set of silos, another pattern of hard sites, another organization of men—almost, they assumed, precisely like theirs. This is no easy knowledge to carry. It is one thing to arm the thermonuclear warhead on an immense missile. It is another to know that another person, with almost the same training, is doing the identical thing—and that he must be thinking of you—and knowing that you are thinking of him thinking of you, and on and on.[47]

Burdick and Wheeler's novel suggested that the effect of handling the bomb was complicated by the public nature of preparing for a nuclear exchange. Workers isolated underground are part of a public that stretched across the Iron Curtain: knowing that when one prepared nuclear weapons to launch that others were doing the same had important psychological effects. Believing that common knowledge exists allows people to think of a certain group as a "we," even if they have never and likely will never meet the other members of the group.

The chemical weapons taboo is a paradigmatic case that emphasizes the importance of plural subjects for intersubjective beliefs to matter in international politics. Every "civilized" state believes that every other civilized state (a plural subject) believes that the use of chemical weapons is taboo (propositional content). The plural subject is crucial. If states do not believe that other civilized states share the taboo, then their behavior may be significantly different because they would not feel as if they are participating in a community with shared beliefs and might not expect reciprocity regarding chemical weapons.[48] The rightly held belief that there is a plural subject—the fact of joint recognition of the public nature of the belief—allows Richard Price to argue that the taboo has the constitutive effect of creating a civilized community.

By separating the subject of belief (public versus private) from the propositional content (shared propositional content from unshared propositional content), we can develop a typology of different types of knowledge or beliefs (summarized in table 1.2). Private knowledge and mutual

TABLE 1.2. Typology of Beliefs

		Subject of belief	
		Plural	Singular
Propositional property	Identical	Intersubjective	Mutual knowledge
	Different	FIB	Private knowledge

knowledge have singular subjects. If two agents have different information and each knows that only it has a piece of information, we refer to that
as private knowledge (Eric: "I have a bomb, and only I know that."). If
two agents share a piece of information and do not know it is shared, then
it is mutual knowledge (Eric: "I know Iran is a threat." Mara: "I know
Iran is a threat." But Eric and Mara do not know what the other thinks of
Iran.). Intersubjective beliefs and FIBs, in contrast, have plural subjects.
An intersubjective belief has a plural subject, and the propositional content
is the same for the subject group (Eric and Mara: "We believe that Iran is
a threat."). In contrast, to count as a FIB, the belief must be public but the
propositional content for group members must be different (Eric: "We believe Iran is a threat." Mara: "We believe Iran is not a threat."). Modifying
Wendt's definition of intersubjectivity, a FIB is a case in which the members of group G wrongly believe that there is a shared proposition that all
other members of group G believe. To believe wrongly, in this context,
means that the propositional content of the two beliefs differs.

FIBs are very common in everyday life. In watching children play chess
when on break during a chess tournament, I am often struck by the number of times children sit down to play, with one believing they are playing traditional chess and the other believing they are playing some variant
(e.g., Crazyhouse). The game begins, a FIB forms, only to be disrupted by
the advent of a move that does not make sense from one child's perspective.
Entire games are played in which such a disruption never occurs, which
makes a disruption that happens in the next game traumatic. A similar
dynamic often happens when children from different elementary schools
meet and play tag. By agreeing to play, they assume that each plays with
the same set of rules. The game begins, only to have arguments soon break
out because the kids play different variants. If we could count the number
of fights over whether I have to go between your legs to unfreeze you,
whether being tagged three times makes you "it," or whether going off the

woodchips on the playground is out of bounds, it would most assuredly outnumber the wars that states have fought.

Similarly, voters may be members of the same political party and in virtue of being members of the same party believe that they share deep normative commitments, only to be surprised when they find that they in fact differ.[49] For example, in the 2008 election, Democratic voters were excited about "change" and felt themselves to be part of a movement. They read their aspirations into their candidate and one another. However, change means different things to different people, and many of their views were directly at odds.[50] One is tempted to argue that part of the art of electoral politics is the encouragement of FIBs among a candidate's constituents, uniting people in a public belief that enables them to read their idiosyncratic propositional content into the beliefs of others.

The central intuition of the cooperation arguments that follow is that, unlike games of tag that degenerate into fights, cooperation may occur when actors wrongly believe that a belief is shared. These illusions can be necessary for cooperation under certain conditions. To show how FIBs are often necessary for cooperation, I discuss the two elements included in any belief about action—principles and expected behavior—so that an assessment of the importance of different types of unfounded public beliefs can be addressed.

Elements of Beliefs

I have defined FIBs as a special class of misperceptions: erroneous beliefs that a belief is shared. I will show how different types of FIBs are able to explain cooperation under different conditions. Before doing so, a typology of different types of FIBs—different ways that public beliefs can be wrong—is necessary to create a more robust theory of cooperation. To generate this typology, I argue that there is a difference in kind from a misperception that the principles, or reasons for acting, are shared and a misperception that expectations for others' behavior are shared.

Many contemporary theories of action propose that every act has two features: an actor and an end.[51] Habermas explains that a social act is an intentional movement through which an "individual changes something in the world."[52] This implies that every act has two related elements, a movement and a belief about the effect of that movement and an intention, a principle or reason that the movement is undertaken. Beliefs about actions, therefore, are usually beliefs about what others will do and why.

Behavior and principles point to different elements of action-oriented beliefs. One element—the behavioral—is the subcomponent of beliefs related to action that involve movement, that is, beliefs about past movements and expectations of future movements. In everyday life, this means that an actor has a belief about what others will concretely do and what affects their own behavior will have on the behavior of others. In game theoretic terms, behavior is observable game play. A behavioral expectation might be that a state will sign a treaty, fire a rocket, or invade a country.

In contrast, beliefs about principles are beliefs about why others will act or, to put it differently, beliefs about the value of the future state of affairs for agents. For Habermas, this is captured by the notion that every action is capable of explanation in relation to values that are sought after.[53] For example, if an action is undertaken because it realizes the values expressed by a community, defends the national interest, permits material gain, or enables a political elite to maintain power, then the action is capable of reason giving. This analysis of principles might seem strange to students of rational choice. Preferences are often exogenous, and rarely do actors have a "reason" for their preferences. Furthermore, preferences are the reasons, strictly speaking, for strategies. Does that make preferences and principles identical?

Principles are not preferences, although the two are intimately connected. Following Kenneth Arrow, preferences are social states that are evaluated in terms of their desirability for an actor, or, as Jeffrey Frieden observes, ranked outcomes of an interaction.[54] For Arrow, preferences are a subjective "taste." The result is that there is no language to explain why actors rank outcomes in specific ways, and therefore language does not capture the subjective reasons for preferring some outcomes over others.

Principles provide the reasons for preferences in two ways. First, *a principle that guides an actor is the reason for the transitive ordering of preferences*. Values are the reason that one preference is preferred to another. For example, one might evaluate the relative values of a set of outcomes by a formula that ranks them in terms of their justness, egocentric benefits, or some other criteria. Here, a principle is not a preference because it is not a state of the world. It is a formula used to evaluate social states in terms of their desirability or appropriateness. Second, in certain cases *a principle that leads to an action in one interaction can, in certain cases, be a preference over outcomes that cannot be reduced to a strategy in another interaction.*[55] That is, sometimes actors are geared toward an endgame that is valued in and of itself. The principle of an action is not that the action places the player in a better position for the next round but that it places the player in a better position for the end result, the final state of the world that the actor is trying to reach.

The important point is that one can misperceive either dimension of a social action. One can have inaccurate estimates for the future behavior of another actor: what another actor will do or consent to do in agreeing to cooperate. One can also misperceive the principles (reasons or values) that cause another actor to decide to do those things. By disaggregating the principled and behavioral dimensions of beliefs, we can classify different types of public beliefs relevant to cooperation.

Types of False Intersubjective Beliefs and Cooperation

Under certain condition, misperceptions of likely future behavior or the reasons for action may generate cooperation. To understand how requires disaggregating FIBs into types of public beliefs by analyzing what happens when the misperception relates to behavior, principles, or a combination of elements of beliefs. By arranging the ways in which public beliefs might be misperceived, four types of public beliefs are distinguishable (summarized in table 1.3). In the table, I use the term "intersubjectivity" rather than "common knowledge." Common knowledge can relate to any proposition (e.g., the sky is blue); intersubjectivity, as I define it, is a belief that is relevant to social or strategic situations. An intersubjective belief is a shared belief by members of a group that contains accurate understandings of the intended future behavior and the reasons for that behavior for members of a socially relevant group.

TABLE 1.3. Public Beliefs

	Accurately perceive behavior	Misperceive behavior
Mutual understanding of principles	Intersubjectivity	Functional overlapping principles
No mutual understanding of principles	Functional incompletely theorized agreements	Imagined intersubjectivity

The other three cases specified in the table are types of FIBs. I discuss each type of FIB and the ways in which it might lead to cooperation. While the empirical argument that follows fully develops only the process through which imagined intersubjectivity leads to cooperation, all three forms may lead to cooperation under different conditions.

Functional Incompletely Theorized Agreements   Functional incompletely theorized agreements are cases in which actors accurately perceive what others will do (their behavior) but misperceive why they will do it (their principles). Two states, for example, might agree to a free trade deal in which they have accurate expectations regarding the rules of the deal and the rates of likely compliance, while misperceiving the principles that underlay the deal. One party, for example, might believe that both have reluctantly reached the deal because of interest-group pressure, while the other believes that both are enthusiastic because free trade promotes growth. These incompletely theorized agreements may promote cooperation in situations where broad ideational conflict might prevent compromise.

Cass Sunstein introduced the term "incompletely theorized agreements" to make sense of important elements in constitutional law. If actors in a multimember institution, such as a court, disagree over fundamental questions, then couching very specific cases in broad principled terms may lead to disagreement.[56] Therefore, incompletely theorized agreements are a mechanism for achieving agreements when principled differences exist: "They agree on the result and on relatively narrow or low-level explanations for it. They need not agree on fundamental principle. They do not offer larger or more abstract explanations that are necessary to decide the case."[57] *Functional* incompletely theorized agreements are different from those discussed by Sunstein directly.[58] Sunstein is primarily interested in cases in which judges intentionally leave decisions incompletely theorized. While this line of analysis may be interesting to explore in international law, for example through the notion of intentional ambiguity, I am interested in cases in which incompletely theorized agreements develop unintentionally but serve a function.[59] In a functional incompletely theorized agreement agents are *unaware* that there are principled differences.

For example, during the Second World War, the US public supported lend-lease aid to the Soviet Union, even though the public and the Soviets had drastically different principled understandings of the fate of Europe after the war. If the US public or US decision makers were aware of the deep ideological divide, cooperation might have been more difficult.[60] Similarly, the United States cooperated with Vietnam in the war against Japan. Ho Chi Minh assumed that the United States and Vietnam, due to shared colonial experiences, also shared a principled understanding of their relationship. This disagreement became apparent after the war, as neither Roosevelt nor Truman supported Vietnamese claims against the French.[61] In both cases, concrete cooperation occurred because the parties believed they knew what behavior to expect of the other with respect to the specific cooperation problem they confronted; if the parties had known that principled differences existed, cooperation might have foundered.

Functional incompletely theorized agreements lead to cooperation by enabling actors to reach agreements that prescribe specific behavior when principled agreement does not exist. Not knowing that there are broad, philosophical differences in the way that others understand the world can promote cooperation by enabling actors to get down to the brass tacks of cooperation without having to resolve fundamental disagreements between worldviews. Cases of cooperation between partners with different worldviews are the most likely places for functional incompletely theorized agreements to exist and function. More important, they are a necessary condition for cooperation in cases in which an actor believes that the principle is more important than expectations of behavior (especially immediate behavior)—for example, cases in which actors are emotionally connected with a principle or identify potential partners for cooperation based on an identity principled belief.

Functional Overlapping Principles   Functional overlapping principles occur in cases in which actors misperceive what others will do but accurately perceive why they will do it. Two actors, for example, might cooperate by creating an institutional architecture to pursue what they believe to be common foreign policy aims without knowing that each favors pursuing those common aims through different concrete policies. Every state in Europe, for example, might rightly believe that solving a dire financial crisis is the most important issue for every state but wrongly believe that every state will adopt some specific policy. Because they agree on the importance of solving an economic crisis, they might cooperate by creating joint institutions, pooling resources, and selling cooperation to their publics. If they knew what other states expected those institutions and resources to be used for they might never cooperate. I use the term "functional overlapping principles" to indicate that there is an overlap in the reasons (principles) for action without a corresponding overlap in accurate predictions about others' behavior.

The term "overlapping principle" is loosely borrowed from John Rawls's *Political Liberalism*. Rawls argues that an overlapping consensus "consists of all the reasonable opposing religious, philosophical, and moral doctrines likely to persist over generations and to gain a sizable body of adherents in a more or less just constitutional regime."[62] Rawls concludes that a pluralistic society can cooperate when there are a few principles held in common. Like Rawls's analysis of liberalism, states in international society may have overlapping, shared principles such as valuing security, sovereignty, rights, and so on. These overlaps are functional when they promote cooperation. Not knowing what others expect to be concretely done about them—especially not knowing what others intend to do in unlikely situations (e.g., an off-the-equilibrium path play) or in the future—might enable cooperation in likely situations and the present.

The relationship between the United States and its Western allies in the early years of the Cold War provides an interesting example. Western European states knew they shared fundamental principles—largely related to human rights, the containment of communism, security, and self-determination—and, as a result, cooperated to create a substantial institutional architecture to support those goals. The origins of NATO, for example, were rooted in a belief that the West shared fundamental values.[63] The specific policies that each expected others to pursue within negotiated cooperative arrangements, however, were drastically different. There were misperceptions about whether NATO would lead to an immediate provision of military aid to Western Europe and about US war plans for defending Western Europe in the case of a Soviet assault. It's likely that the Truman administration would have been more reluctant to agree to NATO if it knew that Europeans supposed that this meant they could expect an immediate defense of Europe in case of a Soviet attack, or the immediate provision of military hardware.[64]

Functional overlapping principles enable cooperation in cases in which actors make agreements in light of knowingly shared principles while being unaware that the other party has different beliefs about the expectations of behavior that stem from that action. Functional overlapping principles are likely to exist in cases of cooperation in which states share similar worldviews, encounter a new issue area (e.g., global warming) or a drastically new situation (e.g., the global financial meltdown). Functional overlapping principles are necessary conditions for cooperation if the discovery of the differences in expected behavior would undermine the agreement. Actors subjectively believe that they are creating agreements to enable policy coordination and to achieve a mutual gain and only discover later that the "FOP" was a flop.

Imagined Intersubjectivity   Imagined intersubjectivity occurs when actors wrongly believe they understand what the other party will do and also wrongly believe they know the principles that guide action. States often choose to cooperate only because they expect that policy coordination will lead to a certain future behavior by all cooperators. If states misperceive the underlying rationale for cooperation, they might also have differing perceptions about what future behavior to expect. Two friends, for example, might cooperate by going to dinner where one friend believes it is a romantic occasion and the other just a friendly one. As a consequence of having different perceptions of the underlying reasons for dinner, they expect different behavior in the future, likely at the end of the date. They cooperate, therefore, only because they neither know what the other expects from them or why they expect it. In the chapters that follow, I trace the impact of imagined intersubjectivity during the US-Soviet détente, showing that it is crucial to explaining the warming of relations between the two powers as well as the successful negotiation of the Basic Principles agreement, the ceasefire resolutions that ended the 1973 Arab-Israeli War, and the conclusion of the Anti-Ballistic Missile Treaty.

The term "imagined intersubjectivity" refers indirectly to the title of Benedict Anderson's *Imagined Communities*. Individuals come to believe in the existence of a "nation" because they believe, often wrongly, that they share common ideas with other members of the group. When reading a newspaper, "each communicant is well aware that the ceremony he performs is being replicated simultaneously by thousands (or millions) of others of whose existence he is confident, yet of whose identity he has not the slightest notion."[65] The public constituted by the shared act of reading a newspaper need not have anything in common: it does not matter what they read but merely that they observe one another reading. For Anderson, this imagined sense of belonging is so strong that "what the eye is to the love—that particular, ordinary eye he or she is born with—language—whatever language history has made his or her mother-tongue—is to the patriot. Through the language, encountered at mother's knee and parted with only at the grave, pasts are restored, fellowships are imagined, and futures dreamed."[66] We fight and die for others within our community because we believe we have something in common with them because we share a language, not because we actually have something in common, something substantive like shared values or expectations for what behavior today will lead to tomorrow.

The power of believing in shared ideas is likely just as important to understanding international cooperation as it is in Anderson's account of society. States frequently misperceive one another, having different expectations for what others will do in the future and different hopes for what the future might look like. In some cases, they are wide awake to these differences; in other cases, they are fortunately half-asleep. Believing that there are substantive common values or expectations for the future might promote cooperation in cases where there are drastic conflicts of interest or dramatic differences in values.

Imagined intersubjectivity enables cooperation by allowing actors to coordinate their behavior with each other through a process of policy adjustments to meet the demands of the imagined other. Each actor subjectively orients itself toward a set of reasons and expectations of behavior that do not exist. Cases of cooperation through imagined intersubjectivity are most likely when actors hold different worldviews and rarely interact in a given issue area. Imagined intersubjectivity is necessary for cooperation in cases in which the discovery of either the true principle or the true expectations of the other's behavior would disrupt the process of policy coordination. It is perhaps the most fragile FIB because it is twice as easy to disrupt as functionally incompletely theorized agreements or functional overlapping principles: revealing the other's actual principles or actual expectations of behavior is a constant threat. I argue that this seemingly *rara avis* of international politics is fundamental to international politics and played a crucial role in superpower cooperation in the 1970s.

These three forms of FIBs and their relationship to international cooperation are summarized by the following proposition:

> Proposition Three: A lack of intersubjectivity contributes to international cooperation. In certain situations, intersubjectivity risks undermining cooperation by revealing ideational divergence or conflicts of interest; a false intersubjective belief can secure cooperation if it masks ideational conflict.

Evaluating the Role of Public Beliefs in International Cooperation

Beginning shortly before Nixon entered office, the United States and Soviet Union entered into one of the most cooperative phases of the Cold War, reaching agreements on a broad range of security, economic, and cultural issues. In the next three chapters, I evaluate the role of intersubjectivity and false intersubjective beliefs on cooperation during détente. Before doing so, I first want to explain how to translate the broad theory addressed in the first half of this chapter to the specific cases of cooperation during détente. Why should we study cooperation during détente? And how can we evaluate the effect of FIBs on international cooperation?

Why Détente?

The dependent variable of interest is international cooperation. I rely on a standard definition: "Intergovernmental cooperation takes place when the policies actually followed by one government are regarded by its partners as facilitating realization of their own objectives, as the result of policy coordination."[67] Cooperation requires actors to do something that they would not do in isolation, and it generally requires a process of negotiation and bargaining to coordinate policy. Furthermore, following the conventional rational choice treatment of cooperation, the concept is theoretically distinct from compliance and effectiveness. By compliance, I mean honoring agreements; by effectiveness, I mean the ability of those agreements, if honored, to enable states to realize their goals.[68]

Separating cooperation from compliance is conceptually important. Cooperation (policy coordination) might establish an institution, but after the institution's creation, cooperation is no longer required for there to be compliance or effectiveness. Two states that share a common border might encounter a coordination problem if their traffic laws differ about what side of the road to drive on. Through cooperation, the states may change their traffic laws to reduce the likelihood of accidents (e.g., all drive on the right). But, after the laws are changed, cooperation ends as there is no incentive to defect from the agreed convention. Compliance (maintaining the convention) and effectiveness (garnering practical results) are assured because successful cooperation turns a coordination problem into a harmony of interests. Treating these as conceptually different issues allows interesting questions to be asked about the effects of different modes of cooperation on long-term effectiveness and compliance. But I focus here only on cooperation.

The superpower détente included key cases of international cooperation. During détente, the United States and Soviet Union cooperated—engaged in policy coordination—on a broad range of issues. In the next chapter, I review the more than 150 superpower agreements reached during the period.[69] The main results of cooperation were arms control, crisis management, and trade agreements. For the first time during the Cold War, the superpowers created limits on the types and numbers of weapons that each side could deploy. In addition, they created an official commercial relationship, heavily benefiting farmers in the Midwest as well as Soviet consumers. Negotiations over conflicts in the periphery—especially the Middle East—sought to establish joint solutions to the kinds of problems that nearly led to war in the preceding decades, such as in Berlin and Cuba.

Détente is an appropriate case to study the role of information or culture because it is a crucial case. Factors pointed to by many theorists of cooperation—international cultural shifts, the development of trust, the creation of international institutions, and so on—all occurred before international cooperation began, making it a most-likely case for theories that highlight the role of mutual understanding for international cooperation.[70] The historical record bears out the logic as to why détente is a least-likely case for a theory of FIBs and a most-likely case for the conventional wisdom that communication and mutual understanding is important for cooperation. Détente sparked the most rigorous discussions between the superpowers during the Cold War. Nixon insisted: "After an era of confrontation, the time has come for an era of negotiation." Nixon followed through on this promise. He met with the Soviets at three summits in three consecutive years, a record for Cold War diplomacy. In addition, he sent his national security adviser, Henry Kissinger, to Moscow on several occasions to engage in direct bilateral talks with the Soviets, and he received Andrei Gromyko, Kissinger's counterpart, many times. Kissinger also entered into direct back-channel negotiations with the Soviet ambassador to Washington, Anatoly Dobrynin. Teams of negotiators met regularly to discuss issues as diverse as arms control, trade, space exploration, the environment, and regional crises.

The cornerstone was the Strategic Arms Limitation Talks (SALT). For more than three years, negotiators met for seven rounds of discussions in Helsinki and Vienna, the longest of which lasted 120 days. These discussions were amiable. The chief negotiators, Gerald Smith and Vladimir Semenov, often discussed business in social settings and had an affinity for each other. They exchanged novels and recited poems, along with presenting their governments' views on arms control.[71] Cooperation moved beyond technical-issue areas, focusing on establishing ground rules for the superpower rivalry in the discussions of the 1972 Basic Principles agreement and the 1973 Agreement on the Prevention of Nuclear War. As Soviet leader Brezhnev summarized, "Probably never before have ties and contacts between the Union of Soviet Socialist Republics and the United States of America in different areas of political, economic, and cultural activity been as lively as they are today."[72]

Theories of cooperation that this book cuts against—those that emphasize ideational or institutional factors—should therefore be well placed to explain détente. In Jack Levy's colorful turn of phrase, there is an "inverse Sinatra inference—if I cannot make it there, I cannot make it anywhere."[73] Détente is therefore an important case because showing that détente was caused by mutual misperception rather than mutual understanding should make us suspicious about what is going on in other cases of cooperation.

Moreover, cooperation during the Cold War is paradigmatic for many institutional and sociological theories of cooperation.[74] The origins of many theories of cooperation emerged from attempts by political scientists to understand how to move the superpowers to a less-aggressive footing. Insights into the role of information for international cooperation stem from interest in Cold War arms control and theories about how to reduce tensions by building trust.[75] Contemporary IR scholars suggest that the insights of these earlier generations of scholars were roughly correct: mutual understanding—through the diffusion of information and common understandings—turned confrontation into cooperation. Deborah Welch Larson argues that the superpowers overcame their distrust to reach agreements during détente.[76] Farrell claims that the language of deterrence and its basic concepts were common knowledge, enabling cooperation between the United States and Soviet Union.[77] Furthermore, Janice Bially Mattern argues that the nature of the relationship in general was intersubjective and that the states understood their respective roles.[78] By selecting a paradigmatic case of international cooperation, I create a fair test of the claim that mutual understanding promotes cooperation. It meets the conventional wisdom head on, and in the case it was partly developed to explain.

In addition to détente being a paradigmatic case for theories of international cooperation, the end of détente is often seen by international security scholars and historians as a clear instance in which misperception led to conflict. The short-term success of arms control and conflict management is often credited to information.[79] Misperceptions, in contrast, are blamed for the demise of détente. Coit Blacker, for example, wrote that the United States and the Soviet Union should "participate in the search for a 'common language' as proposed by Brezhnev in an April 1981 speech. . . . A more active and sustained superpower dialogue on issues of joint concern would not eliminate the confusion, misunderstanding, and tension that has plagued the relationship since its inception; it could, however, facilitate communication and restore an element of predictability to the interaction between Washington and Moscow."[80] Similarly, in *Détente and Confrontation*, Raymond Garthoff concludes that détente failed because of misperceptions: "Each side was unprepared to understand the perspective, and the interests, of the other. Although better understanding would not have removed conflicts of interest, it would have helped to reduce frictions caused or exacerbated by the failure even to recognize the perspective and interests of the other side."[81] In short, the lesson that many historians and political scientists draw from détente is that mutual understanding led to cooperation and mutual misperception drove the parties apart.

This may be the wrong lesson to draw. Détente was certainly accompanied by misperceptions. The central question is whether these misperceptions fueled or dampened cooperation. In contrast to many political scientists and diplomatic historians, I argue that the former is the case: without false intersubjective beliefs, cooperation may have never begun.

Testing the Argument

The superpower relationship before (and during) détente was characterized by conflicting interests and ideologies. I hypothesize that false intersubjective beliefs—erroneous beliefs that the parties held common knowledge—were necessary for cooperation during the early 1970s. Within the context of international negotiations, this means that FIBs were necessary for parties to make the concessions needed to secure cooperation. I use process tracing and, when possible, explicit counterfactual analysis to marshal support for the inference that FIBs promoted cooperation.

International negotiations are processes that occur over time, often including several rounds of concession making in which parties' bargaining positions move closer until agreement is reached. During the process of bargaining, there are crucial turning points in which one party decides to make a concession. One reason for these concessions—familiar to students of cooperation—is that the parties have worked out their differences and reached a mutual understanding. By contrast, a theory of false intersubjective beliefs posits that these concessions are made because the parties have misperceived each other's bargaining positions. The critical question is what types of changes in information prompt parties to change their positions: mutual understanding or FIBs?

To make the causal inference that FIBs were necessary for cooperation during détente, I rely on process tracing to make causal inferences about the necessary conditions for cooperation.[82] Considered in its starkest form, a theory of FIBs hypothesizes that parties make concessions at crucial moments in international negotiations because of misperceptions that precede those concessions. Two types of observations are critical to this analysis. The first type of causal process observation is decision makers' beliefs (the independent variable) that precede an episode of cooperation (the dependent variable).[83] The second type is the process through which a FIB has led to cooperation. I rely on "inductive process tracing" to show different pathways through which misperceptions led to the concessions on which cooperation depended.[84]

Students of qualitative methods note that process tracing is insufficient to make causal inferences about necessary conditions.[85] Tracing a process shows a specific pathway through which one factor causes another; it usually cannot show that, in the absence of the hypothesized cause, another pathway to the same effect may have been trafficked. For example, even if cooperation did not arise in 1972 and 1973, it may have come later after some change in the balance of power. I entertain counterfactuals in conjunction with the process-tracing evidence to show that without a FIB, cooperation would not have occurred. The crucial question asked in the counterfactual analysis section is whether there was a reasonable chance that specific episodes of cooperation—especially the ABM Treaty—would have occurred without misperceptions at three specific moments.[86]

To make the counterfactuals as explicit as possible, I use two types of counterfactual analysis. The first type relates to decision makers' beliefs. I construct extensive game trees to represent beliefs about the negotiations to clarify how beliefs about Soviet behavior influenced the pattern of US concessions in the SALT negotiations. Then, I counterfactually manipulate the game tree: What if the actors had known there were differences in the principles that guided an action, or differences in the behavior that each expected after an action?[87] If the response to these counterfactuals is that the FIB was crucial for a side to make concessions, then I treat the FIB as a necessary condition of cooperation.[88] The second type of counterfactual analysis relates to the timing of concessions. Would cooperation have occurred later if agreements were not reached in 1972 and 1973? And, if so, would cooperation have taken the same form?

This form of counterfactual analysis is necessarily speculative. There are, however, better and worse counterfactuals, and better and worse responses to those counterfactuals.[89] When asking counterfactual questions about decision making, I limit the analysis to other courses of actions that were actively considered, thus providing direct evidence of the counterfactual. Moreover, the evidence used in the counterfactual analysis—like all evidence—can be disputed.

Chapter 4 considers rival explanations. Many scholars who focus on détente argue that cooperation may have been inevitable because of material, economic, and institutional incentives. If these alternative explanations are sufficient to explain cooperation, then FIBs are not necessary conditions. In looking at the decline of détente, I use two methods to assess alternative explanations. The first method is an interrupted time series design. Interrupted time series designs—also called quasi-experiments—test whether changes in the presence or strength of some factor correlates with an outcome of interest over time.[90] For example, if institutions were present before cooperation began and faded before cooperation faded, then it is plausible that institutions helped facilitate cooperation. Interrupted time series designs are often dismissed out of hand because they are not useful tests *for* a theory, especially when one is only investigating one or a few cases of cooperation.[91] When testing a theory against rival hypotheses, however, interrupted time series designs are useful. If there is no correlation between the outcome of interest and factors highlighted by alternative explanations, then those alternative explanations become implausible.[92] In other words, this means that the presence of institutional, cultural, or power-based factors do not correlate well with the rise and fall of cooperation.

The second method is process tracing. The alternative explanations presume that the influence of institutions, trade, or power led policymakers to change their opinions about the viability of cooperation. The observable implication that follows from these theories is that some group changed its perception about the value of cooperation, shifting its policies and votes. The key observations are (a) whether there was a change in policymaker beliefs and (b) whether this change came after some change in the factors highlighted by alternative accounts.[93] These provide basic "hoops tests" that these alternative explanations need to meet if they are to hold water.[94]

Plan for the Study of Détente

The next two chapters explain the rise of détente. Many historians note that détente was accompanied by misperceptions. There is little dispute today that the United States and the Soviet Union never really understood each other, nevertheless, policymakers—especially Nixon and Kissinger—were overly confident that mutual understanding existed. My central disagreement with the mainstream account is the role of misperception in cooperation. One central argument made by political scientists and diplomatic historians is that these misperceptions led to détente's decline. The United States and the Soviet Union had false expectations for what the other would do and, when they realized cooperation was a mirage, they lost interest. Worse, they felt betrayed. I propose the inverse argument. Only because of a false intersubjective belief—an erroneous belief that there was mutual understanding—was cooperation possible. And, when cooperation declined, it was not because the misperceptions were revealed. Instead, new policymakers—especially in the United States—with more conservative views on cooperation began to slowly hammer away at the broad agenda for cooperation formed in the Nixon White House.

The argument is made in three parts. The first part—developed in the next chapter—looks at how misperceptions operated at the macrolevel. What did the Nixon White House and the Brezhnev Kremlin believe characterized their relationship in the broadest dimensions? Did they agree on how the superpower conflict should be managed (the BPA)? Could they develop a common approach to dealing with hotspots they thought might spin out of control (the 1973 Arab-Israeli War)? The second part—developed in chapter 3—investigates cooperation in a more specific case: the ABM Treaty negotiations. During the course of a negotiation, specific concessions are necessary to reach agreement. In the case of the ABM Treaty, at least three concessions by the United States stand out: Kissinger's decision to offer to limit antiballistic missile systems, the timing of negotiations over defensive and offensive arms control (an important political and strategic issue), and the decision to attend the summit in 1972 after an escalation in Vietnam. What drove Nixon and Kissinger to make these decisions? Did mutual understanding lead them to make the concessions necessary to get to international cooperation? Or were these concessions based on misunderstandings—false intersubjective beliefs—about the Soviet position? The final part—developed in chapter 4—looks at the relationship in its broadest form. Political scientists and diplomatic historians—as noted earlier—often argue that cooperation was inevitable but that it was undone by misperceptions. Were the misperceptions that were built into cooperation the reason cooperation largely ended by 1979? Or were other factors relevant to the decline of cooperation?

2

DÉTENTE

There will be much talk about the necessity for "understanding Russia";
but there will be no place for the American who is really willing to
undertake this disturbing task. The apprehension of what is valid in
the Russian world is unsettling and displeasing to the American mind.
He who would undertake this . . . the best he can look forward to is the
lonely pleasure of one who stands at long last on a chilly and inhospitable
mountaintop where few have been before, where few can follow, and
where few will consent to believe he has been.

GEORGE KENNAN, SEPTEMBER 1944

During the early 1970s, the United States and the Soviet Union began a remarkable process of cooperation intended to develop an enduring relationship that would end the excesses of superpower competition. Superpower cooperation was so successful that many prognosticators predicted the end of the Cold War. Perhaps most impressive was the timing. Détente occurred less than ten years after the Cuban Missile Crisis, at the height of the Vietnam War, and nine years before the Soviet incursion in Afghanistan. What enabled the United States and the Soviet Union to improve relations? Was the change from what Richard Nixon called an "era of confrontation" to an "era of negotiation" premised on mutual understanding?

Kennan's statement in the epigraph to this chapter—that one who understands Russia is of no use in American foreign policy and the effort to do so will leave such a person alone "on a chilly and inhospitable mountaintop"—may seem strange to students of diplomacy and international politics. In the previous chapter, I showed that IR theorists often explain peace and cooperation as a product of mutual understanding. In particular, constructivists might argue that the shift in this case from mortal enemies to cooperative rivals was the result of a change in the superpowers' social relationship.[1] The early years of the Cold War, rooted in enmity and ideological warfare, gave way to rivalry and coexistence. These scholars highlight the importance of shared ideas—intersubjectivity—in managing the superpower rivalry.[2] In their view, Kennan is wrong: "understanding Russia" or "understanding America" is useful and likely played an important role in superpower diplomacy.

I argue, in contrast, that the superpowers improved their relationship only because of misperceptions: détente succeeded only because mutual understanding failed. Even though the leaders of both superpowers thought they understood each other in the early 1970s, détente was not the result of intersubjectivity. To paraphrase Kennan, neither Brezhnev nor Nixon really grasped what was valid in the world of the other. Nixon and his foreign policy team, especially Henry Kissinger, thought that an understanding had been reached about the nature of US-Soviet relations that emphasized political competition, linkages, and threats. Brezhnev and his foreign policy team also thought the fundamentals of the superpower relationship were shared: the United States had been compelled to accept Soviet political equality and the danger of political competition and threats, and the United States accepted Russian influence in sensitive parts of the Third World. Both wrongly thought that their public beliefs were shared, a phenomenon I refer to as false intersubjective beliefs. FIBs encouraged détente and cooperation by enabling the leadership in both states to overlook their fundamental differences. In this chapter I examine the general relationship between the Soviet Union and the United States during détente. I show that constructivist accounts capture a turn from enemy to rival that was indicative of the period. However, the underlying idea of détente was not shared. Soviet and US decision makers had two very different understandings about what détente meant. The change in the superpower relationship was premised on imagined intersubjectivity— an inaccurate belief that both sides shared principles and expectations for future behavior. The existence of this imagined intersubjectivity was productive. Because each side believed that the other recognized the meaning of the relationship, each was willing to engage in cooperative actions that might not have been taken had either side recognized the extent of their differences.

Let me be clear at the outset what I am not arguing. I am not arguing that every misperception during détente produced cooperation. During the 1973 Arab-Israeli War, as I show later, some misperceptions contributed to conflict and others contributed to cooperation. Nor am I arguing that misperceptions, on balance, are more likely to produce cooperation than conflict. I suspect that most cases of both conflict and cooperation are produced, in part, by misperceptions. The balance does not play a role in the argument. My argument is that a specific set of misperceptions— a group of imagined intersubjective beliefs concerning détente—made cooperation possible during the 1970s.

I first outline Wendt's account of the relationship between rivalry and cooperation so as to draw a sharp line against theories that claim that shared ideas constitute cooperation. Then, I summarize the beliefs of US and Soviet decision makers to show that détente was premised on imagined intersubjectivity. Finally, I show how imagined intersubjectivity enhanced the prospects for the Basic Principles agreement and the resolution of the 1973 Arab-Israeli War.

A brief digression is warranted to explain the relationship of this chapter to its successors. This chapter traces the importance of imagined intersubjectivity at the macrolevel; chapter 3 discusses the microlevel by examining the specific issues at play in the negotiation of the ABM Treaty; and chapter 4 shows that variation on the independent variable— decision makers' beliefs—alters the prospects for cooperation by tracing the causes of the decline of détente and evaluating alternative explanations. Whereas the next chapter relies heavily on archival documents, this chapter relies more heavily on secondary sources. The major empirical claim concerning different interpretations of détente is documented by a number of historians and political scientists and is consistent with firsthand accounts.[3] In addition, when major turning points are discussed or there is tension in secondary source material, I rely on archival documents. In the effort to cover such a long period in detail, I have been forced to rely primarily on secondary sources, but the consensus adds weight to each author's claims.

Constructivist Explanations of Détente

While few constructivist scholars have examined superpower relations during détente, it is an exemplary case to detect the causes of a shift from enmity to rivalry, the sort of shift that lies at the heart of Wendt's seminal *Social Theory of International Politics*.[4] Wendt argues that shared ideas make cooperative (or conflictual) behavior possible by creating social regularities that enable states to pursue specific patterns of behavior.[5] In the case of enmity, the international system is characterized by a culture that prescribes behavioral rules, such as nonrecognition of perceived enemies and prescribing no limits on violence, that are constitutive of conflict.[6] In a culture of rivalry, which is exemplified by détente, shared ideas constitute the social basis for cooperation.[7] Rivals differ from enemies in that rivals do not believe others will attempt to conquer or dominant them.[8] Rivals accept, at least in principle, that opponents have legitimate interests within their borders, are sovereign, and therefore will not engage in unlimited violence to destroy them. When states accept others' sovereignty, there are fewer security fears; this enables states to pursue cooperative gains because there are socially recognized limits on the use of violence.[9] A shift in international culture from enmity to rivalry, in sum, enables cooperation.

At first glance, détente appears to bear out Wendt's insight. Cooperation during the early 1970s was an emerging pattern. Between 1969 and 1980, the United States and the Soviet Union met at five summits, arranged eleven bilateral commissions, and reached 150 agreements.[10] The ABM Treaty, often referred to as the most important arms control treaty in history, was the crown jewel of the first SALT round. This was quickly followed by the limitation of offensive weapons and the agreed code of conduct in the BPA. Further, Nixon and Brezhnev established a joint commercial commission and agreed to enhance cooperation in science and technology, medicine, public health, the environment, space, and the avoidance of naval accidents.[11] At a second summit, the Agreement on the Prevention of Nuclear War was signed, and four joint committees were established related to oceanography, transportation, agriculture, and atomic energy. The superpowers also agreed to expand air service, cultural and scientific exchanges, and to establish a joint chamber of commerce.

This pattern of cooperation was accompanied by a shift in the super-powers' perceptions of each other. In 1973, Brezhnev declared, to a group of American businessmen no less, that the Cold War was over. Two days later, in a televised address to American viewers, Brezhnev remarked, "Mankind has outgrown the rigid 'Cold War' armor which it was once forced to wear."[12] The Nixon administration's rhetoric closely paralleled the Soviet attitude. In his inaugural address, President Nixon made his intentions dramatically clear: "And now to the leaders of the Communist world, we say: After an era of confrontation, the time has come for an era of negotiation."[13]

During détente, US public opinion regarded the Soviet Union more positively than at any other time during the Cold War. In 1973, 45 per-cent of the public had a favorable impression of the Soviet Union. In con-trast, this shrank to only 13 percent in 1980, when the "second Cold War" began.[14] The Soviet Union experienced a similar shift. At the Twenty-Fourth Congress of the Communist Party in 1971, the ideological content of Brezhnev's speech was toned down, and class antagonisms were hardly mentioned in his discussion of superpower relations.[15] The Soviet leader-ship began to prepare its public for détente. Politburo members' speeches changed remarkably: the theme of détente was referenced 7,075 times between 1972 and 1979, compared with only 217 references to class strug-gle.[16] Beyond the politburo, the tone of Soviet publications shifted, with a dramatic move toward favoring improved relations.[17]

The elements of rivalry highlighted by Wendt were emphasized by the leadership in Washington and Moscow. Before Nixon entered office few in power in the United States believed that the Soviet Union was willing to respect US sovereignty or that it would limit its use of violence. In 1967 Nixon himself promoted the image of a Soviet Union bent on the destruc-tion of the United States: peace with the Soviets was unlikely "until they give up their goal of world conquest."[18] By 1969 Nixon's tone had changed in his public speeches and private correspondence. No longer did he use the language of enmity to describe the Soviet Union; instead, it became an actor with legitimate interests. Writing to his secretary of defense, Melvin Laird, shortly after taking office, Nixon explained that the basis of rela-tions "is a mutual recognition of our vital interests. We must recognize that the Soviet Union has interests; in the present circumstances we cannot but take account of them in defining our own."[19] This was the cornerstone of the era of negotiation. The Soviet Union had reached the status of a world power, and, to ensure peace, the United States would have to take account of it when conducting foreign policy.[20] The superpowers must become rivals, not enemies.

Détente is a likely case for constructivist theories that highlight the importance of shared ideas. There is a shift from a culture of enmity, in which the parties do not believe that the other respects its sovereignty, its interests, or that it will restrict its use of violence, to a culture of rivalry, in which cooperation becomes possible. The intuitive appeal of arguments premised on international cultures is that they capture the underlying deep ideational changes that appear to be necessary for success in changing long-standing patterns of foreign relations. It is certainly plausible that détente was premised on new ideas and that these ideas were shared. Indeed, in the 1970s, there was a buzz about the sudden bridging of worlds occurring in the wake of the Vietnam War, the surge in public support for the Soviet Union in the United States, and the softening Soviet tone concerning the United States. In fact, I believe that a constructivist study that seeks to understand the consequences of ideational change from the late 1960s through the 1970s would largely follow the line of argument pursued here thus far.

But this type of constructivist account is only partly right. On the one hand, the shift from enmity to rivalry was important for cooperation. This confirms the claim that anarchy is "an empty vessel and has no intrinsic logic; anarchies only acquire a logic as a function of the structure of what we put inside them."[21] During détente, factors other than material ones mattered, and, in particular, the death of enmity mattered quite a bit.[22]

Rivalry, however, is too ambiguous a notion to provide the full ideational basis for cooperation. Two "best friends" might have very different understandings about what is required to be friends, believing that because they call themselves best friends, the other consents to a specific set of responsibilities. This relationship might quickly degenerate into rivalry or even enmity if the two discover that what each meant by friendship— the content of the responsibilities—is different. Not knowing can bring the bliss of friendship, but only to the happily ignorant.[23] Similarly, "rivalry" is an empty term, devoid of a concrete set of practices necessary to sustain a pattern of relations. Rivals, with two very different conceptions of the rules of the rivalry such as the disparate conceptions held during détente, may quickly degenerate into enemies. Perhaps there was no bliss in becoming rivals during détente, but at least there was a sense of relief that enmity had been overcome, a collective exhale as everyone pulled back from the brink. During détente, this breath was possible only because it was premised on a misunderstanding, a false intersubjective belief.

One objection to this characterization of Wendt's theory is that it conflates dyadic with systemic analysis. Wendt argues that the international system as a whole can be characterized through patterns of enmity, rivalry, or friendship. By concentrating on dyads, one risks missing the systemic effects. While Wendt focuses on systemic effects, however, he also argues that subjective beliefs about self and other—bilateral relationships—are "a micro-foundation for cultural forms."[24] Once many bilateral relationships shift toward rivalry, only then do macrocultural roles supervene on states' individual beliefs. Until then, bilateral relationships matter.[25]

Imagined Intersubjectivity and Détente

In the 1970s, détente referred to a diverse set of policies pursued by the United States, the Soviet Union, and Germany.[26] In diplomatic parlance, détente, or the Russian term *razryadka*, means a relaxation of tensions. Despite its use to describe the policy of all three governments, the term meant different things to each. This section shows that the overarching relationship between the United States and the Soviet Union was a FIB. The leadership of both the United States and the Soviet Union believed that their image of détente—their understanding of the meaning of the relationship—was shared. Both superpowers were wrong. This belief was premised on a misperception; neither party accurately understood the other's principles of détente (the values each side sought to realize from the relationship) nor their expectations for behavior (the policies the other would likely pursue). Imagined intersubjectivity, not mutual understanding, led to cooperation.

In this section, I show that the meaning of détente—how the rivalry was supposed to be conducted—was different for each superpower. The emergence of strategic parity was the event that triggered each side to rethink its pre-existing beliefs. The brute fact of strategic parity was common knowledge; what it meant for the relationship was not. The Nixon administration, in particular the president's influential aide Henry Kissinger,

TABLE 2.1. Summary of Beliefs Related to Détente

		Principles		Behavior	
	Military parity	Political parity	Linkage and threats	Safe Third World competition
United States	Yes	No	Yes	No
Soviet Union	Yes	Yes	No	Yes

continued to seek political dominance. Strategic parity had reshaped the means away from arms and toward diplomacy, but political dominance remained the end. The Soviets, in contrast, believed that by reshaping the means, strategic parity had changed the ends. Military parity meant the United States had been compelled to accept the Soviet Union as an equal meriting equal prestige and that it would no longer rely on linkages or threats or prevent the Soviets from enjoying influence in the Third World. Table 2.1 summarizes these differences.

To establish the value of the independent variable (the beliefs of actors), I analyze the beliefs of US and Soviet decision makers, their beliefs about the other side, and whether, if their beliefs differed, they were aware of those differences. If their beliefs differ in meaningful ways and they are unaware of those differences, then I classify the belief as a case of imagined intersubjectivity.

Military Parity

Détente began with a mutual recognition of the emergence of Soviet military and strategic parity with the United States. Brezhnev and others in the Soviet leadership, along with Nixon and Kissinger, accepted this fact.

The road to parity began in the mid-1960s when Leonid Brezhnev and Alexei Kosygin came to power in the Soviet Union. In response to the perceived Soviet failure during the Cuban Missile Crisis, as well as US interventions in Southeast Asia and the Dominican Republic, the Soviet Union began a rapid expansion of its strategic and conventional arsenals.[27] Statistics vary, but at a minimum from 1964 to 1970 the Soviet arsenal increased from 472 strategic weapons to 1,470, annual production of tanks grew by 25 percent, and their stock of armored vehicles almost doubled.[28]

The Soviets were intent on reaching military parity and pursued it despite the economic damage such a large diversion of resources to the military required. This formidable addition to Soviet military strength, especially in strategic weapons, reinforced in both the United States and the Soviet Union the belief in the importance of mutually assured destruction, the impossibility of winning a nuclear war.[29]

Brezhnev held a deep conviction that strategic parity meant that global war was unthinkable.[30] The horrors of the Second World War deeply impressed themselves on Brezhnev, who continually referred to the experience in foreign policy discussions. Soviet policy was geared toward ensuring that a world war would not recur and reducing the chances of nuclear conflict.[31] Military parity was a key step toward obtaining that goal. Raymond Garthoff's analysis of the reception of military parity in the Soviet Union during the period shows that its implications were widely shared and understood in the Soviet government.[32] At the Twenty-Fourth Party Congress in 1971, for example, Vladimir Semenov, the deputy foreign minister, remarked that "the political significance of a stable strategic balance is indisputable; it is the guarantee not only of the security of the two sides, but of international security as a whole," and "the existing military-strategic parity undoubtedly exerts a stabilizing effect on the international situation."[33] In the 1970s, Soviet strategic power grew enough that the Soviets did not need to be concerned about American strategic threats.

Not only did the Soviet leadership believe it had reached military parity but it believed (rightly) that the US foreign policy leadership also believed that parity had been reached. Soviet analysts noted that "by the beginning of the 1970s not only the fact of the absolute vulnerability of American territory, but also the inevitability of a crushing retaliatory strike if the United States delivered a nuclear missile strike against the USSR, had become completely evident to everyone in the American ruling class."[34] The Soviet Union knew that the Nixon administration knew that the Soviet buildup meant that "winning" a nuclear war was impossible.

The Soviets were right that strategic parity was common knowledge. Nixon and Kissinger knew the strategic world they met on entering office was significantly different from that which greeted their predecessors in the mid-1960s. By 1969, the Soviet Union had reached, or would soon reach, strategic parity. In the United States, the media reported almost weekly stories warning that the Soviets were closing the missile gap and might soon move ahead of the United States.[35] This became a campaign issue in the Nixon-Humphrey contest as Nixon pledged to prevent the Soviets from closing the gap.[36] If American decline is the catch phrase in the foreign policy community today, parity was the buzzword in the late 1960s and early 1970s.[37]

Nixon and Kissinger understood it would be impossible to restore nuclear superiority over the Soviet Union. This led to a drastic shift from "superiority" to "sufficiency" as the foundation of US defense policy.[38] Sufficiency was intended as a middle position between deterrence and dominance. Dominance was unobtainable and costly: the effort would lead to arms races, instability, and perhaps war. At the same time, relying on assured destruction was insufficient because it limited military options to retaliation against civilian targets. In the effort to restore flexibility to US strategic policy, the doctrine of sufficiency meant the United States should be able to strike civilian targets, military assets, or both, but without the capacity to overwhelm the Soviet nuclear arsenal.[39] Like the Soviets, Nixon's team understood that establishing strategic dominance was impossible and that parity had set in.[40] The existence of strategic parity was common knowledge. However, what parity *meant* was not.

Principle: Political Parity

In the previous chapter, I divided public beliefs into two component parts: beliefs about principles (reasons) for action and beliefs about expectations for behavior. The United States and Soviet Union unknowingly held different principles for cooperating as well as different expectations for behavior.

The superpowers' reasons for cooperation relate to their views on political parity; the principles of détente were not shared because each side thought the reason for cooperation implicated political equality differently. The Soviet view was that détente meant *the United States had accepted the Soviet Union as a political equal*, whereas the American understanding was that through negotiations détente was *a competition for political supremacy with limited risks*. The Soviet Union acted as if Nixon and Kissinger had accepted political equality; the United States acted as if Brezhnev knew that there was a continued geopolitical contest for political supremacy.

From the Soviet perspective, détente was, in large part, a way to convert Soviet strategic parity into political parity.[41] Brezhnev and others believed that the Soviet Union had suffered a significant decline in prestige under Nikita Khrushchev. The emerging Brezhnev clique was concerned that Khrushchev's reckless conduct, especially during the Cuban Missile Crisis, unnecessarily risked war and damaged Soviet prestige.[42] In the meetings in which the leadership overthrew Khrushchev, they lectured him for hours on the damage he had done to the Soviet image. The leadership shared the belief that Khrushchev had attempted to bluff from a position of weakness, rather than establishing a position of strength, and that the bluff was called.

The Soviet weapons buildup in the mid-1960s and early 1970s was therefore intended to secure more than Soviet safety. The aim of this buildup was not to generate a first-strike capability, as many US conservatives supposed, but to obtain political equality. As Melvyn Leffler, a noted Cold War historian, explains, "they yearned for American respect, despised America's strength, and demanded equal security."[43] Khrushchev's failures were compounded by those of his successors later in the 1960s, which included the failure of Soviet clients to win a war against Israel in 1967 and the slaughter of Communists in Indonesia. The Soviets decided to build their way out of the morass of US global dominance.

As Soviet military power grew, the Brezhnev leadership expected political parity. At least by 1968, with the Soviet intervention during the Prague Spring, Soviet leaders began to comment on their renewed political prestige and its relationship to military parity. The Soviet Union believed the United States had meddled in Czechoslovakia, and the lack of a strong US reaction to the Soviet intervention was attributed to mounting Soviet military and political strength.[44] Andrei Gromyko, the Soviet foreign minister, remarked that before the Prague Spring, "the politburo had to think carefully time and again, before taking any foreign policy step—What would the US do? What would France do? This period is over. . . . Whatever noise they can make, the new correlation of forces is such that they no longer dare to move against us."[45]

Political parity was the Soviet principle for cooperation during détente. Military parity meant that the United States could no longer negotiate from "positions of strength" and the Soviet Union could enjoy influence in the periphery and an equal seat at negotiations.[46] The Soviets pursued détente to help "manage the transition of the *United States* into a changing world, one no longer marked by American predominance but by a political parity of the Soviet Union with the United States that matched their military parity."[47] In short, equal power should translate into equal prestige.

Not only were the Soviets convinced that political parity was achievable, but they also believed the United States was prepared, however reluctantly, to accept it. Brezhnev and others believed military parity had compelled the Nixon administration to accept political equality. For this reason, they frequently discussed peace in militant terms: "the Soviet view was that a 'struggle to *compel*' the imperialists to accept peaceful coexistence was required."[48] For example, arms control talks were designed to compel the United States to negotiate from a place of equal standing, not from a position of strength.[49]

Unsurprisingly, the Soviets were wrong to assume that the United States was ready to cede political equality. For the Nixon administration, military parity did not mean equality but rigidity. Kissinger thought a bipolar system turned international politics into a zero-sum game.[50] In a nuclear world, if every issue is a zero-sum issue and thus matters to the overall strategic balance, then every issue is related to the prospects for survival. The Nixon team's approach to foreign policy was designed to find a way of moving in a world of strategic bipolarity, to reinstate creativity in a world that otherwise might remain static. A creative foreign policy would provide the United States with the diplomatic tools to retain political dominance in a world of strategic parity.

The solution to the dangers of military bipolarity was suggested by the emergence of political multipolarity. For Nixon and Kissinger, political multipolarity emerged during the Kennedy and Johnson administrations because other states, concerned about their own security, were driven to seek agreements with both superpowers to enhance their status and ensure their security.[51] This created flexibility because the balance of power might be managed through creative diplomacy, that is, through forming alliances with former enemies, such as China. Kissinger intended to rely on this flexibility to increase US political power.[52]

The trick was to increase US influence without alienating the Soviet Union. Kissinger analyzed this problem extensively before entering office. He begins his study of nineteenth-century European diplomacy, *A World Restored*, by making a distinction between legitimate and revolutionary international orders. States in a legitimate international order are satisfied because every state accepts certain rules of the game for the resolution of conflicts. As Kissinger explained, "diplomacy, in the classic sense, the adjustment of differences through negotiation, is possible only in 'legitimate' international orders" because every state has a stake in the present international system. Revolutionary international orders, by contrast, are systems in which one or more states want to reinvent the "system itself." In a revolutionary system "only absolute security—the neutralization of the opponent—is considered a sufficient guarantee, and thus the desire of one power for absolute security means absolute insecurity for all others. Diplomacy, the art of restraining the exercise of power, cannot function in such an environment."[53]

Kissinger was concerned that continued competition without a strategy for managing the Soviet rise to power risked alienating the Soviet Union, turning it into a revolutionary power.[54] The Soviet rise to parity needed to be managed, ensuring that the Soviets were satisfied while US political dominance was maintained. "Nixon and Kissinger were clear about the meaning attached to détente," according to the noted historian John Lewis Gaddis. The Nixon administration "viewed it as yet another in a long series of attempts to 'contain' the power and influence of the USSR, but one based on a new combination of pressures and inducements that would, if successful, convince Kremlin leaders that it was in their country's interest to be 'contained.' "[55] Linkages and threats, I suggest later, were the tools to maintain dominance.

The differences between the US and Soviet views are, in retrospect, quite apparent. But in the confusion of the 1970s, policymakers on both sides believed they fundamentally understood the other's worldview. The Soviet Union believed that a world of political equality was developing and that the Nixon administration accepted it. As Garthoff summarizes, the Soviet Union believed that "American acceptance of parity meant a readiness to accept a degree of shared and equal power by the two superpowers, which carried implications of cooperation—or even condominium—in avoiding challenges to each other's vital interests, even while competing."[56] In the United States, the Nixon administration believed that Brezhnev had accepted the dangers of mutually assured destruction and prepared to enter a competitive period of negotiations in a multipolar world. Kissinger and Nixon did not understand the Soviet motivation; they believed the Soviet Union, like the United States, was motivated by the desire to seek unilateral and relative political advantages and assumed the Soviets understood that the United States would not willingly cede political equality.

These two disparate understandings of the effect of cooperation on political parity betray the lack of intersubjective agreement on the principles that would guide the superpower relations during détente. The aims of each—the purposes of cooperation—were different. These misunderstandings over principle imply that the agreement was based on a false intersubjective belief. I have described two types of false intersubjective beliefs that contain disagreements over principles: functional incompletely theorized agreements and imagined intersubjectivity. If these differences over the principles of détente led to differences in the concrete sets of policies that each state expected the other to pursue, then the relationship is characterized as imagined intersubjectivity.

Behavior: Linkages and Threats

The superpowers' differences over détente's principle—political parity—led them to pursue and to expect different patterns of behavior. In particular, this was manifested in differences in the negotiation strategies each expected the other to pursue, addressed here, and the relationship of the superpower conflict to the Third World, discussed in the next section. Kissinger sought to use his toolkit for détente—linkages and threats—to obtain political dominance over the Soviet Union. By contrast, the Soviet Union expected negotiations to proceed without linkages or threats, tools used to undermine political parity by forming negotiating advantages. These disparate expectations of behavior followed from the two states' different formulations of détente's principles. In the context of negotiations over the Basic Principles agreement and the 1973 Arab-Israeli War I flesh out the details, but here I focus on the abstract picture.

The differences in the parties' views of political equality and linkages are subtle, so taking a brief bird's-eye view is helpful. Figure 2.1 describes the differences in the US and Soviet expectations for negotiations in an analytic way. The more nuanced understanding in both capitals reflects the underlying logic. The line in figure 2.1 represents all of the cooperative arrangements that realize maximum gains within an issue area (the Pareto frontier).[57] The Soviets "knew," and "knew" that the Americans "knew," that cooperation implied mutual gains. Not cooperating in a world of strategic parity meant a dangerous competition that damaged both parties' interests. Brezhnev believed that the United States' and Soviet Union's equal

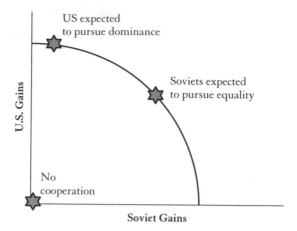

Figure 2.1. US and Soviet expectations for bargaining strategies

strategic power meant that they should cooperate in a way that took each other's interests mutually into account (the midpoint of the arc). Attempts to obtain more favorable bargains—by trying to obtain leverage or making threats—risked undermining the gains from cooperation. The United States also thought that cooperation was mutually beneficial. The Nixon administration, however, tried to steer cooperation toward arrangements that benefited US political interests more than Soviet interests (moving the agreement point as far up figure 2.1 as possible). Kissinger, in particular, thought that the Soviets were engaged in negotiating behavior to pursue the same strategy, trying to move the agreement point as far right as they could. The United States, in short, intended to use issue linkages to reap higher political gains than the Soviet Union, whereas the Soviet Union expected issues to be discussed in isolation from one another, ensuring equality.[58]

The Nixon administration sought to use issue linkages to maintain US political supremacy. Shortly after he entered office, Nixon announced his intention to link progress with the Soviet Union in some areas to progress in others.[59] This strategy of linking negotiations was the cornerstone of his Soviet policy. As Nixon recalled:

> Since US-Soviet interests as the world's two competing superpowers were
> so widespread and overlapping, it was unrealistic to separate or compart-
> mentalize areas of concern. Therefore we decided to link progress in such

areas of Soviet concern as strategic arms limitation and increased trade with progress in areas that were important to us—Vietnam, the Mideast, and Berlin. This concept became known as linkage.[60]

Linkage, for the Nixon administration, was détente—it enabled the United States and the Soviet Union to negotiate and, through negotiation, to reach agreements that led to common gains. Linkages were intended to manage the Soviet rise to power, giving them a stake in the status quo, preventing them from becoming a revolutionary power. Linkage meant granting the Soviets some increased influence and explicit demonstrations of respect without sacrificing US dominance. This was the meaning of the "era of negotiation"—the use of linkage and diplomacy to ensure political superiority.[61]

The Nixon administration thought and acted in these terms.[62] On the one hand, détente was intended to enhance mutual gains. By working together, the United States and the Soviet Union could obtain gains that were not possible without cooperation.[63] More important, the United States sought to use linkages to enhance US power without alienating the Soviet Union. While both parties would benefit from cooperation, the United States should always benefit more by negotiating from positions of strength. The Soviets would gain more from cooperating than not cooperating, but always less than the United States. Kissinger intended "to build the Soviet stake in maintaining cooperative relationships and in eschewing confrontations that would imperil or disrupt them."[64] It was a strategy of competitive coexistence, one that sought to contain Soviet power without alienating it. According to Garthoff, "Détente was expected to provide leverage for managing the emergence of Soviet power, and in doing so would draw the Soviet Union into de facto acceptance of the existing world order."[65] It was in this context that seemingly unimportant agreements, such as joint space missions, commerce commissions, technical exchanges, and cultural programs mattered. Deborah Welch Larson suggests that these agreements added up, albeit in small increments, on a balance sheet that the Soviets would see as a cost if they backed out of détente to pursue a revolutionary foreign policy.[66] Each link drove another Soviet stake into the existing order that would need to be pulled up to pursue a belligerent policy.[67]

The desire for unilateral gains through negotiation became most apparent when Nixon and Kissinger linked threats to expected gains. By threatening no cooperation, Kissinger intended to hold hostage all of the gains from cooperation. This darker element was expressed in a dangerous pattern of brinksmanship. In 1969, Nixon secretly conducted strategic exercises designed to force the Soviets into dealing on North Vietnam. Brezhnev resented the US threats, and the linkage failed.[68] Similarly, Nixon raised the readiness level of US nuclear forces in October 1973 to convince the Soviets not to intervene to save the Egyptian Third Army during the October War.[69] In both cases, the United States threatened to pursue a strategy of confrontation rather than cooperation, potentially undermining mutual gains in order to obtain favorable settlements. These are only two dramatic episodes in which the administration tried to obtain increased political influence with the threat of upsetting the process of cooperation. Kissinger expected the Soviet Union to understand the superpower game in the same way as he did. He expected the Soviets to use negotiations to obtain unilateral advantages and did not understand that the Soviet belief that political equality was inevitable led them to expect different negotiation strategies.

The Soviet leadership had a fundamentally different understanding of appropriate negotiating behavior. Because Soviet foreign policy emphasized equality instead of dominance, negotiations should proceed with the parties on an equal footing, in specific areas (not linked complexes of issues), where mutual gains were possible. The Soviet Union, therefore, sought negotiations that were independent of other issue areas, with one set of negotiations on trade, another on arms control, and another on science.[70] They rejected attempts to link issues or to create positions of strength by relying on bargaining advantages.[71] Even within an issue area, the Soviets tried to delink issues, negotiating a treaty on freezing offensive weapons separately from defensive weapons or insulating concerns over the emigration of Russian Jews from the rest of the bilateral relationship.

Avoiding a return to positions-of-strength diplomacy was central to the Soviet image of détente. A brief glance at the leading Soviet foreign policy journals bears out the negative connotations given to the US position. Between 1969 and 1979, *International Affairs*—the journal of the ministry of foreign affairs—published at least eighty-two articles that discussed "positions of strength" and détente. The Soviet press more widely had countless more. The Soviets had always believed that building positions of strength was dangerous. In the 1960s, before détente, the United States,

West Germany, and NATO in general were accused of trying to obtain leverage or positions of strength over the Soviet Union by fomenting arms races and developing alliances. After détente, the United States was described as having returned to this position.[72] Only during détente itself was the United States usually described as having been forced to negotiate on an equal footing.

Furthermore, unlike in the Khrushchev era, during détente the Soviet Union did not rely on nuclear threats, and they were puzzled by US threats. There is no evidence they used perceived leverage in Vietnam to obtain beneficial deals from the United States in other areas or that they threatened increased competition on the periphery to win favorable trade terms. Brezhnev believed the United States recognized that parity meant equality in negotiations and did not expect US policy to continue to rely on linkages. Military parity, in the words of one Soviet commentator, had "knocked the imperialists 'policy of strength' off its very foundation."[73]

As the United States and the Soviet Union moved to negotiate with each other, neither had its eyes wide open. Kissinger thought the Soviet Union would and did attempt to make unilateral gains through negotiations. Brezhnev believed his relationship with the Nixon administration portended some measure of equality in negotiations. One reason for this misperception may have been that public statements made by the Nixon administration said that it would not pursue linkages.[74] Regardless, Brezhnev interpreted Kissinger and Nixon's behavior through this lens. Neither came to grips with the position of the other; neither understood that, in the future, their behavior would diverge remarkably.

Behavior: The Third World

The Nixon administration's and the Brezhnev politburo's expectations about each other's conduct in the Third World also differed. For Nixon and Kissinger, détente meant continued geopolitical competition in the Third World and the use of linkages and threats to reduce Soviet influence. For the Soviets, détente meant the superpowers would work cooperatively to resolve conflicts that risked undermining US-Soviet relations and that Soviet political prestige would be considered equal in relation to global settlements.

The Soviet attainment of military parity had important political consequences for how the Soviets expected to be treated in the Third World.

Czechoslovakia was the first instance of a trend in which the overcoming of strategic inferiority meant that the Soviet Union had become a global power. Brezhnev, especially after Nixon's hands-off approach in Eastern Europe and the continued US entanglement in Vietnam, believed he had secured the safety of Soviet competition with the United States in the Third World in "national liberation movements." Brezhnev believed military parity meant political parity in terms of global influence.[75] The United States could not, and should not, hold US-Soviet relations hostage to prevent Soviet involvement in peripheral conflicts where Soviet interests were at stake.

During the 1970s, the Soviet Union increased its global influence.[76] The 1970s saw a global quest for influence, with sub-Saharan Africa playing as important a role as Southeast Asia and the Middle East. The competition in the Third World, which was a corollary of peaceful coexistence between the superpowers, meant that Soviet influence could safely increase. Indeed, from the intervention in Angola to less direct entanglements, the Brezhnev leadership believed that Soviet assertiveness on the periphery risked neither damaging US-Soviet relations nor escalation.[77] Robert Kaiser, the *Washington Post* correspondent in Moscow during the period, described the Soviet attitude: "The idea that the United States and Soviet Union could someday share responsibility for managing the entire world, perhaps even divide it up between them, appeals enormously to Soviet leaders. Originally, détente looked in Moscow like a first step toward just such an arrangement."[78]

The Nixon administration did not understand the Soviet view of the Third World. It did not intend to allow the Soviet Union to pursue increased global influence, at least not without a challenge. "In retrospect, the Soviets were wrong in their evaluation that the United States was ready to accept the changed correlation of forces as they appeared to Soviet leaders in the early 1970s," according to Garthoff. Kissinger actively attempted to reduce Soviet influence, refusing to acknowledge that his efforts risked undermining détente; he continually attempted to use carrots and sticks to limit Soviet influence in the Middle East, Angola, the Horn of Africa, and elsewhere. For Kissinger, linkages were compatible with détente, not with increased Soviet influence. Garthoff continues, "The Soviet leaders harbored illusions not only that the United States was ready to accept changes in the Third World but, even more, that it would regard active Soviet support for 'progressive' changes in the Third World as compatible with Soviet-American détente."[79] This false Soviet optimism, that the United States had accepted political parity, translated into a false optimism that the United States anticipated and would not attempt to curtail increased Soviet influence across the Third World.

These differences in how the two sides viewed competition in the Third World affected US-Soviet relations and had practical consequences. Later in this chapter I discuss these differences in relation to the 1973 Arab-Israeli War. However, the importance of this difference is not limited to the Middle East. For example, in 1976, Kissinger was concerned about growing Soviet influence in Angola. He suggested to Brezhnev that Angola was a dangerous situation that, if left unresolved, would sour US-Soviet relations. This was not a subtle threat; he linked Soviet policy in Africa with arms control, threatening to end cooperation in areas where mutual gains were being made to obtain unilateral advantages in other issue areas. Brezhnev resisted connecting Angola to SALT, noting that he did not believe the United States would risk a war over Angola. Brezhnev separated the issues, asking, "Are we here to discuss SALT? Or Angola?"[80] Brezhnev believed that the United States had accepted Soviet influence broadly enough to ensure that Soviet participation in peripheral conflicts did not risk damaging détente. The same sort of episode repeated itself throughout the 1970s, especially in the case of the Ogaden War between Ethiopia and Somalia, in which the Carter administration, taking a page from Nixon's team, attempted to link SALT to Soviet influence in the Horn of Africa, with much the same result.

Summary of Beliefs

The beliefs of Soviet and US decision makers constituted a FIB. The principles that guided US and Soviet foreign policy (their views on political parity) were not intersubjective, nor did the parties understand the differences between their positions. Consequently, both were unjustifiably confident that they understood the foreign policy of the other. Both mistakenly believed they could predict the types of actions the other would pursue in negotiations and in the quest for global influence.

This is an example of imagined intersubjectivity: Kissinger, Nixon, and Brezhnev believed they were engaged in an intersubjective relationship in which they understood the principles that guided the other power's foreign policy and could predict what types of behavior would stem from that principled understanding. However, they were wrong. The leadership of each superpower held an idiosyncratic view that was read into the position of the other power, creating a mirror image of their beliefs in their opponent.

Imagined Intersubjectivity and Two Cases of Cooperation

I have argued that Soviet and American understandings of détente were premised on imagined intersubjectivity. Here I show how these misunderstandings did not stand in the way of cooperation but were integral to it. The confusion over détente led to the successful conclusion of the BPA in 1972 and contributed to crisis management during the Arab-Israeli War in October 1973. In both cases, the parties cooperated, in part, because they believed the other agreed to the rules of the superpower rivalry. In both cases, the Soviet Union thought that the United States had accepted it as a political equal and was willing to cooperate because this guaranteed equal access to political power. By contrast, the United States thought that because of strategic parity, the Soviet Union was willing to let complex negotiations, including threats and incentives, decide their respective political status, with the inevitable result that the United States would retain political dominance over the Soviet Union, particularly in the Middle East.

The BPA and the 1973 Arab-Israeli War are examples of two classes of agreements. The BPA is an example of a broad philosophical agreement.[81] The BPA sought to lay out what détente meant, what each party expected of the other in the broadest sense, and to lay the groundwork for cooperation. Broad philosophical agreements, such as the BPA, should be easy cases for constructivist theories because actors are intentionally trying to develop an explicit account of their relationship. This broad agreement is theoretically interesting because it shows that FIBs can explain agreements in which actors believe they are explicitly codifying an intersubjective set of rules. That is, even when actors try to reduce misperceptions and create intersubjective rules of the road, they might come up far short of their goal because of a false confidence in mutual understanding—imagined intersubjectivity.

In contrast, attempts at cooperation during the 1973 Arab-Israeli War, including Brezhnev's efforts to prevent war and pass ceasefire resolutions, are examples of specific agreements. Imagined intersubjectivity not only plays a role in the broad contours of the relationship but in agreements that are specific, suggesting concrete policies and expectations for specific future conduct. The ability of imagined intersubjectivity to explain both classes of agreements shows the myriad ways in which unshared ideas can constitute cooperation.

The Basic Principles Agreement

Reciprocal misunderstandings were enshrined in the Basic Principles agreement, signed in Moscow in 1972. The BPA is an interesting case because it shows how two rivals can agree to two different sets of rules to rivalry without realizing it. An analysis of the BPA is a particularly important empirical test for the comparative role of intersubjectivity and false intersubjective beliefs in détente. During the BPA negotiations, the central issue was what the roles of the superpowers would be vis-à-vis each other and the world. It is, therefore, a likely case in which an intersubjective understanding of rivalry could develop. The negotiating history of the BPA is not long, and the brief account that follows agrees with the consensus of historians and political scientists as to the misperceptions that were instrumental to the agreement.

The Basic Principles agreement was signed at the 1972 summit in Moscow. Anatoly Dobrynin, the Soviet ambassador to Washington, raised the possibility of a BPA with Kissinger in early 1971. The Soviets had already signed similar declarations of principles in the preceding years with France and Turkey, and reached similar agreements with Canada and Germany.[82] The aim of each of these agreements—including the agreement with the United States—was to provide ground rules for political and military competition, create mechanisms for consultation in crises, and highlight the importance of cooperation.[83] In one of their first meetings, Brezhnev described the BPA as a "very great achievement," remarking to Nixon that it was "the most important document" that they would sign at their summit.[84] During the BPA's negotiation, Brezhnev was explicit. He wanted no room for confusion in the document. He told Kissinger that even a misplaced comma might cause confusion, using a Russian anecdote about a confusing comma that made a tsar's order in a capital case obscure.[85] After the agreement was signed, the United States and the Soviet Union would both point to it as a clear explanation of the ground rules for competition. As confrontation replaced cooperation later in the decade both would cite the BPA as providing clear norms that the other had violated. Was the BPA a product of intersubjectivity, providing a route from enmity to rivalry? Or was it the product of imagined intersubjectivity?

Every historian and political scientist who has discussed the BPA has reached the same conclusion: the BPA meant different things to each superpower. The Soviets wrote the first article of the agreement, which unsurprisingly reflected the Soviet understanding of the political principles and expected behavior guiding détente. The Americans wrote the second article, which also unsurprisingly reflected the American understanding of the principles and expected behavior underwriting détente.

The first article highlighted the three elements of the Soviet understanding of détente. It states that there is a "common determination that in the nuclear age there is no alternative to conducting mutual relations on the basis of peaceful coexistence. Differences in ideology and in the social systems of the US and the USSR are not obstacles to the bilateral principles of sovereignty, equality, noninterference in internal affairs, and mutual advantage."[86] This "had special significance for Soviet leaders," explains Alexander George, because it was "an acknowledgement by the United States that Soviet achievement of strategic military parity entitled the Soviet Union to be treated by the United States as a political-diplomatic equal as well."[87] The Soviets also believed that the first article suggested that neither superpower would use linkages to negotiate from positions of strength by promising that sovereignty and equality were the cornerstones of the relationship. Moreover, the first article implied that the Soviets could safely support national liberation movements—the ideological element of the superpower struggle—and explicitly claimed that this would not affect bilateral relations.[88] The first article thereby tacitly approved the Soviet doctrine of "peaceful coexistence," permitting Soviet influence in the Third World.[89]

The second article, drafted by Kissinger, reflected the American understanding:

> The USA and the USSR attach major importance to preventing the development of situations capable of causing a dangerous exacerbation of their

relations. Therefore, they will do their utmost to avoid military confrontations and to prevent the outbreak of nuclear war. They will always exercise restraint in their mutual relations, and will be prepared to negotiate and settle differences by peaceful means. Discussions and negotiations on outstanding issues will be conducted in a spirit of reciprocity, mutual accommodation and mutual benefit.[90]

The second article is significantly different from the first. The second article makes no reference to political equality, sovereignty, or noninterference, the Soviet principles of détente. It highlighted reciprocity—the linking of issues in a tit-for-tat way—instead of mutual advantage, thus approximating the spirit of linkage. Perhaps most important, the second article suggested a different approach to the Third World. The superpowers should prevent dangerous situations from erupting that might risk souring US-Soviet relations. As noted earlier, for Kissinger, this implied that Soviet attempts to aid progressive struggles would damage relations.

There are two reasons for these ambiguities. Procedurally, the successive drafting of the proposal, with the Soviets taking the lead on the first article and Kissinger on the second, is a problematic method of developing an agreement. Moreover, the parties were overconfident that a mutual understanding had been reached. Garthoff, who was a participant at the summit, notes that "there was too little attempt at the time and later to understand the views of the other side and to seek to reconcile, or at least identify, differences in understanding."[91]

Not only did this document rely on two different meanings, but its importance was different for each party. For Brezhnev, the agreement was fundamentally important. Brezhnev described it as "the most important document" to be signed at the summit, making it more important than the ABM Treaty.[92] The recognition of political equality was enshrined in the document and signified the drastic change that the Soviets felt had accompanied the achievement of parity—a goal sought since the founding of the Soviet Union.[93] One cannot overstate the degree of enthusiasm with which the BPA was greeted in the Soviet Union. Half of the department involved in drafting the language of the BPA was given an immediate merit promotion, and media accounts and public statements focused heavily on the BPA.[94] It was publicly touted as evidence that the United States accepted parity and equal security and had placed US-Soviet relations into a juridical setting; peaceful coexistence had been enshrined in international law.

For Nixon and Kissinger the agreement was less important. Nixon, who played no role in negotiating the document and was only sparingly briefed on it, may never have read the short agreement.[95] When the BPA was first raised by Dobrynin before the summit, Kissinger did not find it important enough to even record in his memorandum of the meeting.[96] The entire US negotiating effort entailed Kissinger and a few of his staff spending only a few hours going over the Soviet draft. Kissinger's assessment was that "if any of these principles is flouted, we will not be able to wave a piece of paper and insist that the illegality of the procedure will, in itself, prevent its being carried out."[97]

The result was not an agreement on a "roadmap," as Kissinger and Nixon later publicly claimed, nor did the BPA establish a successful juridical foundation for international relations, as many Soviet commentators thought. The BPA was, in Alexander George's terms, a "pseudoagreement": an agreement that prevented the parties from understanding the extent of their disagreement. George explains that "it gave an erroneous impression that the United States and the Soviets were in substantial agreement on the rules of the game and the restraints to be observed in their competition in third areas."[98] However, this did not make the agreement unimportant; when these differences became known, as the 1970s moved along, "this ambiguity later contributed to the unraveling of détente, as each side accused the other of violating its conception of the Basic Principles Agreement."[99]

The BPA is theoretically fascinating because it shows that FIBs can occur even when two parties sign a piece of paper that is intended to document a change in international norms, that is, a document intended to produce an intersubjective agreement concerning either a roadmap or a legalistic basis for understanding great power relations. This document preserved a misunderstanding, thus enshrining imagined intersubjectivity in international law. The actors cooperated because of a misunderstanding, a false intersubjective belief: imagined intersubjectivity. The Basic Principles agreement is a hard case for a theory of FIBs to explain. The parties sought to outline the basis of their intersubjective relationship, a rarity in great power politics. The actual agreement, however, required little policy coordination.

The 1973 Arab-Israeli War

The first dramatic challenge to the superpowers' ability to moderate their competition occurred during the Arab-Israeli War in 1973.[100] Egypt and Syria, two Soviet clients, along with limited assistance from Jordan, Saudi Arabia, and others, launched the war against Israel on the Jewish holiday of Yom Kippur. The attack, which largely took Israel and the United States by surprise, led to one of the tensest standoffs of the 1970s.

Decision makers thought the conflict had enormously high stakes. On the one hand, both superpowers worried that the failure of a client might undermine the credibility of its patron. On the other hand, both were acutely aware that an overwhelmingly successful client would damage its patron's position in the region. For the United States, too much Israeli success risked alienating Arab friends, which would stall a future peace process and create tension with the Soviet Union.[101] Similarly, too much Egyptian success might lead Moscow to lose control over its client and jeopardize US-Soviet relations.[102] This paradoxical situation presented a unique set of strategic dilemmas. For Kissinger, who had reached the pinnacle of his power as Nixon became embroiled in Watergate, and for Brezhnev, who tightly controlled decision making in the Kremlin during the conflict, the Arab-Israeli War became a crucial test for détente.[103]

The following analysis of US and Soviet decision making during the 1973 Arab-Israeli War shows the role of imagined intersubjectivity in crisis management in two ways. First, imagined intersubjectivity played a crucial role in negotiating the critical ceasefire resolution (UN Security Council Resolution 338). During negotiation of the resolution, Kissinger thought the Soviets felt backed into a corner and had agreed to reduce their influence in the settlement of the conflict; Brezhnev, however, believed the United States had agreed to accept the Soviets as equals during implementation of the ceasefire and at a future peace conference. These differences in understanding the meaning of Resolution 338 mirrored the differences in their understandings of détente in general. Imagined intersubjectivity was, therefore, crucial for explaining cooperation during the crisis. Second, during confrontational moments—the outbreak of war and the nuclear alert—each party interpreted the other's behavior as operating within the bounds of détente. For the Soviets, the nuclear alert was explained by domestic politics (Watergate), whereas for Kissinger, the outbreak of the war and the suggestion of unilateral Soviet intervention in the conflict were evidence that the Soviets were playing for dominance. Because neither side's behavior contradicted the spirit of détente, as understood by each, détente acted as a restraining influence, channeling competition into cooperation.

To isolate US and Soviet decision makers' beliefs at different stages during the war, I discuss four moments during the crisis—the outbreak of the war, the Moscow visit (ceasefire negotiations), the nuclear alert, and the resolution and end of the war. One limitation in the following analysis is that some of the crucial documentation remains classified; however, a circumspect judgment is possible because of the confluence of sources. The following account draws on already declassified documents, memoirs, and the historical and biographical literature that sets the crisis in the context of US-Soviet relations.[104]

The Outbreak   The surprise Egyptian and Syrian offensive began on October 6, 1973, and was immediately seen by policymakers in the United States and the Soviet Union as a crucial test of détente. For US decision makers, the central question was how to use the Middle East crisis to obtain increased political influence. For the Soviets, the crucial question was how to use the crisis to preserve political parity without jeopardizing US-Soviet relations.

At first, many in the United States believed the war was a Soviet plot. Initial intelligence reports received by the Washington Special Actions Group, the committee chaired by Kissinger to respond to crises,[105] indicated that the Soviet Union knew Egyptian and Syrian intentions in advance and intended to provoke a showdown in the Middle East.[106] To many critics of détente, especially conservative journalists, this demonstrated Soviet failure to abide by détente and required a show of force to stand up to aggression.[107]

Kissinger publicly and privately disagreed with the conservative assessment of the situation. The Soviets might be behind the Egyptian and Syrian attack, but this was consistent with American-style détente. The aim of détente was not to prevent a crisis but to limit Soviet influence in the Third World, in particular the Middle East.[108] Détente did not require the Soviets to abandon the effort to exert pressure on the United States by unilaterally reducing their influence in the Third World. Rather, through diplomacy, détente was to provide for stakes in the status quo that would cajole the Soviet Union, over time, to reduce their footprint in areas such as the Middle East.

In the early days of the war, Kissinger's read on the Soviets was that they were trying to gain influence in the Middle East.[109] As Kissinger remarked to a Chinese official, "our strategic objective is to prevent the Soviet Union from getting a dominant position in the Middle East" and "to demonstrate that whoever gets help from the Soviet Union cannot achieve his objective, whatever it is."[110] On October 6, Kissinger told Nixon that the Soviets knew about the impending war. He said, "They knew about it or knew it was possible. They did not warn us."[111] His initial strategy was to ferret out Soviet involvement. He told Gen. Alexander Haig and President Nixon that the United States should propose a ceasefire resolution, saying, "This is designed in part to smoke them out. If they want the fighting stopped this will stop it fast. If they refuse to do this then we have to assume some collusion."[112]

Later that day, the Soviets rejected the ceasefire overture, arguing that a ceasefire would be difficult to get if neither party asked for it. A UN Security Council debate would lead to a shouting match instead of a settlement.[113] Kissinger decided that the Soviet rejection of a ceasefire resolution might provide an important opportunity. If the United States offered a ceasefire resolution that Israel could accept, then the Soviets would not "get the credit" for bringing peace.[114] Moreover, Kissinger began to think through the use of issue linkages to cajole the Soviets. He told the Special Actions Group, "If the Soviets get themselves into an anti-US or an anti-Israel position, they can kiss MFN [the trade agreement] and the other things goodbye."[115] In conversations with the Soviet ambassador, he subtly threatened to sink détente if the Soviets refused to cooperate, citing serious consequences in the Congress and with the public if the Soviets did not use private influence to end the fighting.[116] The efforts of the US and the Soviets to use their clients to obtain political dominance in the Middle East, and the developing of issue linkages, were part and parcel of the US understanding of détente.

In contrast to the American impression of Soviet belligerence, Brezhnev attempted to warn the United States about the potential for war and tried to prevent Egyptian president Anwar Sadat from beginning the war. Victor Israelyan, a member of the small Soviet taskforce assigned to make recommendations to the politburo during the 1973 Arab-Israeli War, recalls that Egypt's decision to attack Israel was unpopular.[117] First, the success of such an attack against a superior Israeli military was unlikely and an Egyptian failure might be an embarrassment to the Soviet Union. Furthermore, Sadat's decision to expel Soviet military advisers from Egypt upset Soviet-Egyptian relations. Most important, Brezhnev worried that an Egyptian attack might disrupt détente. According to Israelyan, "a military confrontation with the West, and in particular with the United States, was by no means on the Kremlin's political agenda. A war in the Middle East could only worsen relations with the West, which is why the Soviet leadership tried to steer the Arabs toward a political solution to the problem."[118]

Brezhnev tried to avert the war and maintain détente. On at least four occasions Brezhnev and others attempted to persuade Sadat not to attack.[119] Further, Brezhnev personally warned Nixon and Kissinger about the likelihood of another war in the Middle East.[120] When Soviet dependents were evacuated from Egypt before the crisis, the Soviet leadership made no effort to disguise their removal, providing forewarning that an attack might be coming.[121] Brezhnev showed no interest in allowing the conflict to disrupt the gains expected from détente.

While neither Kissinger and Nixon nor the Israelis appreciated the Soviet warning and thus did not head off the crisis, the Soviet Union did try to avert the conflict. There were several attempts in the early days at limited cooperation. The superpowers agreed that it would damage the interests of both sides if the crisis were raised at the UN General Assembly where the nonaligned movement might undermine superpower influence. They also agreed to keep their collaboration secret. Both worried that if US-Soviet cooperation became public, it would create the appearance of Soviet collaboration with Israel, undermining its position with its Arab clients. This would force the Soviets to adopt a more confrontational tone with the United States and Israel, leading to a ratcheting up of tension.[122]

Détente provided the best chance for cooperation to avert the war before it began. Not only did concerns about rupturing their new relationship prompt both to engage in limited collaboration at the beginning of the crisis—by ensuring a private back channel remained open, coordinating their strategies at the United Nations, and beginning to talk about a way forward—but détente provided the best chance to avoid war. Concerned about their relationship, Brezhnev repeatedly warned Nixon about the risk of war in the Middle East, tried to alert the United States that it was about to begin, and immediately made diplomatic overtures to Washington after the war began. US-Soviet cooperation failed to prevent the war—it's unclear how the superpowers could have stopped it if Egypt was bent on fighting—but it provided critical opportunities for peace.

The Ceasefire Negotiations   By October 18, Brezhnev began to circulate a draft proposal for a ceasefire, and after two days of stalling, Kissinger agreed to travel to Moscow on October 20 to discuss it.[123] The ceasefire negotiations created a new opportunity for international cooperation. Throughout the negotiations, Kissinger sought a settlement that would use linkages and threats to enhance US influence while expecting the Soviets to engage in similar behavior for similar reasons. The Soviets, in contrast, sought to reach a joint settlement that ensured superpower political equality in the Middle East.

The Soviet team decided, before the negotiations began, to try to obtain US cooperation for a settlement that ensured that US and Soviet interests were both respected in any final settlement. Shortly before Brezhnev's meeting with Kissinger, the politburo agreed that a ceasefire resolution should concentrate on an immediate ceasefire, be a joint US-Soviet action, and provide provisions for the Soviet Union and the United States to enter the peace process with equal standing.[124] The final element of the Soviet position, that it be involved in the eventual outcome, would play a dramatic role in the coming weeks. With Sadat appealing to Brezhnev for assistance, given Egypt's precarious military position, the Soviet Union was eager to work out a settlement.[125]

Whereas the Soviet Union sought a joint approach toward the Middle East, Kissinger sought to exclude the Soviets from the region. He also wanted to avoid the appearance of a joint US-Soviet condominium in the Middle East.[126] To increase US postwar influence in the region, Kissinger wanted to ensure that the United States played the crucial role in whatever peace process occurred. This meant that, in the interim, he had to avoid the appearance of collusion with the Soviet Union, which would lead Egypt and Israel to resent the United States and damage its political influence.

To obtain these aims, Kissinger used two tactics to put the Soviets into an inferior bargaining position. First, he wanted to stall as long as possible, delaying the deadline for the actual ceasefire so that Israel could continue to make gains.[127] This would place pressure on Moscow. In addition, before leaving for Moscow, Kissinger increased US aid to Israel so that he could have bargaining chips against the Soviets, telling the deputy assistant for national security affairs that "the negotiations I am about to undertake will be tough, and I will need to have some bargaining chips to give up should the occasion warrant. We could use it to get the Soviets to stop their airlift."[128]

At the meeting, Kissinger proposed the basis for what would later become UN Security Council Resolution 338. The first two articles of Resolution 338 call on the parties to cease firing within twelve hours and to begin to implement Resolution 242, the resolution passed at the end of the 1967 Arab-Israeli War. The third article was the most important for US and Soviet decision makers. It stated that "immediately and concurrently with the cease-fire, negotiations shall start between the parties concerned under appropriate auspices aimed at establishing a just and durable peace in the Middle East." The phrase "under appropriate auspices" is, to say the least, ambiguous.[129] Did appropriate auspices mean under the Security Council's, under the United States', or under both superpowers' authority? Neither party was content to leave "appropriate auspices" without qualification. At Soviet insistence, Kissinger and Soviet foreign minister Gromyko signed the Understanding, which clarified that "the negotiations between the parties will take place with the active participation of the United States and the Soviet Union at the beginning and thereafter in the course of negotiations when key issues of a settlement are dealt with."[130]

The term "understanding" was a misnomer. Similar to the BPA, each party unknowingly read its own understanding of détente into the agreement. For Kissinger, the Understanding implied a significant US presence in the negotiations, first by excluding Europe because "appropriate auspices" called only for a joint US-Soviet role. In addition, the document meant that the Soviets should only be allowed to give an opinion of the substance of the negotiations; there was no promise of a direct role in the settlement.[131] During the war, Egypt began to negotiate directly with the United States. If the Soviets were excluded from the peace process, Egypt might be brought into the US orbit. When combined with Israeli battlefield success, this promised enhanced US influence. The Understanding, by promising

Soviet influence in the early stages and a Soviet a seat in the final conference, was Kissinger's carrot to prevent the Soviets from attempting to revise
the new status quo. This is fully consistent with Kissinger's understanding
of détente: the careful management of the balance of power in the region,
combined with a carefully selected set of incentives to ensure the Soviets
did not rock the boat, maintaining US superiority.[132]

The Soviet understanding of the third article was very different. As
Israelyan recalls, the interpretation in the Kremlin was "crystal clear." The
third article provided the United States and the Soviet Union with a special role in the peace process throughout its life cycle, guarantees of Israeli
compliance with Resolution 242, and a commitment to ensure compliance
with the agreements of the superpowers. This meant that if a party violated the ceasefire, active US and Soviet pressure might be used to return
the parties to their original positions. The Soviet Union saw a more thor-
ough role for the superpowers, in which they jointly managed the crisis on
an equal footing.[133]

This is consistent with the Soviet impression of détente. They would
negotiate with the United States if political parity in the process was assured
in order to reduce the chances of great power conflict. Their goals were
realistic. As Garthoff explains, so long as each state enforced the ceasefire,
"the Soviet objectives were modest: to retain and if possible recoup lost
Arab confidence, and to bank on the possibility that the new collaborative
relationship with the United States would allow the USSR to share in the
peace process."[134] When the resolution was approved on October 22, the
misunderstanding was codified into international law.[135]

These misunderstandings were based on imagined intersubjectivity.
The Soviet Union thought the principle behind Resolution 338 was that
the United States had agreed that the Soviet Union merited political parity
and that the United States was willing to reduce superpower competition.
By contrast, for Kissinger, it was part of an elaborate set of linkages, the
culmination of a strategy that painted the Soviets into a corner in the Middle East. He thought the reason the Soviets accepted Resolution 338 was
a preponderance of US political power: they were granted the bare minimum to prevent them from undertaking a revisionist policy in the Middle
East. The Soviets, who did not understand that Kissinger believed they
were boxed in, could not understand his interpretation of the agreement.

The Nuclear Alert   The differences in Kissinger's and Brezhnev's under-standings of the Understanding had important consequences when Israeli forces continued to fight after the deadline, surrounding the Egyptian Third Army on the bank of the Suez Canal. Cut off and without food or medical supplies, the Third Army needed rapid resupply. This became the most dramatic moment of East-West confrontation during the war. As the Third Army was encircled, Sadat requested assistance from both the United States and the Soviet Union.[136] The Israeli offensive risked hijacking US-Soviet relations and undermining détente by alienating the Soviet Union. As Kissinger recalled, "there were limits beyond which we could not go, with all our friendship for Israel, and one of them was to make the leader of another superpower look like an idiot" for accepting a ceasefire that would not be enforced.[137]

On October 24, with the crisis mounting, Brezhnev sent Nixon a brief letter. In the note, Brezhnev wrote that Israeli violation of the ceasefire was a violation of the will of the superpowers. He requested US assistance in implementing the ceasefire through a joint mission: "Let us together, the Soviet Union and the United States urgently dispatch to Egypt Soviet and American military contingents, with their mission the implementation of the decision of the Security Council." Finally, and for Kissinger threaten-ingly, he wrote, "I will say it straight that if you find it impossible to act jointly with us in this matter, we should be faced with the necessity urgently to consider the question of taking appropriate steps unilaterally."[138]

Washington read the letter as a threat because it implied that the Sovi-ets were considering deploying combat troops. From the Soviet perspec-tive, however, the proposal did not mean a large-scale joint intervention. The phrase "military contingents" did not mean massive intervention. Premier Kosygin's recommendation was that 200 to 250 observers be sent to monitor the ceasefire, and Kuznetsov, an influential adviser, thought that, by convention, the term "contingents" meant personnel with limited functions.[139]

The Soviets thought the proposal was consistent with détente. As Israe-lyan recalled, the politburo met on October 23 and 24 to discuss the viola-tion of the ceasefire, and there was near unanimous agreement that the political agreements reached in 1972 and 1973 indicated that both parties needed to constrain their clients. In addition, they read the text of Nixon's and Brezhnev's correspondence, which indicated that each power needed to use its influence over its clients, implying that Nixon accepted the need for joint action. Furthermore, the Kremlin leaders came to believe that the correspondence indicated that each party had guaranteed that its client would honor the ceasefire. This implied, to them, that military force would be used if necessary. Finally, this interpretation fit with what they were hearing in other bilateral channels, where Sadat and third parties suggested that this notion was in the spirit of a proper resolution to the crisis:[140] "This language served to meet Sadat's appeal for help regardless of the US view. . . . At the same time, in urging Washington to act jointly in accordance with the ideas shared by the superpower leaders, the Kremlin was fostering détente. Everything looked very nice, certainly from the Kremlin's point of view."[141]

Unfortunately, everything did not look nice in Washington. The United States read the letter as an overt threat to send Soviet combat troops to the Middle East to contain the Israeli army.[142] That evening, the decision was made to raise the readiness of US nuclear forces to Defense Condition III.[143] Kissinger was convinced the Soviets intended to intervene in the region to increase their influence.[144] He recalled, "I attached a very high probability to Soviet intervention."[145] In the middle of the night the meeting was grim. General Haig thought the Soviets would move in at dawn. The secretary of defense thought the crisis was a ruse for the introduction of Soviet troops. And Kissinger thought the threat might mean that Soviet hawks had ousted Brezhnev.[146] Kissinger, who was not familiar with the nuanced Soviet position on the meaning of "military contingents," read Soviet intentions through the lens of US intentions as a bid for influence through the use of force.

For Kissinger, the consequences of either forming a joint deployment with the Soviet Union or allowing the Soviet Union to deploy troops in Egypt were equally unsavory. His aim throughout the conflict was to reduce Soviet influence in the region; if Kissinger caved in to the Soviet threat, the United States risked being locked out of the peace process. Kissinger recalled:

> If Soviet forces appeared dramatically in Cairo with those of the United States—and even more if they appeared alone—our traditional friends among Arab moderates would be profoundly unnerved by the evident fact of US-Soviet condominium. The strategy we had laboriously pursued in

four years of diplomacy and two weeks of crisis would disintegrate: Egypt would be drawn back into the Soviet orbit, the Soviet Union and its radical allies would emerge as the dominant factor in the Middle East, China and Europe would be dismayed by the appearance of US-Soviet military collaboration in so vital a region.[147]

The meeting of the Washington Special Actions Group concluded that a nuclear alert designed to deter the Soviets from placing troops in the Middle East was necessary. Kissinger told the meeting that "he had learned, finally, that when you decide to use force you must use plenty of it."[148]

Kissinger did not believe that either the Soviet threat or the US nuclear alert were inconsistent with détente. Soviet behavior was similar to US behavior. He thought Brezhnev was threatening to sink détente in order to gain influence. And the United States threatened to up the ante, risking a war to obtain a more favorable bargain. Each was an effort to link issues and threats in bids for influence—to create favorable positions in future rounds of cooperation. Detente was "partly a tranquilizer for Moscow as we sought to draw the Middle East into closer relations with us at the Soviet's expense."[149] In the coming days, Kissinger highlighted the fact that the United States, despite the nuclear alert, was not seeking a confrontation with the Soviet Union but was leaving the door open for cooperation. At a press conference, Kissinger explained, "We are not seeking an opportunity to confront the Soviet Union. We are not asking the Soviet Union to pull back from anything it has done. The opportunity for pursuing the joint course in the Security Council and in the diplomacy afterward is open."[150] By providing avenues through which the Soviet Union could hope to gain future access, Kissinger hoped to provide the Soviets with enough of a carrot that, when combined with the stick of the nuclear alert, cooperation would follow. Even if some may consider his strategy absurd, it was intended to generate cooperation.[151] He wanted to pressure Brezhnev to comply with the US proposal, but he wanted to do so without creating a direct public confrontation with the Soviet Union. As he wrote, "a public challenge could provoke the Soviets to dig in beyond what the politburo might consider prudent. Many wars have started because no line of retreat was left open. Superpowers have a special obligation not to humiliate one another."[152]

The Resolution of the War   Surely the nuclear alert should have disrupted imagined intersubjectivity as it directly contradicted the Soviet understanding of détente. However, the 1973 Arab-Israeli War demonstrates the resiliency of preconceived beliefs about relationships. Fortunately for the Middle East and US-Soviet relations, Brezhnev ignored the US threat. At a politburo meeting on October 25, every participant expressed outrage at the US overreaction. Most Soviet officials believed the nuclear alert was caused by Nixon's domestic problems. As Richard Ned Lebow and Janice Gross Stein explain, "many Soviet officials saw the alert as so inconsistent with the ongoing negotiations and the frequent communication between the two capitals that they could find no explanation other than Watergate." When it was suggested that Brezhnev's letter provoked the American response, the politburo could not understand. Brezhnev asked, "What has this to do with the letter I sent to Nixon?" Nikolai Podgorny, the Soviet head of state, commented, "Who could have imagined that the Americans would be so easily frightened?"[153]

Despite being angry over the nuclear alert, Brezhnev chose to ignore it. While several politburo members recommended a reply by force, Brezhnev disagreed. Brezhnev asked, "What about not responding at all to the American nuclear alert? Nixon is too nervous—let's cool him down."[154] The politburo agreed that because they had provided Nixon with no pretext for the alert, they should wait for an explanation. Brezhnev decided on this option, in part to prevent escalation, but more importantly to safeguard détente. As Israelyan recalled, Brezhnev worried about the risk that a response to the alert would pose for US-Soviet relations. During the meeting, he argued, "No matter how complicated the situation might be, our wish is to develop our relations with the United States." The decision was welcomed by several members because of its consistency with détente.[155]

Even though US behavior was inconsistent with the Soviet understanding of détente, imagined intersubjectivity was maintained because the Soviet leadership was able to place the blame on Watergate. The Soviet Union then relied on its own understanding of détente to deescalate the conflict. By contrast, Kissinger surely would have reacted to a Soviet threat. To do nothing was inconsistent with Kissinger's understanding of détente. When Kissinger believed the Soviet Union was trying to bargain, he raised the US nuclear alert level, creating a stick to prevent Soviet involvement in Egypt.

On October 25, Kissinger penned a letter for Nixon to Brezhnev.[156] It rejected joint action as well as the unilateral ceasefire. It did not directly explain the nuclear alert, although Nixon (Kissinger) remarked that we should act with "cool heads." The politburo found the call for calm ironic, coming from the power that threatened nuclear escalation. However, the letter called for joint US-Soviet participation in a United Nations force. Nixon (Kissinger) wrote, "If that is what you mean by contingents, we will consider it." From the Soviet perspective, this letter was perplexing, in part because it provided no explanation for the alert, but even more so because the letter indicated that Nixon was willing to jointly send personnel to monitor the ceasefire, which is what the Soviets had proposed in the letter that triggered the alert.[157]

In the end, the crisis was fortunately anticlimactic and resolved faster than it started. UN Security Council Resolution 340 created an emergency force without the aid of US or Soviet troops, and the ceasefire, which was soon enforced, made joint US-Soviet action unnecessary.[158] The crisis was over.

The crisis is often depicted as a confrontation; for the participants, however, it was an example of cooperation. As Garthoff notes, "during the October War both powers sought—in addition to maneuvering for political advantage—to defuse the crisis and to end the war."[159] Détente provided incentives for Brezhnev to warn the United States on four occasions about the risk or war, providing an opportunity for cooperation before the war began. Moreover, throughout the crisis, both parties refused unilateral action, and each eventually ensured that its ally stopped fighting and maintained the ceasefire, however belatedly. The superpowers initialed two ceasefires that led to two Security Council resolutions, navigated a nuclear crisis and a naval standoff in the Mediterranean, and managed a war without escalation. Each party, through its own idiosyncratic understanding of the nature of the rivalry, adjusted its policies to ensure that the "rules" of détente were obeyed. As Nixon opined, "without détente, we might have had a major conflict in the Middle East. With détente, we avoided it." Or, as Secretary of Defense James Schlesinger put it, "to work out in collaboration with the Soviets the arrangement for two cease-fires is, I think, a tribute to the strength of détente—the communications that existed."

Moreover, for the Soviets, "the experience of détente *had*, in their view, helped to regulate the American-Soviet competition at a time of potential danger."[160] Cooperation during the 1973 Arab-Israeli War occurred, not despite imagined intersubjectivity, but in part because of it. Two different understandings of rivalry laid the groundwork for cooperation.

Explaining Cooperation

The analysis of détente tested constructivist theories that highlight the importance of norms and identities. Because the advent of détente marked a cultural change in relations between the United States and the Soviet Union—a shift from enmity to rivalry—intersubjectivity, broadly defined, should play a role in explaining cooperation. Did intersubjectivity play a role in the creation of détente? Or was détente premised on a false inter-subjective belief—a belief by both the Brezhnev leadership and Nixon and Kissinger that there were new rules of the road that were shared by both sides, an imagined intersubjectivity?

No part of this chapter should be construed to imply that there were no intersubjective ideas during the 1970s. The superpowers began a process of consultation that relied on a pattern of behavior (norm) that would yield consistent results concerning the form that diplomacy was to take. When a crisis broke out, Kissinger talked to Ambassador Dobrynin; Nixon and Brezhnev exchanged correspondence; and, at significant junctures, there were direct conversations in Moscow between Kissinger and Brezhnev. Moreover, common knowledge of military parity, at the very least, appears to have been necessary for the growth of détente. Yet, one should be careful in ascribing shared strategic concepts to the superpowers because of the significant difference between Kissinger's nuclear brinksmanship and Brezhnev's attitude toward nuclear weapons. While the fact of military parity was common knowledge, what it meant for the superpowers was wildly different for Washington and Moscow.

There is less evidence that a common identity played a role in détente. The identity of rivals, as described by Wendt, was not understood inter-subjectively except in the most abstract sense. The rules of rivalry were not shared, and each superpower understood the logic of rivalry in different terms. The rules concerning violence varied, with Kissinger believing in the efficacy of nuclear threats and Brezhnev believing that such threats risked war. The rules of sovereignty and legitimacy—regarding US and Soviet equality and the relationship between influence and violence—also varied. This is described more in depth in chapter 4. Thus, it is unlikely that a single shared identity played a role in cooperation during détente.

Of course, not every misperception during détente produced cooperation. If Nixon and Kissinger knew that the Soviets were warning the United States of the prospects for war, cooperation might have ensued to stop the war before it began. Or, if Kissinger had known that the Soviets did not intend to send troops to Egypt, the 1973 Arab-Israeli War might have ended sooner, with less of a chance for escalation. Misperceptions can be dangerous. I have shown, however, that they can also produce cooperation. The actual causal pathways through which agreements were actually reached—the BPA, the ceasefire resolutions that ended the 1973 Arab-Israeli War, SALT, as well as many other agreements reached during détente—relied on misperceptions.

Imagined intersubjectivity played a crucial role in creating and sustaining détente. In chapter 1, I defined imagined intersubjectivity as an instance in which actors unknowingly rely on different principles and unknowingly expect different patterns of behavior to stem from an action. For the Soviets, the principle of détente included the importance of political parity, and for the United States, détente was intended as a relationship that would enable the United States to continue competing with the Soviet Union to ensure US political primacy. These principled differences led the parties to expect different patterns of concrete behavior. Kissinger expected linkages and negotiating ploys, the use of nuclear threats, and Soviet competition in the Third World. In contrast, Brezhnev expected to be treated as an equal in negotiations, the abandonment of linkages and threats, and US acceptance of Soviet influence in the periphery.

The best evidence indicates that the turn to cooperation depended on imagined intersubjectivity. Imagined intersubjectivity was enshrined in the Basic Principles agreement and employed with some success in gaining a ceasefire resolution during the 1973 Arab-Israeli War. These differences enabled cooperation because neither superpower would have accepted the other's understanding. Kissinger likely would not have accepted political parity, and Brezhnev certainly would not have conceded to a position of inferiority. Détente was therefore a success because imagined intersubjectivity allowed the superpowers to look past their principled differences to cooperate.

Changing patterns of interstate relations are, therefore, not necessarily the product of an intersubjective understanding of a relationship. The label "détente" was an empty signifier for the superpowers' relationship: a shared word, not a shared idea. The false confidence—a false intersubjective belief—that they shared an understanding of their relationship was crucial for cooperation. The sense of "we-ness" that developed was more imagined than real as the parties projected their own self-image onto their rival. But, this artificial we-ness—this FIB that tricked the superpowers into believing that there was a common understanding of detente—allowed the parties to cooperate by enabling them to overlook principled differences and conflicts of interest.

3

THE ANTI-BALLISTIC MISSILE TREATY

Brezhnev: There is an anecdote about the Tsar who had before him a case
of an arrested man. The question was, would he be executed or
pardoned? The Tsar wrote out a piece of paper with only three
words on it: "Execution impossible pardon." . . . It should have
read: "Execution impossible, pardon." . . . The Tsar wrote it
without commas and then the lawyers had to decide which he
meant.

Kissinger: What happened to the man?

Brezhnev: I will tell you that at the end of our discussions, before you go.
My answer will depend on how our talks go.

Gromyko: Maybe the answer should be given only at the Summit.

Brezhnev: No, Dr. Kissinger has to leave Moscow with clear answers to all
his questions. Because you might want to tell the president this
story. He will want to know the ending. If you don't know it,
he will wonder what you were talking about here.

Kissinger: From my experience with bureaucracies, they probably did
both.

I never did receive the answer.

HENRY KISSINGER, *White House Years*

The story about the tsar, recited by Brezhnev during Kissinger's secret
trip to Moscow in the spring of 1972, is indicative of the stumbling path
that culminated in the Anti-Ballistic Missile Treaty later that year. Despite

seeming clarity, like the tsar's order, the superpowers' signals, beliefs, and aims were misinterpreted throughout the ABM Treaty negotiations. The most remarkable part of the ABM Treaty negotiations was the circuitous path they took. The process was plagued with misjudgments, misunderstandings, and simple mistakes. Whereas many theories in International Relations maintain that these should stand as a barrier to cooperation, I argue that imagined intersubjectivity—a false belief that the parties know what others will do and why they will do it—promoted cooperation. Neither Nixon and Kissinger nor Brezhnev and other Soviet decision makers understood the reasons for or the patterns of the other side's negotiating behavior. The result was a more-or-less clumsy set of negotiations in which actors were frequently surprised as they limped their way toward the ABM Treaty. These misunderstandings were an important part of the process. Consistently, misunderstandings of the other side's position led to important concessions that made the treaty possible.

In this chapter, I test whether the rational-choice concept of common knowledge—information that every party knows, knows that every other party knows, and so on—may in certain cases stand in the way of cooperation. In Chapter 1, I divided common knowledge into three types: strategic or information about the structure of the game, linguistic or shared communication systems, and situation specific or additional elements such as focal points. During the ABM Treaty negotiations, there were moments when common knowledge was lacking in regard to certain pieces of crucial information concerning all three species of common knowledge. In these cases, Nixon, Kissinger, Brezhnev, and others held imagined intersubjective beliefs, and these beliefs were crucial for cooperation.

I focus on the ABM Treaty because arms control agreements are often treated as a paradigmatic case for the importance of information in international cooperation. Schelling's initial insights about common knowledge, especially regarding the importance of focal points, the credibility of signals, and other issues, were in part developed to solve problems related to arms races and arms control.[1] Many discussions of tacit bargaining strategies and the production of information in regimes use arms control as a critical case.[2] In particular, the ABM negotiations are often treated as an example of common knowledge leading to regime success. Condoleezza Rice, for example, argues that the ABM Treaty was a product of shared knowledge of the link between defensive and offensive weapons.[3] Emmanuel Adler and Matthew Evangelista similarly stress the shared strategic knowledge held by US and Soviet opponents of ABM systems.[4] The Strategic Arms Limitations Talks were, in Nixon's language, a "getting to know you" experience, and the agreements reached were supposedly the result of the successful feeling out of each side's negotiating positions.[5] This means that the success of the negotiations for the ABM Treaty should be a hard case for a theory of false intersubjective beliefs.

In what follows, I set the stage for the ABM negotiations, briefly rehearsing the history of the ABM debate in the United States and the Soviet Union before SALT. Then, I recount the beliefs that the actors had at three key moments in the negotiations—April 1970, May 1971, and May 1972—showing how these beliefs conditioned cooperation and explaining why they are examples of imagined intersubjectivity. I demonstrate that imagined intersubjectivity was a necessary condition for the ABM Treaty through a counterfactual analysis, by showing that more information would have led to less cooperation. I only consider counterfactuals intended to test FIBs against the rationalist conception of common knowledge; other alternative explanations are assessed in the next chapter.

The US and Soviet ABM Programs

The domestic debates that preceded the ABM Treaty negotiations are an important background for the arms control process. On entering office, President Nixon quickly entered into one of the most divisive political debates in American politics: whether to build an ABM system. While in retrospect it may seem strange, the ABM debate was more divisive than the Vietnam War in the halls of the Capitol in 1969.[6] The August vote to approve Nixon's Safeguard ABM system was harrowingly close for the new administration; an amendment that would have blocked Safeguard was defeated by a dramatic 51–50 Senate vote in which Vice President Spiro Agnew broke the tie.[7]

The tenacity of the ABM debate during Nixon's first term was a dramatic reversal of the debate during the Johnson administration. Under Johnson, Congress and the Joint Chiefs of Staff ardently pushed a reluctant administration to deploy an ABM system capable of damage limitation for cities in the event of a Soviet strike (a "thick" system). In 1966,

Congress approved $167 million for an ABM system that the Department of Defense neither requested nor wanted. Secretary of Defense McNamara telephoned a committee chairman after the vote, "making clear in the bluntest possible language that he had no intention of spending one dime of the appropriated funds."[8] The ABM debate under Nixon was dramatically reversed. Johnson's system was unpopular in the Senate because of a diminishing Chinese nuclear threat, spending on the Vietnam War, and cost overruns on other major weapons programs.[9] Nixon wanted to build an ABM system, and the Senate opposed it.

To build support for an ABM system, Nixon renamed it Safeguard and reworked the manner in which it would be deployed. The program was to be deployed in two phases. Safeguard would first be deployed around Minutemen missile fields to defend against a Soviet first strike.[10] This enabled Nixon to argue that the ABM would be relatively inexpensive and not destabilizing. By securing only Minutemen fields, and not cities, the ABM would not be a threat to the Soviet Union because the majority of the US population would not survive a nuclear attack, leaving the Soviet deterrent intact. The second phase was intended to meet the needs of hawks and satisfied Kissinger and Nixon's preference for defense: it expanded Safeguard to provide area defense against a Chinese threat or even a thick defense against a future Soviet threat.[11] The phased deployment, which met several challenges from both Republican and Democratic critics, managed to eke out a slim majority in the Senate.

While the United States was considering developing an ABM system, the Soviet Union had already produced a partial one. On February 9, 1967, the Soviet Union announced the deployment of an ABM system around Moscow "and boasted of the ease with which incoming American missiles would be knocked down."[12] As the Soviet Union built Galosh, public statements signaled their intention to complete the buildup. At a London news conference, Premier Kosygin suggested that these defensive systems were less destabilizing than offensive systems and that he did not favor limitations on them.[13] Perhaps more influential for Western analysts, Maj. Gen. N. Talensky argued in *International Affairs* that "it would hardly be in the interests of any peace-loving state to forgo the creation of its own effective systems of defense against nuclear-rocket aggression and make its security dependent only on deterrence, that is, on whether the other side will refrain from attacking."[14] Until 1964, or perhaps even as late as 1967, "an effective ballistic missile defense was plainly a must" and "a major task" for the Soviet military.[15]

However, the ABM debate pursued a different trajectory in the Soviet Union than in the United States. While the Nixon administration pushed for an ABM expansion, Soviet decision makers began to delay and eventually cancel their program after only two-thirds of the launchers were completed.[16] The reason was in part financial, but in larger part technical. Dmitri Ustinov, the chairman of the politburo commission tasked with deciding the Soviet approach to SALT, held a meeting on the ABM project, and there was a consensus that the project was a failure.[17]

The ABM debate in the United States and the Soviet Union set the stage for the ABM Treaty. On the Soviet side, a decade-long effort to develop ABM systems was running aground in light of technical and financial problems. On the US side, a new administration was trying to push an unpopular ABM system through a reluctant Senate at the height of the Vietnam War.

Imagined Intersubjectivity in Three Periods in the Negotiations

It is against this backdrop that US and Soviet negotiators sought to develop a framework for arms control. Nixon wanted to wring support for ABM systems from a reluctant Senate, and the Soviets hoped to negotiate an end to a system that would not work. Moreover, beyond complicated domestic politics and technical issues, the ABM negotiations were the first serious bilateral arms control negotiations that required extensive technical expertise, political management, and consultation reached between ideological enemies. To understand the negotiations, rather than thinking of them as a continual process, it is better to think about them as water moving through a clogged hose, gaining pressure until it spurts through one clog, only to encounter another one a foot down the hose. I concentrate on three of these spurts forward: Kissinger's offer to negotiate a deal that limited ABMs to defense of capitals or National Command Authority (NCA)–only, concessions made by both parties to reach the May 20 agreement in 1971, and Nixon's decision to not cancel the Moscow summit despite pressure to do so. At each of these three moments, imagined intersubjectivity led to cooperation.

I trace this process using a series of "smoking guns" tests. In order for the ABM Treaty to be reached it was necessary (1) that it be tabled as a point of discussion, (2) that it be delinked from other arms control issues that would prevent cooperation, and (3) that it would make political sense to sign the agreement.[18] If the evidence shows that mutual misperceptions were necessary for these three elements of the negotiations to proceed, then there is clear evidence (a smoking gun) regarding the role of misperceptions in the negotiations. To complement this analysis, the final portion of this chapter uses counterfactual analysis to ask what may have occurred if the causal condition—imagined intersubjectivity—were not present.

The National Command Authority–Only Offer

In 1970, Henry Kissinger offered to negotiate an ABM Treaty with the Soviets. Kissinger was convinced the Soviets would refuse to negotiate over ABMs. He was wrong. Within a week the Soviets accepted the offer. Why did Kissinger offer to negotiate over ABMs? And how did this contribute to the final form of the ABM Treaty?

The negotiation of the ABM Treaty officially began in Helsinki in the winter of 1969 but did not become substantively interesting until April 1970, when the United States tabled proposals in Vienna. In the first few days of the Vienna round, Kissinger authorized Gerald Smith, the head negotiator of the US SALT delegation, to make a comprehensive offer to the Soviet Union limiting offensive and defensive weapons.[19] The defensive component required that both states limit ABM systems to the defense of capitals, which was designated "National Command Authority–only" because it limited missile defense to defense of governments in the capital. Kissinger later referred to this offer as "a first class blunder."[20] He did not predict that Moscow would accept it.[21] The offer was a blunder because it was based on a misunderstanding of the Soviet position and was intended as an offer the Soviets would surely reject. Once it was accepted, both parties committed themselves firmly, albeit in principle only, to an ABM agreement, the first major bilateral arms control effort of the Cold War.[22]

Within a week, Soviet negotiators accepted Kissinger's NCA-only offer.[23] The welcome surprise, from the Soviet perspective, was not that an agreement was possible to limit defensive weapons but rather that

Kissinger's offer was so generous. Not only was the United States willing to limit defensive weapons, but the NCA-only alternative allowed the Soviet Union to maintain the Galosh system around Moscow while the United States did not have plans to build a similar system to defend Washington. This handed the Soviet Union an asymmetric advantage. This appeased Soviet hawks because it meant that they would not have to dismantle an expensive existing weapons system.[24] In short, Kissinger's offer required only that the Soviet Union abandon a thin nationwide ABM deployment that was not planned, that was technologically impossible, and that was likely unaffordable.

The US offer to limit defense to NCA-only is a puzzle. In their memoirs, Nixon and Kissinger both argue that the entire ABM effort—pushing Congress to build it and then negotiating over it with the Soviets—was an effort to enhance their bargaining position at SALT.[25] The evidence against this explanation is decisive. If Kissinger and Nixon sincerely wanted to preserve only a limited ABM program, they would not have offered an NCA-only deal because that would require moving sites, something that the Senate showed no intention of allowing and the Department of Defense and Joint Chiefs considered unworkable.[26] As Kissinger put it, while blaming the SALT team for the mistake, "we would have to tear down the only thing we are building with the right to build something that Congress will never appropriate . . . and they can continue to keep what they already have."[27] If the ABM were a bargaining chip that was never intended to be built, then Kissinger should have offered to ban ABM systems altogether, not to limit them. Yet neither Nixon nor Kissinger was sincerely interested in banning ABMs: at one point, Kissinger authorized Gerard Smith to privately probe an ABM ban, a position he was "sure the Soviets would reject."[28] When the Soviets showed a willingness to accept, the probe was abandoned. Additionally, when Kissinger notified Dobrynin of Nixon's push for ABMs in 1969, he argued that ABMs around Minutemen fields were stabilizing, in an attempt to reduce Soviet fears, not augment them, so as to push them to negotiate.[29] The claim that NCA-only was a bargaining move vis-à-vis the Soviet Union was a post hoc justification for a mistake.

Kissinger and Nixon believed that ABM development was important for strategic and political reasons. The ABM could defend Minutemen fields from the growing threat of the large Soviet SS-9 missiles and intercept accidental or third-party strikes. Nixon told his National Security Council, "We want area defense."[30] Even during the summit, Nixon continually reiterated that the US had no interest in reducing ABMs; it was at best a concession to the Soviet Union to control offensive weapons as US national security interests were best pursued through the development of defensive weapons.[31] These concerns were underscored by Nixon's selection of Kissinger as national security adviser, which was in part due to his emphasis on defense.[32] The ABM was also politically important. As the debate over whether to build the ABM system heated up, Nixon came to consider it a decisive test of his political leadership. As Robert Dallek explains, "Nixon saw the battle for congressional approval as more a test of his political strength and prospects for reelection than of the country's future safety against attack. Senator Edward Kennedy's opposition to ABM was seen as a first confrontation in a likely contest with Nixon for the presidency in 1972."[33] The Nixon administration never intended its NCA-only offer to reduce the chances of ABM deployment.

Kissinger made the NCA-only offer because he was convinced that the Soviets would reject it.[34] "Kissinger and probably the president (although he displayed a remarkable indifference) expected that the Soviet side would take the lead in proposing an ABM level higher than NCA," explains Garthoff. This mistaken assumption was based on an inaccurate reading of Soviet statements supporting ABM systems.[35] Nixon continued to hold this view in his memoirs: "We knew that even as the debate in Congress over an American ABM was raging, the Soviets had initiated work on more ICBMs and ABMS, as well as major new radar systems in conjunction with their deployment."[36] Neither he nor Kissinger paid sufficient attention to later signals that the Soviets were reducing their ABM commitments and were willing to trade.[37] Thus, they were convinced the Soviets would reject an NCA-only offer, a serious misjudgment.[38]

Instead, they reasoned that if the Soviet Union took the lead in rejecting the NCA-only offer, "that move would place the onus on the Soviet Union and could then be used against congressional opponents of Safeguard."[39] That is, the anticipated rejection of an ABM component in the SALT process by the Soviets would force the Senate to either approve the Nixon administration's ABM program or to contemplate unilaterally ending a US program in an area of traditional American strength (technological development). As Gerard Smith put the issue to Nixon, "If SALT fails,

Congressional support for strategic weapons programs in the future may depend in good part on the nature of United States SALT offers that the Soviets would not accept."[40] This insincere use of the ABM as a bargaining chip was the beginning of a trend in which Nixon, and later Ford, used negotiations as a "reverse bargaining chip," that is, they claimed that a weapons program was needed as a bargaining chip but clandestinely had no intention of trading it away.[41]

This "first class blunder" had enormous consequences. At Vienna, the Soviets were passive and did not table any offers. This meant that Kissinger could pick which issues were to be discussed, and the NCA-only offer placed ABMs at the center of the table. This committed the United States, in principle, to a future ABM agreement. While this did not make the ABM Treaty inevitable, it did place the burden on the American side to either make the most of it or find an uncomfortable way to withdraw the offer.[42] In the rest of the negotiations, the US side attempted to make the best of the accidental concession by attempting to win offensive limitations and to move the ABM sites away from Washington.

This misjudgment was the result of imagined intersubjectivity. As explained in Chapter 1, imagined intersubjectivity exists when actors wrongly believe an intersubjective consensus exists and, as a consequence, they cannot predict the behavior of the other or understand the reasons for that behavior. Kissinger misunderstood the principles that guided Soviet behavior at SALT. He thought the Soviet Union would reject an NCA-only ABM offer because he thought that the Soviet Union's military culture emphasized defense over arms control.[43] While believing that ABM defenses were strategically and politically important for Nixon, Kissinger also thought the Soviets wanted to build ABMs. The Soviets, unaware of Kissinger's mistake, thought the US offer to reduce ABMs was sincere. By following the public debate within the United States, Ustinov, Gromyko, and Brezhnev all thought that the US attempt to reduce defensive systems was in accord with popular strategic and technical arguments. Misperceptions of the principles of action led to failed predictions for the other's behavior. Kissinger did not predict that the Soviet Union would accept the NCA-only offer, especially in only one week; and the Soviet Union did not predict that once the offer was accepted, the Americans would later make four additional offers to move off the NCA-only position. If Kissinger has not offered a defensive agreement, there is no evidence that the Soviets would have proposed one, which would have prevented an ABM deal.

Kissinger's surprising offer to limit NCA-only systems undermines the important claim of Evangelista and Adler that the ABM Treaty was the product of "common knowledge" of strategic concepts. Adler and Evangelista argue that new US strategic ideas, emphasizing strategic stability and the dangers of ABM systems, convinced US and Soviet policymakers to acknowledge the dangers of building ABMs. Advocates of arms control put their concern on the agenda in the United States through a public campaign and then likely convinced Soviet leaders that arms control was in the Soviet national interest.[44] Certainly, public awareness of the value of arms control was important. It was, however, neither common knowledge nor decisive. Neither Kissinger nor Nixon was aware of the shifting Soviet ABM position. In fact, if the epistemic community was common knowledge—if Kissinger knew that Brezhnev favored limiting ABMs—cooperation would have become less likely. Moreover, while an epistemic community might put arms control on the agenda, it does not ensure that a treaty will be signed. Evangelista is careful: he notes that there is some circumstantial evidence that Western ideas reached the ears of some in the Soviet politburo. On balance, Evangelista concludes, there is good evidence that Brezhnev accepted the ABM for political reasons.[45]

The May 20 Agreement

In 1971, with the SALT negotiations in a deadlock, the parties made a fundamental breakthrough in the form of the May 20 agreement. Once the deal was reached, the parties began to quickly work on what they thought were the final details and to arrange a summit meeting, and then go public to sell the benefits of détente. Was the May 20 agreement the result of information transmission? Did the parties mutually understand its terms? And how did the May 20 agreement grease the wheels of the negotiation of the ABM Treaty?

The NCA-only offer, while committing the superpowers in principle to an arrangement that limited ABMs, did not easily lead to a workable agreement, for two reasons. The steadfast US position was that any defensive agreement be accompanied by a comprehensive agreement on offensive weapons, in particular modern large ballistic missiles such as the SS-9.[46] The critical problem with limiting Soviet missiles was that the Soviet position required that US forward-based systems (FBS), such as light aircraft capable of carrying a nuclear payload, be included in any offensive deal.

US negotiators consistently refused to include FBS, which stalled not only agreements on offensive limitations but also defensive agreements.[47] Moreover, the NCA-only offer was itself a problem. The Senate had approved funding for the development of ABM sites around several Minutemen fields, most importantly at Grand Forks, North Dakota where construction had already begun. Yet at SALT, Kissinger proposed an NCA system with a site near Washington, D.C. Kissinger and Nixon believed, rightly, that shifting ABM construction to a new site near the capital would have been politically impossible.[48]

After the first round, SALT was stalemated.[49] Unknown to either the public or the negotiators at SALT, Kissinger was secretly negotiating an agreement with Ambassador Dobrynin that became known as the May 20 agreement. At noon in Washington and seven in the evening in Moscow, Nixon and Kosygin publicly and simultaneously read the agreement that was to end the deadlock:

> The Governments of the United States and the Soviet Union, after reviewing the course of their talks on the limitation of strategic armaments, have agreed to concentrate this year on working out an agreement for the limitation of the deployment of anti-ballistic missile systems (ABMs). They have also agreed that, together with concluding an agreement to limit ABMs, they will agree on certain measures with respect to the limitation of offensive strategic weapons.[50]

Note the phrase "together with" as it becomes important in what followed. The May 20 agreement created the general form that the ABM Treaty and interim agreement would take. It separated the ABM from an interim freeze on new silo construction, disentangling the ABM from the more difficult work on offensive weapons.[51] This was a significant breakthrough. In exchange for the May 20 agreement, the Soviets dropped their demand that FBS be included and that ABMs be limited to NCA-only, and Kissinger dropped the demand for a comprehensive offensive treaty.[52] After May 20, Kissinger and Dobrynin believed that the principled issues had been resolved and that they could leave the technical details to the SALT delegations.

Perhaps even more important, the May 20 agreement publicly committed Brezhnev and Nixon to a workable SALT agreement as part of their respective peace agendas. Since the close Senate vote in 1969, support in Congress for ABM systems was waning.[53] The agreement temporarily disarmed critics of Safeguard; it was praised by liberal and conservative media as well as the dovish arms control experts who were Nixon's chief antagonists in the debate.[54] Nixon was ecstatic about making a prime-time television announcement.[55] As Kissinger told Nixon, the agreement would "break the back of this generation of Democratic leaders," to which Nixon replied, "That's right. We've got to break—we've got to destroy the confidence of the people in the American establishment."[56] After the May 20 agreement, it would have been enormously difficult for Nixon and Kissinger to not conclude an ABM Treaty, especially because they were on record in support of it and had begun the difficult job of explaining to the public why a system that was once so vital to national security was being traded away.[57] The situation was similar for Brezhnev, who declared in March that he was committed to a policy of détente and arms control.[58] As Melvyn Leffler explains, "Brezhnev put the full imprimatur of the party leadership behind the policy of relaxing tensions with the West and negotiating arms-reduction treaties with Washington and NATO."[59] By issuing the statement that the parties were prepared to negotiate an agreement, Brezhnev invested the process with a sense of purpose that had hitherto been lacking.[60]

Was this breakthrough the result of more information being shared between Kissinger and Dobrynin? Did the development of common knowledge allow a breakthrough toward the first significant arms control treaty of the Cold War? In short, no. Concessions were made to reach the agreement because of its ambiguity. The critical issue was what was meant by the phrase "together with." The guidance Kissinger gave the US delegation was that "together with" meant simultaneously. As Smith interpreted that instruction, it meant spending a few weeks discussing ABMs, and then a few weeks on offensive limitations, and back and forth.[61] Vladimir Semenov, the chief Soviet negotiator, held a different view. The Russian translation used the word "pri," which is much weaker than "together with." He concluded that the agreement implied that an ABM deal and the freeze should accompany one another in the final version but that the ABM Treaty would come first in the negotiations. It was this ambiguity that led each side to publicly back the May 20 agreement.[62]

The ambiguity of the agreement was developed by Kissinger and Dobrynin unintentionally after months of back-channel discussions. The back channel began discussions of a limited agreement in the spring of 1970, when Kissinger floated the idea of letting the SALT negotiators attempt to reach a comprehensive agreement while he and Dobrynin secretly worked on a limited agreement. After the Soviet team accepted the NCA-only proposal at SALT, Dobrynin asked whether a limited agreement might quickly be reached over ABMs.[63]

On January 9, 1971, Kissinger agreed to begin work on an ABM-only agreement, but only if the Soviets agreed to a freeze on new starts on missiles.[64] This agreement—the interim agreement—was a concession by Kissinger. He was dropping the demand that any ABM agreement be accompanied by a comprehensive offensive agreement. In February, Dobrynin came to Kissinger with good news: the politburo accepted Kissinger's offer of a separate ABM Treaty but, in exchange for a freeze, the US would have to include FBS.[65] Despite the continued demands on FBS, Kissinger was enthusiastic about the progress. He told Nixon that these meetings were "most constructive" and that Dobrynin "fell all over himself."[66] On March 13, Dobrynin said that the politburo would accept his offer to link an ABM agreement to an offensive freeze, suggesting that they were willing to negotiate the ABM first, followed by the freeze. In addition, Dobrynin said because a freeze would be temporary, FBS was not essential, and suggested they would negotiate other limited ABM deployments beyond Washington and Moscow.[67]

Despite these concessions, Kissinger balked. He believed this was an effort by the Soviets to secure an ABM-only agreement; once the ABM treaty was in place, the Soviets would have no incentive to finish negotiating a freeze.[68] As Kissinger told Nixon, "they are asking us to dismantle our ABM while they keep theirs and build like crazy while they do nothing."[69]

The problem was sequence. Kissinger wanted ABM plus freeze, whereas Dobrynin wanted ABM followed by freeze. As the negotiations moved along, both became convinced that the other had accepted their position. The minutia is important because it shows the source of confusion. On March 26, when Dobrynin offered to allow Kissinger to move off of the NCA-only offer, Kissinger suggested that Nixon would quickly agree so long as the freeze was discussed "simultaneously" with the ABM Treaty. Dobrynin, trying to interpret Kissinger's meaning, replied, "simultaneously concluded on separate agreement and freezing at the same time," after which Kissinger said, "exactly." Dobrynin refined this as "discussion of the details will be discussed simultaneously with the conclusion of the agreement," to which Kissinger exclaimed, "That would be fine. See how easy I am to get along with."[70] They both hung up the phone convinced they had come to a mutually acceptable agreement.

However, Dobrynin's interpretation did not mean "exactly" what Kissinger meant. Dobrynin's wording implied that discussions of the freeze would come with the conclusion of the agreement, not its inception. This meant there would be an ABM-only agreement on the table and almost complete before the negotiation of the freeze. The Soviets wanted this because it would prevent links between specific elements of the ABM Treaty and specific elements of the freeze. In return, the Soviets were willing to change their NCA-only position and to not include FBS.[71] In contrast, when Kissinger suggested simultaneity, he meant that the two agreements would be worked on "side-by-side."[72] This would allow the US delegation to link the elements, increasing US negotiating leverage over Russian offensive missiles by enabling ABM trades for missiles. There is no evidence that they understood each other.[73]

Dobrynin returned from Moscow in April with a draft copy of the Soviet response agreeing in principle to a freeze, and this "could be discussed before the work on the separate ABM agreement is complete."[74] The ABM negotiations would come first, but before the treaty was signed and finalized, the freeze negotiations would begin. Despite last-minute discussions on the language, Kissinger believed that Dobrynin had folded on the sequence, and he told Nixon, "We got everything we asked for."[75] In contrast, Dobrynin believed Kissinger was conceding that the ABM would be negotiated before offensive weapons limitations. On May 20, when Nixon and Kosygin read the public announcements, neither was aware of the fundamental differences in their interpretations of the text.

The ambiguity of "simultaneous" and "together with" was built into the back-channel diplomacy. When the diplomatic record and negotiating instructions were forwarded to the SALT negotiators, the difficulties became apparent and the process stalled. As Smith recalls, the sequence issue was not resolved until late September, only a few months before the summit. In the meantime, Smith and Semenov read and reread the joint announcement and the letters, rehearsing the instructions provided by Gromyko and Kissinger that they stand fast to their positions. Smith wrote, "Our discussions of the sequence issue became more or less a dialogue of the deaf.... I had the impression that we were just repeating what

Dobrynin and Kissinger had said to each other months ago."[76] Yet each had invested political capital in the misunderstood agreement.

May 20, 1971, despite the tortuous path leading to it, was a critical date in the process of reaching an ABM agreement. Similar to the NCA-only offer, the May 20 agreement was the product of imagined intersubjectivity. Kissinger and Nixon thought that the Soviet Union shared their interpretation of the agreement and that the concessions were sufficient to ensure compliance. For Kissinger, the Soviets had dropped their demands over FBS and allowed the United States to move off its NCA-only position because Kissinger had separated the two agreements. Kissinger presumed that his concessions were sufficient; he did not imagine that sequence was also considered a key concession by the Soviets. Kissinger neither understood the meaning of the May 20 agreement for the Soviet Union nor predicted the resulting deadlock later in 1971 over the text of the agreement. For Dobrynin and the Soviet leadership, Kissinger had agreed to drop his demands for a comprehensive agreement because the Soviet Union had agreed to a freeze that would come later, which was sufficient for Nixon to show a limit on offensive weapons. There is no evidence that the Soviet leadership predicted the dispute over the sequence or that they understood the reasons for Kissinger's concessions. The agreement was premised on imagined intersubjectivity because neither actor understood the behavior of the other or the reasons for that behavior. If imagined intersubjectivity did not exist, neither Nixon nor Brezhnev would have publicly committed themselves to a separate ABM Treaty and possibly not have made the concessions necessary to reach one.

The Moscow Summit

The May 20 agreement did not resolve any of the technical details that surrounded SALT; those took an additional year of negotiations to hammer out. Both delegations worked quickly though, once the United States and Soviet Union decided to sign the agreement at a summit in Moscow on May 22, 1972. As the Moscow summit approached, most of the details of the ABM Treaty had been resolved. Yet, two weeks before the summit, the enterprise was at risk. In a dramatic turnaround, Nixon told his National Security Council on May 8, "There will be no summit."[77] Then, just as quickly, Nixon changed his mind again, deciding to go to Moscow and sign the ABM Treaty.

Did Nixon gain accurate information about Brezhnev? Was the near breakdown in cooperation the result of misperceptions and was its restoration the result of common knowledge? I argue that Nixon decided to go because he believed Brezhnev would not. Imagined intersubjectivity, not common knowledge, led Nixon to cooperate.

Earlier that year, North Vietnam had begun its Easter Offensive, a massive invasion of the South. Nixon was enraged. The Easter Offensive occurred during troop withdrawals and negotiations with the North.[78] Nixon saw both détente and his reelection at risk. He told Kissinger, "If the ARVN collapses? A lot of other things will collapse around here. . . . We're playing a Russian game, a Chinese game, and an election game." Kissinger responded, "That's why we've got to blast the living bejeezus out of North Vietnam."[79] As Seymour Hersh observed, this was "war by temper tantrum."[80]

I argue that Nixon did not himself cancel because he believed Brezhnev would cancel. Between May 1 and May 8, Nixon (a) did not want to go to the summit if the United States was losing in Vietnam, and (b) believed the solution to this problem was to let Brezhnev pay the political cost of cancelling. These two claims are crucial to my argument because Nixon's misperception of the Soviet position—that they would cancel instead of attend—led him to pursue a cooperative course (not cancelling) even though he preferred not to cooperate.

Even before the May 8 announcement the summit was at risk. Nixon thought it would damage his chances for reelection if he met with Brezhnev at the height of the offensive. As H. R. Haldeman explained to his diary, "how can we have a Summit meeting and be drinking toasts to Brezhnev while Soviet tanks are crumbling Hué."[81] In mid-to-late April, Nixon ordered Kissinger to prioritize Vietnam over the summit in his negotiations with the Soviets, implicitly linking a solution in Vietnam to the success of SALT.[82] In a meeting at the White House on May 1, he reiterated to Kissinger that "under no circumstances would the P[resident] go to the Summit while we're in trouble on Vietnam."[83] On April 29, 1972, Nixon ordered Kissinger to cancel the summit, an order that Kissinger chose to ignore until Nixon cooled off. At the same time that Nixon was contemplating cancelling, he was also suggesting that Haig plan for calling up reserves and seizing Haiphong and Hanoi.[84] As Nixon told a close friend, "It will of course, probably, most people think it will sink the Russian summit, but if it does, what the hell."[85] SALT was much less important than Vietnam. The previous month, Nixon had remarked, "We have got to give up the Summit in order to get a settlement in Vietnam. . . . Vietnam is ten times more important than the Summit. . . . Tell him no discussions of the Summit before they settle Vietnam and that is an order!"[86]

At first, Nixon planned to cancel the summit. On May 2, he and Haldeman met to plan how to word a statement to cancel the summit.[87] But Nixon soon changed his mind. Haldeman had done a poll on the summit, finding that it was popular despite the situation in Vietnam.[88] This created a dilemma: How could Nixon cancel without risking a public backlash? That evening, Nixon called Kissinger to discuss reevaluating his decision on account of the polls.[89] Should Nixon cancel the summit or let the Soviets cancel so that Nixon could obtain the peace dividend?

To be clear, Nixon thought Brezhnev would cancel. The preponderance of conversation between May 1 and May 8 clearly shows that most of the major actors in the Nixon administration expected Brezhnev to cancel. This contrasts with Haig's claims that Nixon was always planning on going to the summit and that Nixon believed the Soviets would not cancel if Nixon escalated in Vietnam.[90] Haig claims that the administration thought Nixon could be tough nosed in Vietnam and look like a peacemaker in Moscow. In contrast to Haig's interpretation of events, the historical record clearly shows that Nixon had his doubts. He agreed that he needed to escalate in Vietnam but thought the price of escalation was no summit.[91] He could not be seen in Moscow while Russian military equipment was being used to overrun US positions. The historical record gives Haig's interpretation of events little credence; days later, Nixon continued to remark, "I cannot be in Moscow at a time when the North Vietnamese are rampaging through the streets of Hue."[92] Appearing at the summit would make Nixon look weak, and not going would make him seem like a hawk.

A Brezhnev cancellation, however, would provide Nixon with a political advantage. As John Connally explained to Nixon, "It is better for the Soviets to cancel the summit than us."[93] Haldeman argued that the last time a summit had failed dramatically—Eisenhower's summit with

Khrushchev—it had enhanced Eisenhower's popularity; Nixon, apparently convinced, made the same argument to Kissinger two days later.[94] Like Eisenhower, if Nixon did not cancel, then he could look tough nosed in Vietnam and like a peacemaker, but only if he did not actually need to follow through on meeting with Brezhnev. If they met, then Nixon might look weak, running to Moscow to sign arms deals while the North Vietnamese were making gains. Kissinger explained in a conversation the next day, "So be it. We will have the record of having tried."[95]

When Nixon opted to blockade North Vietnam, therefore, he believed one side-effect would be that Brezhnev would cancel the summit.[96] In a sense, Nixon decided to play a game of chicken. He would unswervingly move head-on toward a summit because whichever leader veered first would pay a political cost. Nixon chose not to cancel so as to force the Soviets to call off the meeting. After the commencement of the bombings, Nixon waited for the inevitable cancellation. While they were waiting, the administration and the public scoured the Soviet press, diplomatic exchanges, and public statements for clues about the Soviet response.

For several days, the Nixon administration wrongly assumed the Soviets would cancel. The Soviet media assailed the bombings in Vietnam but did not include official statements about the summit.[97] The back channel was also silent except for an ominous message that an attack on Soviet ships would be considered an act of war, after which US pilots accidently struck a Soviet ship.[98] Only on May 11 did Kissinger suspect that he and Nixon had erred in believing the Soviets would cancel. At a meeting with Dobrynin, to which he brought a note from the Soviet leadership that condemned the Vietnam bombings, Kissinger repeatedly asked whether the note was intended to communicate something about the summit. Dobrynin consistently said no, the letter was just a letter condemning the United States and did not take a position on the summit.[99] The following morning, Kissinger spoke to Nixon on the telephone, pointing out that if the Soviets were going to cancel, their best opportunity had been the previous night. He now thought the odds of having a summit were better than a coin toss.[100] Later that afternoon, after discussing the exchange of gifts in Moscow, Kissinger was sure. "We can count on the summit," he reported to Nixon.[101]

One interpretation of Nixon's vocal statements that he wanted to cancel the summit is that he was playing devil's advocate.[102] This position, first elaborated by Haig and recently endorsed by Robert Dallek, suggests that

Nixon wanted to go to the summit but worried that a Soviet cancelation might damage Nixon's foreign policy and chances for reelection.[103] If true, then Nixon's misperception that Brezhnev would cancel was not crucial for cooperation because Nixon would agree to go whether or not Brezhnev planned on attending. The evidence in support of this claim is not persuasive.[104] Dallek cites a note from Haig to Kissinger claiming that Nixon was playing devil's advocate. It's unclear, however, how Haig formed this impression. In two meetings alone with Haig on May 2, Nixon continually asserted that attending the summit was politically impossible.[105] In fact, his strongest language about cancelling was reserved for these occasions: "But then you come to this. How can you possibly, how can you possibly go to the Soviet Union and toast to Brezhnev and Kosygin and sign a SALT agreement in the Great Hall of St. Peter when Russian tanks and guns are kicking the hell out of our allies in Vietnam? Now that's—I ask you, how in the hell can you do it?" Haig's reply—"It's impossible to do if there's that kind of a decisive battle still underway"—does not track with the claim that Nixon believed it politically advantageous to go to the summit.[106]

In contrast to Nixon's conviction that the summit would not occur, Brezhnev worried about the political reaction but continued toward the summit. When the Soviet leadership met, Brezhnev resisted pressure to cancel.[107] North Vietnam had launched the Easter Offensive without Soviet knowledge and refused Soviet offers to mediate. The leadership would not allow North Vietnam a veto over Soviet foreign policy.[108] Brezhnev was still nervous about the reaction of Central Committee members and convened a secret Central Committee plenum in the following days, but his fears were unfounded as several important members vocally supported the summit.[109]

Nixon thus agreed to go to the summit, in part, because he believed that the Soviets would cancel. Brezhnev, having no intention of canceling, did not consider it likely the United States would cancel. Nixon thought the Soviets shared the principles of his actions, that the political reality of meeting while bombs were falling was untenable for both parties. He thus expected Brezhnev to exhibit the same behavior he would: Brezhnev would undertake the action that Nixon could not because of public opinion. Brezhnev, however, did not know that Nixon would like to cancel the summit; he believed that Nixon shared his belief in the domestic and international importance of the summit and thus would not seriously contemplate canceling. The meeting happened because of imagined inter-subjectivity, not common knowledge. If Nixon had chosen to cancel, it likely would have enraged hardliners in the politburo, making future summit meetings difficult, and removed Nixon's chief incentive to meet—the coming 1972 elections. The history of failed Cold War summit meetings does not leave one optimistic about future prospects for cooperation.

The US-Soviet relationship was rooted in a FIB at all three moments of the negotiations. All three are examples of imagined intersubjectivity; neither party knew the reasons for the other's negotiating behavior, nor could they accurately predict what the other would do. At each of these three critical junctures, as the parties stumbled one step closer to the ABM Treaty, policymakers in both countries learned about the other side. These cases of imagined intersubjectivity were extinguished quickly. When a party reacted unpredictably to a negotiating offer, it was revealed that the offer was based on a misperception. But this series of FIBs moved the parties closer, step by step or stumble by stumble, until the signing of the ABM Treaty. The role of FIBs in this process shows that tripping can move someone forward in the same way that stepping does, so long as one is willing to trip again and again.

Counterfactuals

In the previous section, I traced the process through which the ABM Treaty was reached. Kissinger offered to negotiate ABMs because of a mistaken assumption that the Soviets would reject the offer. The pattern of concession making that led to the May 20 agreement, which broke a deadlock in the negotiations, resulted from a critical ambiguity that led each party to publicly commit to the treaty. At the eleventh hour, when Nixon considered canceling the summit and the signing of the treaty, a misperception of Brezhnev's position led him not to cancel. In each case, imagined intersubjectivity was useful in moving the superpowers toward cooperation.

The evidence from process tracing has shown the role of imagined intersubjectivity in reaching the ABM Treaty. Process tracing can show the process through which a cause leads to an effect; however, to demonstrate that the cause is a necessary condition requires counterfactual analysis to show that other pathways to the same effect are improbable. To provide more evidence that imagined intersubjectivity was a necessary condition, I engage in two forms of counterfactual analysis. First, how would the negotiation of the ABM Treaty have been affected by more information at these three critical moments in the process? Second, if the negotiations had stumbled at any of these three moments, would cooperation on ABMs have occurred later, perhaps in the second half of the 1970s?

In asking these questions, I primarily focus on US decision makers. My earlier analysis traced the process through which largely American concessions were made, and these concessions promoted cooperation. The Soviet Union usually responded to American offers; only the May 20 agreement involved Soviet offers to which the United States needed to respond. Moreover, there is enough of a historical record within the Nixon administration to show the likely results of counterfactual levels of information; there is not an equivalent body of work on Soviet decision making, and therefore I have less confidence in potential counterfactuals on the Soviet side.

NCA-Only Offer

Kissinger's decision to offer an NCA-only ABM component of a future arms control treaty was the result of a complex calculation intended to play the US Senate and the Soviets off against each other. Kissinger offered NCA-only ABM defenses, not because he preferred those defenses, but because he believed the Soviets would reject the offer. If Kissinger had had more information about the Soviet position, would he have offered to negotiate an ABM agreement? And, if Kissinger had not made an offer to negotiate ABM defenses, would a treaty have emerged later in the Nixon administration, or perhaps even later in the 1970s?[110]

To respond to these questions, it is helpful to depict the interaction as it was understood by Kissinger. Kissinger's understanding of the likely course of the SALT process is depicted in figure 3.1. Kissinger wanted to build an ABM system for domestic and strategic reasons, and he preferred that a full system be built to a partial build, and a partial build to cancelling the program or a Soviet acceptance of the offer.[111] Kissinger believed that the Senate's payoffs would vary as a function of the offers he might make. If Kissinger offered to negotiate a limited but still full system, such as a negotiated level of ABMs that would allow them to be dispersed across the United States, then the Senate would likely favor cancelling the ABM program. This offer is not a sincere effort to limit ABMs, meaning

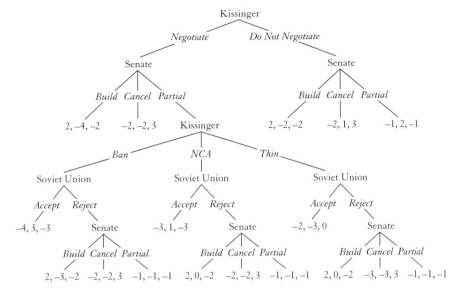

Figure 3.1. Kissinger's perspective on the NCA-only offer. The payoffs, reading from left to right, are for Kissinger, the Senate, and the Soviets. In this depiction of Kissinger's understanding of the NCA-only offer, the payoffs are largely ordinal, with 1 representing a slight gain, 2 a larger gain, and 3 a maximal gain (along with the corresponding negative payoffs). This game, and those that follow, are solvable through backwards induction, are subgame perfect, and the payoffs are estimated, although, any permutation that maintains the ordinal values works.

that Kissinger did not attempt to deal with Senate concerns through negotiations.

The crucial question was whether to propose an ABM ban or an NCA-only offer. Kissinger decided that an NCA-only offer would provide more leverage over the Senate. If he offered a ban and the Soviets rejected it, the Senate could build a partial system in response. If he offered a partial system, and the Soviets rejected it, then the Senate would need to build a more complete system in response. Therefore, the equilibrium path led Kissinger to offer a NCA-only deal in order to pressure the Senate to build a more complete ABM system.

If Kissinger knew the Soviets would accept a NCA-only offer or an ABM ban, would he have made the offer? This counterfactual requires changing the Soviet preferences, making the Soviets prefer accepting a NCA-only offer or an ABM ban to rejecting them.[112] These counterfactual changes are indicated in figure 3.2, where the changes relevant to the outcome are represented by bolded lines. In the counterfactual case,

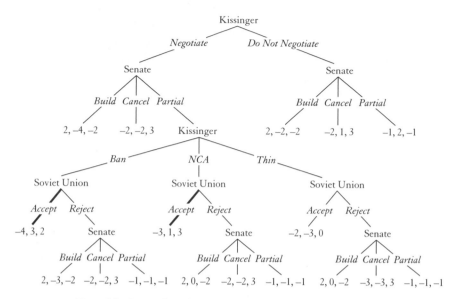

Figure 3.2. Counterfactual: Kissinger with information on Soviet position

Kissinger recognizes that his three potential negotiating strategies will leave him worse off because no strategy would persuade the Senate that the United States needed a defensive system. If Kissinger offered to ban ABMs, the Soviets might accept the deal, preventing ABM deployment. If Kissinger offered to limit weapons to a more complete system, the Senate would cancel the ABM program because Kissinger would have made no serious attempt to limit the unpopular weapons system, and therefore could not argue that Soviet refusal to limit weapons meant that the United States needed to build weapons. By choosing to not negotiate, Kissinger would allow the Senate to continue funding a partial system. Therefore, Kissinger's belief that the Soviets would refuse the NCA-only system is a necessary condition for cooperation because that belief is central to his making any ABM offer at SALT.

If Kissinger had not made an offer to negotiate with the Soviet Union in 1970, would ABMs have made it onto the negotiating table in the SALT process? Would cooperation have occurred in 1973 or 1974 instead of 1972? A delay in the ABM negotiations likely would have ended the chance for cooperation. If the Senate eliminated the ABM program before a treaty was signed, the Soviet Union would have no incentive to formalize the deal in a treaty. Recall that Soviet hawks were happy to continue research and development of the Galosh system, and there is little reason to believe that doves would have supported unilaterally limiting Soviet programs for no apparent gains. Furthermore, a major incentive for the Soviets to agree to an offensive freeze was preventing the growth of the American ABM program. With no ABM proposal on the table in 1970, it is difficult to see what the substance of SALT would have become, who would have tabled an ABM proposal—the Soviets rarely suggested topics for discussion—and where momentum in the process would reside. More important, the climate for cooperation with the Soviet Union was positive in the early 1970s (discussed in the next chapter), and attempts at cooperation became more difficult as a growing conservative shift in foreign policy occurred later in the decade. There are substantial reasons to believe the first Nixon administration had a window of opportunity for cooperation that was quickly closing. Therefore, imagined intersubjectivity was a necessary condition for the NCA-only offer, and the NCA-only offer was the only offer that would have led the United States to negotiate an ABM Treaty.

May 20 Agreement

Due to the ambiguous wording of both the negotiations and the written text of the May 20 agreement, the parties were able to reach agreement because each believed that the other was making a concession over the sequence of the negotiations. Since each believed the other made a concession, the Soviets dropped their demands that both NCA-only and FBS be included in the final agreement, and Kissinger gave up the demand for an immediate and comprehensive limitation on offensive weapons. The agreement also publicly committed both sides to arms control, increasing the political costs of not reaching an agreement.

Two sets of counterfactual questions are relevant to the inference that misperceptions led to the May 20 agreement and that the agreement was necessary for cooperation. First, if either Nixon or Kissinger understood that the Soviets were not making the concession of linking the offensive and defensive elements of the treaties together within the negotiation process, would they have signed the May 20 agreement? Second, if the Soviets had understood that the United States intended to maintain a link between the defensive and offensive elements after the May 20 agreement, would they have signed? Would they have dropped their demand that the United States include forward-based systems?

The historical record clearly shows that only through misperception was the agreement reachable. Before the misperceptions that led to the May 20 agreement emerged, Kissinger repeatedly rejected Dobrynin's offer to conclude a separate ABM agreement. Kissinger argued that the only leverage the United States had to limit the SS-9s that worried US policymakers was the ABM. He explained to Nixon, "If they're not willing to give us a freeze before an ABM agreement, they sure as hell aren't going to give it to us after," to which Nixon responded by saying that a Soviet attempt at a "Hanoi tactic" (asking for a concession first) was inadequate for US concessions.[113] This steadfast negotiating position was maintained when the agreement was later disputed. During the debate at SALT over the ambiguities of May 20, Kissinger never backed down. After several months, the US position prevailed and the Soviets agreed to conduct both negotiations simultaneously.

If there was room for movement, it was on the Soviet side. If the Soviets knew that Kissinger would insist on negotiating the freeze and the ABM agreement simultaneously, would they have dropped their demands related to FBS and NCA-only? In May 1971, the answer was clearly no. After the ambiguities were discovered, it took months for the Soviet position to change. There is no evidence that the Soviets would have considered changing the sequence earlier, and the repeated efforts to craft ABM-first language in the May 20 agreement is indicative that it mattered. The negotiators at SALT were stalled because the Soviets refused to concede their interpretation of the agreement.

However, the Soviets eventually met Kissinger's demand to negotiate the agreements simultaneously. Does that mean the misunderstanding was unimportant, as the Soviets were willing to make concessions on FBS, NCA-only, and sequence in the final bargain? This is unlikely. First, recall that until progress was made on the ABM, there was little impetus to have a summit meeting, but once there was movement in that direction, Brezhnev was interested in linking the progress in arms control talks to his enhanced position in the Soviet Union. Without the May 20 agreement, the summit might not have been forthcoming, and thus there would have been less impetus to meet US demands over sequence. More important, Brezhnev might not have publicly linked the ABM Treaty to his peace agenda. Instead, he could have linked his agenda at the Twenty-Fourth Party Congress to the Incidents at Sea Agreement, grain sales, or the Basic Principles agreement. Highlighting the importance of these agreements might have met the political demands for cooperation with the United States without needing an ABM treaty. Additionally, if sequence had been delayed for too long, it might have become linked to more thorny issues, especially Vietnam. There was little chance for new American concessions during the Easter Offensive, and the negotiators still had to resolve complex issues such as limits on submarine-launched missiles and the grain deal. Reaching agreement in 1971 was therefore important before the dilemmas of 1972.

If the May 20 agreement had not occurred, would the ABM Treaty have been reached later? The short answer is that it is unlikely. Before the May 20 agreement, there was no progress at SALT. The Soviet Union was not willing to meet the US demand for a comprehensive offensive weapons agreement, and the Americans were not willing to meet the Soviet demands that FBS and NCA-only be included in the agreement. In the early 1970s, Kissinger was not ready or willing to reduce the US presence in Europe for the sake of SALT, and the Soviets were not willing to abandon the modernization of their missiles. Progress happened because of the agreement; it is unclear where else it may have been made. Furthermore, as noted, if an agreement was not forthcoming before the 1972 elections, and especially before the controversy over Watergate began, it is doubtful that Nixon would have had the political capital to reach an agreement with the Soviet Union.[114]

Therefore, imagined intersubjectivity was a necessary condition for the May 20 agreement. Had either party understood the principles of the other, or realized that future negotiating behavior would not be altered because of the agreement, they would not have made the concessions necessary for the May 20 agreement to occur. This would have fatally undermined progress toward a summit, prevented the ABM from becoming linked to Brezhnev's peace agenda, and led to the sequence issue being injected into the troublesome calculations that immediately preceded the signing of the ABM Treaty.

Moscow Summit

I have shown that during the Easter Offensive in Vietnam, Nixon decided to cancel the summit and not to sign the ABM Treaty. The evidence from process tracing shows that Nixon decided not to cancel the ABM Treaty signing because he expected Brezhnev to cancel, allowing Nixon to obtain political and strategic gains without having to handle the embarrassment of meeting with the Soviets while Americans were taking losses in Vietnam.

If Nixon had more information about Brezhnev's motivations, would he have cancelled? And, if Nixon cancelled in the spring of 1972, would the ABM Treaty have been agreed on in the near future? There is clear evidence that Nixon would have cancelled the summit if he had more information about Brezhnev's intentions. As explained earlier, one can understand Nixon's decision not to cancel the Moscow Summit of 1972 as a game of chicken. Figure 3.3 depicts Nixon's perspective on the decision. Nixon was confronted with two options. First, he could cancel the summit, although he believed that he would be punished in the 1972 election because the upcoming meeting with Brezhnev was popular. The payoff would be negative, but only slightly negative because it would avoid the larger problem of meeting with Brezhnev during a North Vietnamese offensive. Second, he could agree to go to the summit, forcing Brezhnev to cancel. If Brezhnev canceled, which Nixon thought was a certainty because of the US bombing of the capital of a Soviet ally, then Nixon would have avoided the political fallout of having to meet with Brezhnev and he would not have to take responsibility for the collapse of the summit.

If Nixon had known that Brezhnev preferred not to cancel the summit, would he himself have canceled? Nixon's decision, including accurate information about Brezhnev's preferences, is represented in figure 3.4. In the counterfactual, Nixon knows that Brezhnev prefers to continue rather than to cancel. The bold line shows the variance between Nixon's

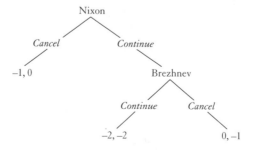

Figure 3.3. Nixon's perspective on the 1972 Summit Decision

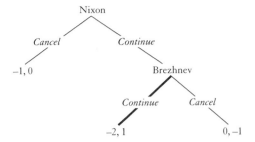

Figure 3.4. Counterfactual: Nixon understands Brezhnev's preferences

definition of the situation and the counterfactual: Brezhnev prefers that both parties continue rather than having either party cancel.

If Nixon had known that Brezhnev would not cancel, Nixon would have cancelled the summit. As already noted, Nixon had ordered Kissinger to cancel only two weeks earlier, but Kissinger had ignored the order. Before Haldeman ordered public opinion polling in early May, Nixon told his National Security Council that the summit was off. The evidence presented earlier shows that the meetings that changed Nixon's mind were those that presented the argument that Brezhnev would cancel. Therefore, if the bargaining situation had remained the same, and the only addition in the counterfactual case is added information, the summit would not have occurred.

If the summit had not occurred, would the ABM Treaty have been concluded later, or would it have been scrapped? It is likely that if either party cancelled, the prospects for the ABM Treaty would have been dim. One critical reason for pushing toward the ABM Treaty was the 1972 elections.[115] The summit was scheduled for May, and it is unlikely that a summit held later would occur before Nixon hit the campaign trail. Thus, one of the major impetuses toward concluding the ABM Treaty would disappear if the summit was delayed. In addition, any significant delay would have reduced the momentum toward the agreement.[116] Progress toward the summit dictated progress on arms control.[117] While the ABM Treaty was largely worked out by April 1972, the interim agreement still had several unresolved issues over which there were hurried negotiations as the May deadline approached.[118] Even after Nixon arrived in Moscow there were days of frantic negotiations, in particular over the definition of "heavy missile," to resolve the thorny issues related to offensive weapons. It is, at best, unclear whether progress on offensive weapons would have been made without the danger of a failed summit looming over the negotiators, and it is very clear that if the interim agreement was not reached, the ABM Treaty would have been doomed. Furthermore, extended delays might also have prevented the conclusion of the ABM Treaty. As discussed in the next chapter, there was a window of opportunity for US-Soviet security cooperation that ended when Jimmy Carter entered office. SALT II was contentious and never ratified, and the ABM Treaty likely would have fared just as badly with conservatives in the US Senate.

In sum, if Nixon had understood Brezhnev's position on the summit, he would likely have preemptively cancelled. If he had done so, cooperation on ABMs would at least have been significantly delayed, and more likely not occurred at all. Therefore, imagined intersubjectivity was a necessary condition for the summit meeting and the successful signing of the ABM Treaty. If Nixon had understood the principles or could have predicted the direction of Brezhnev's behavior, he would have either cancelled the summit or likely linked the summit to impossible improvements in Vietnam. This would have delayed and probably ended the movement toward the ABM Treaty.

Assessing Common Knowledge

The argument advanced so far, that imagined intersubjectivity played an essential role in the ABM Treaty process, does not deny that intersubjectivity also played a role. It might be necessary that actors understand some things in identical ways, even if imagined intersubjectivity exists in regard to one fundamental belief. This appears to be the case in the ABM Treaty process. The findings that emerge from studying the ABM negotiations show mixed results for the role of common knowledge.

Strategic common knowledge was in some respects crucial for the success of the ABM Treaty. The United States and the Soviet Union understood who their primary partners were in the SALT process. They negotiated with each other. The Soviet Union also understood the importance of the US Congress, and close votes in the Senate, to the SALT process. However, there were also central misunderstandings related to the identification of players. The Soviet Union never grasped the relationship between Vietnam and the SALT process, and there were frequent disagreements over the role of NATO allies on the issue of FBS in Europe. It is unclear, in the end, whether all sides understood the roles that other states played.

There is less evidence to support the existence of strategic common knowledge about the payoffs for each of the players. Neither the Soviet nor the American negotiators successfully understood the payoffs of their interlocutors, no matter how certain they were that their guesses were right. Moreover, the counterfactual analysis shows that these misperceptions were necessary for cooperation.

Linguistic common knowledge also shows mixed results. On the one hand, it was crucial that each party was able to communicate clearly with the other in certain cases. The Soviet Union needed to understand the meaning of the NCA-only offer in 1970 and that Kissinger was dropping the demand that an agreement be comprehensive in 1971. Similarly, the Nixon administration needed to know that the Soviet Union was no longer pushing for the inclusion of limits on FBS in 1971 and that the Soviet Union's condemnation of US conduct in Vietnam was not tantamount to a summit cancellation. In fact, each side generally communicated quite clearly with the other, and each caught the right meaning in many cases.

Yet the May 20 agreement shows that there are cases in which linguistic common knowledge can stand as an impediment to cooperation. If the United States and the Soviet Union had understood the meaning that the other imparted to "together with," "pri," "simultaneous," or other language, they would not have made the concessions necessary to reach the ABM Treaty. There are cases in which linguistic common knowledge is not necessary to, but stands in the way of, international cooperation.

There is some evidence that there was a role for situation-specific common knowledge in the ABM Treaty negotiations. A significant amount of technical know-how was common knowledge. Neither party disputed how specific types of missiles, submarines, radars, or other weapons work. Furthermore, both parties understood specific negotiating rules, such as the importance of site alternation, protocol, and other diplomatic procedures that may have stood in the way of the negotiation process. An institutionalist scholar who studied the ABM Treaty process would likely find other situation-specific elements of common knowledge that also played a role.[119]

In conclusion, this chapter provides decisive evidence that, at least in the case of the ABM Treaty, imagined intersubjectivity was a necessary condition for cooperation. Kissinger only offered to negotiate an ABM Treaty because he misunderstood the Soviet position; he and Dobrynin only agreed to a crucial compromise because each misunderstood what the other was offering; and Nixon only agreed to travel to Moscow to sign the agreement because he thought that Brezhnev would cancel the summit before he left. At each moment in the process, each party believed that it *knew* what the other side would do, and they were often wrong. They imagined that the other side made or would make concessions, and they were wrong. The ABM Treaty was the product of imagined intersubjectivity, not common knowledge.

4

The Decline of Détente

The President [Ford]:	I should tell you, Mr. General Secretary, and you may have already heard this from your Ambassador and Foreign Minister, that I intend to be a candidate in 1976. I believe it most important, therefore, to have coordination of our foreign policies, coordination which I am convinced benefits not only the United States and the USSR but also the entire world. I am apprehensive that if others were elected the policy of 72–76 could be undercut. [...]
General Secretary Brezhnev:	I'm for Jackson.
The Secretary [Kissinger]:	Our intelligence reports say so.

Vladivostok meeting, November 1974

I have traced the process through which imagined intersubjectivity promoted cooperation in the early 1970s. The shift from enmity in the early Cold War to rivalry during détente was caused by misperceptions. The Soviets believed that the United States was ready to accept political equality and some Soviet influence in the periphery and would no longer try to obtain positions of strength in negotiations. The United States, in contrast, believed that the superpower contest remained a competition for political dominance and tried to use issue linkages and nuclear threats to prevent the Soviets from enlarging their area of influence. This false intersubjective belief—the erroneous belief that there was common knowledge or shared ideas—smoothed the path for cooperation by allowing the superpowers to overlook differences and disagreements.

Skeptics might point to two traditional historical claims about the period to show that false intersubjective beliefs did not matter or in fact damaged cooperation. The first argument is that some form of cooperation was inevitable, even if it did not take the specific form of an agreement on basic principles, an ABM treaty, or cooperation during the 1973 Arab-Israeli War. These skeptics might point to structural pressures on the United States and Soviet Union that encouraged cooperation: domestic pressures in the United States to find a way out of Vietnam and in the Soviet Union to reduce defense costs, as well as economic incentives in the Soviet Union to create a trade partnership with the United States. False intersubjective beliefs, in short, may have smoothed the path to cooperation, but other pressures might have led to the same results.

The second argument—most forcefully advanced by Raymond Garthoff—is that misperceptions damaged détente, leading to its eventual decline.[1] In his view, misperceptions plagued the superpower relationship, leading them to read the worst into each other's behavior. On balance, therefore, misperception damaged rather than promoted cooperation. These arguments challenge the main claims of chapters 2 and 3 of this book. If structural pressures were sufficient for cooperation, than FIBs were not necessary. And, in the long run, FIBs may have unraveled cooperation by creating mistrust when parties "broke the rules" by behaving in ways that the other side did not expect.

Neither of these traditional arguments is satisfactory. The same structural, economic, and domestic political pressures that these theories claim led to cooperation were also present during the decline of détente, making their sufficiency to explain deep cooperation unlikely. If détente was inevitable because of these overpowering forces, why did cooperation decline when these structural pressures were the strongest?

At the same time, the argument that misperceptions about détente contributed to its demise may be too simplistic. Hawkish Democrats in the United States (and some hawks in the Soviet Union several years later) gained increasing power and used that influence to reduce the prospect for cooperation. This group—including key figures such as Henry "Scoop" Jackson and Zbigniew Brzezinski—had always opposed cooperation. Jackson, whom Ford, Brezhnev, and Kissinger were joking about in the epigraph to this chapter,[2] was an early and very vocal critic of détente. In the early 1970s, however, these hawks did not have sufficient political power to challenge the Nixon White House and to collapse détente, although they tried. As they gained increasing influence over foreign policy, they fought tooth and nail to end US-Soviet cooperation, to pressure the Soviets on human rights, and to combat Soviet influence on the periphery. The rise of these figures—not the misperceptions that contributed to détente—led to détente's early demise. Neither their anti-Soviet views nor their growing power was related to the misperceptions underwriting détente. In short, the set of false intersubjective beliefs that contributed to the rise of détente does not also explain its decline as Garthoff and others suggest.

In the first section of this chapter, I briefly describe three accounts of the origins of cooperation during détente that are related to power, institutions, and trade. I develop a set of predictions about how these factors relate to the decline of détente. In the second section, I discuss in detail détente's decline. There are two parallel themes. The first is whether shifts in power, institutions, or trade expectations preceded changes in cooperation, or whether changes in decision-makers' beliefs preceded changes in cooperation. The second is whether the decision to be increasingly confrontational during the 1970s was the result of misperceptions created during détente or due to hostile images that preceded détente. I argue that decision makers who gained power did not develop hostile images of the Soviet Union because they were "tricked" into cooperation ; instead, the group of conservatives who undermined cooperation always held anticooperation views before cooperation began. In the final sections, I analyze alternative explanations for the decline of détente and show that cooperation was not inevitable because of structural, economic, and other pressures.

The Case That Détente Was Inevitable

Many IR theorists do not think of détente as much of a puzzle because the conventional wisdom is sufficient to explain cooperation. Changes in the balance of power, international institutions, and internal economic conditions all pointed toward cooperation. Structural realists may concentrate on the changing distribution of power to show that as the powers approached parity, cooperation became likely. And liberal scholars may

argue that the development of an arms control regime promoted cooperation and trade provided strong incentives for warming relations.

Power

Realists focus on power-based considerations to explain the rise of cooperation and institutions.[3] I consider two realist explanations for cooperation.
The first view is that cooperation is more likely when great powers reach
parity. When powers reach parity, their relative security fears are less intense
because there are fewer opportunities for war, which allows for cooperation. For example, E. H. Carr argued that parity was the foundation for the
Locarno Treaty.[4] In 1922, Germany could not convince France to agree to a
security deal because France was more powerful than Germany. Two years
later, cooperation was possible because the French began to fear Germany's
growing power. For Randall Schweller and William Wohlforth, "the moral
of Carr's story is straightforward: the ideational and interest convergence
required for the Locarno Treaty was simply a product of Germany's achievement of relative power parity with France." Focusing on parity also provides
an explanation for the decline of cooperation. When parity ends, so too does
cooperation. Shortly after the Locarno Treaty was signed Germany became
stronger than France. The treaty became ineffective when Germany had no
interest in cooperation with the French, whom they no longer feared.[5]

A realist might argue that US-Soviet détente was similar to Locarno.
As shown in chapter 2, a fundamental element of détente was the recognition of strategic parity. This clarified the bipolar nature of the international
system and redcuced the chances of conflict.[6] Limited cooperation therefore may have become possible because concerns about relative gains were
less acute in a period in which neither side thought dominance possible.
Hypothesis 4.1, the balance-of-power hypothesis, summarizes the applica-
tion of balance-of-power theory to détente:

> H4.1: The shifting balance of power is sufficient for explaining détente.
> As the superpowers approached parity, cooperation became possible,
> especially in areas that did not implicate their relative security. When
> parity ended, cooperation was reduced.

Power-transition theory also furnishes useful hypotheses for explaining the decline of détente. For power-transition theorists, in general,

parity leads to conflict, not cooperation as suggested by Carr, Schweller, and Wohlforth.[7] The logic of power-transition theory is that war is likely when a rising power approaches or obtains parity because declining powers worry about their future security and influence. In the case of détente, power-transition theorists might argue that as the Soviet Union reached parity and was seen to be moving ahead, the United States increasingly adopted confrontational policies. Thus, power-transition theorists might advocate Hypothesis 4.2:

> H4.2: The perceived power transition between the United States and the Soviet Union is sufficient for explaining the decline of détente. As the superpowers approached parity, cooperation became impossible because of mutual security fears.

Institutions

Liberals, unlike realists, have concentrated on explaining specific agreements reached during détente. Liberal IR scholars highlight the importance of institutions, democracy, and trade for international cooperation.[8] Several scholars argue that two features of liberalism, institutions and trade, explain the achievement of cooperation during the Nixon administration.

Liberal institutionalists often posit that cooperation in international politics is complicated by a lack of information, absence of a centralized enforcement agent, and high transaction costs.[9] Therefore, there is a demand for international regimes to provide information, reduce transaction costs, and provide consequences for defection from international agreements. International regimes resolve these problems by enabling actors to develop reputations through continual processes of cooperation, allowing side payments to promote cooperation, and permitting information sharing.[10]

Détente may be a strong case for a liberal institutionalist explanation because the central features of successful regimes were developed during the period.[11] Security cooperation was part of a fledgling security regime. As noted in chapter 2, the ABM Treaty was preceded by the Strategic Arms Limitation Talks, which comprised seven rounds of diplomacy, in which each state invested political capital. The process became heavily institutionalized. Delegations met over a period of years, shared information, developed negotiating rules, and tried to make deals that each could live with. In addition, the superpowers thought of détente as a package and attempted to link improved relations to arms control; trade; and cooperation in space, science, technology, the environment, and conduct in the Third World. Indeed, development of linkages was an integral part of Kissinger's strategy for managing the rise of Soviet power. Joshua Goldstein and John Freeman's *Three-Way Street* is representative of a body of work that suggests that these elements of cooperation in the 1960s and early 1970s were part of a pattern of strategic reciprocity that culminated in détente.[12] This argument is summarized in Hypothesis 4.3:

> H4.3: Détente and the ABM Treaty developed because of the establishment of a security regime. The security regime provided information, established reputations, enabled issue linkages, and ensured reciprocity. The development of the regime was sufficient for the improvement in relations and the treaty.

Trade

A second liberal approach to explaining détente is the commercial peace.[13] Many scholars argue that trading partners rarely fight. Dale Copeland extends this to explain cooperation during détente. During the 1970s, the superpowers engaged in little trade, but expectations for future trade were high.[14] Trade, especially the importation of American grain, provided economic incentives for reaching agreements in other issue areas.[15] Trade was, therefore, the sweetener that made cooperation possible. The evidence for Copeland's claim is especially strong because it can also explain the decline of détente. As discussed later, the undermining of trade deals in 1973 was an important step to undermining cooperation later in the decade. Hypothesis 4.4 summarizes Copeland's view:

> H4.4: Cooperation during détente was caused by high Soviet expectations for trade with the United States. These expectations were sufficient to explain cooperation, and when expectations declined, cooperation ended.

The Decline of Détente

International Relations scholars, whether they focus on power, institutions, or trade may believe that cooperation during détente was inevitable. While

IR scholars tend to disagree about which factor best explains cooperation, there is a consensus that cooperation is not a puzzle. In contrast, I argue that cooperation—at least deep cooperation—was *not* inevitable in 1972. One key factor needed to explain détente is individual decision-makers' beliefs. Within both superpowers, influential political elites opposed détente before it even started. As détente declined, these groups obtained political power—due to political circumstances removed from the US-Soviet rivalry—reducing the prospects for continued cooperation. The simple fact that US conservatives hated cooperating with the Soviet Union, and when they came to power cooperation was reduced, makes structural explanations for cooperation dubious. It seems reasonable to conclude that when decision makers are opposed to cooperation, cooperation is less likely, regardless of structural factors, especially when decision-makers' beliefs precede structural change.

In this section I criticize both structural arguments and the argument about misperceptions unraveling détente. Many observers of détente credit its decline to misperceptions that arose during its formation. The logic of the argument is that détente was premised on a misperception and when that misperception was revealed cooperation became difficult because both parties thought the other side "cheated" on the original deal. In *Détente and Confrontation,* Garthoff gives the primary cause for failure as the gap in their understandings that "led to unrealistic expectations that were not met and that undermined confidence in détente."[16]

To test the merit of the claim that the misperceptions that led to détente also explain its decline, I analyze the decline of détente, especially in the United States. Two observable implications follow from this argument. First, some decision makers changed from being pro-cooperation to being anti-cooperation. Second, the moment at which these decision makers changed their views and behavior is related to behavior by the other superpower that increased mistrust. I focus on the United States because US decision makers were largely responsible for the reduction in cooperation during the period. US political elites undermined trade arrangements, shifted US arms control positions, and consistently threatened to sink détente because of Third World confrontations. A parallel process—if it did exist in the Soviet Union—was much slower and less effective in curtailing pressures for cooperation.

To unpack the importance of the decline of détente, I break the decline—between 1972 and 1980—into three periods. The first establishes a baseline by analyzing the beliefs and influence of antidétente forces in 1972 at the height of cooperation and. In the second, I focus on changes in their beliefs and influence during the remainder of the Nixon administration and the Ford administration (1973–76). And finally I look at end during the Carter administration (1977–80).

Opposition Groups in 1972

When Nixon and Brezhnev met in 1972, détente was at its high point. There was a broad agenda for cooperation from arms control to trade to science to crisis management. During this period, an influential minority in the United States and the Soviet Union opposed cooperation.

Shortly after the successful Moscow Summit of 1972, a growing concern began to mount within the Nixon administration about conservatives from both parties in the US Senate. In particular, Henry Jackson, a conservative Democrat from Washington state, and his influential adviser, Richard Perle, were outspoken critics of détente. While Nixon was in Moscow, Jackson began to argue that the SALT agreements would enable the Soviet Union to gain strategic superiority, claiming that the accords contained "a series of loopholes as big as a 25-megaton bomb."[17] When Nixon returned, Jackson continued to argue against ratification of the SALT agreements, declaring that Nixon had reached "secret" agreements in Moscow that would undermine US security.[18]

Jackson had deep reservations about cooperating with the Soviets. His key argument was that cooperative moves by the Soviets were a ruse to expand Communist power. The Soviets, he argued, had no intention of honoring their SALT obligations and were using arms control to prevent the United States from anticipating Soviet buildups. Furthermore, Jackson believed that Kissinger's policy of selling détente to the public risked undermining popular support for containing the Soviet Union, propped up a failing Soviet economy, and was amoral because it ignored human rights.[19] Jackson's strategic concerns were augmented by political motives. As a socially liberal Democrat who planned to run for president, Jackson had a political incentive to attack Nixon from the right on foreign policy.[20]

Jackson and his allies could not prevent cooperation in 1972 because they did not have sufficient political strength, but they were influential enough to take important shots at détente. Nixon, worried about SALT's ratification, tried to placate Jackson by dismissing most of the SALT negotiating team, including Gerard Smith, the chief negotiator.[21] Since Jackson argued that the SALT team was too soft on the Soviet Union, this was intended as a way to win Jackson's support for the SALT process. Moreover, Nixon agreed to the Jackson amendment, which declared that the United States must not negotiate an arms control treaty that would leave it worse off in any category of weapons.[22] This amendment became an enormous barrier in future arms control negotiations. Because the Jackson amendment measured US dominance system by system, arms control treaties could not take into account the overall balance.[23] These measures did not stop SALT, but they heralded problems down the line.

Understanding the beliefs and influence of antidétente forces in 1972 is important for two reasons. The first relates to the argument that misperceptions formed during détente contributed to its demise. The anti-cooperation preferences of many conservatives pre-existed détente. If these groups are implicated in the collapse of cooperation, then misperceptions formed during détente are likely less important than the antidétente policy preferences that pre-existed cooperation. Moreover, if antidétente forces already had anti-cooperation preferences in 1972, then later shifts in the balance of power, institutions, or expectations of trade cannot explain why these groups held anti-cooperion positions because these positions preceded structural change. In other words, détente was only inevitable so long as a group of prodétente policymakers were in office.

Growing Opposition after Nixon

After Nixon resigned from office in August 1974 cooperation with the Soviet Union began to decline. The first set of pressures on détente emerged in economic and trade issues: conservative critics shaped the legislative debate in the United States toward reducing grain shipments to the Soviet Union and placed restrictive conditions on trade relations with the Soviet Union. In addition, they put political pressure on the Ford administration to condemn Soviet conduct on the periphery, especially in Angola. They also began to inflate the extent of the Soviet strategic and military threat to make arms control look less attractive. Even before President Carter took office cooperation was reduced from a broad agenda to just arms control. This increased hostility to détente arose from tactical decisions made by détente critics and was not the result of changes in structural or economic pressures or the realization of a misperception.

In 1972, however, there was widespread interest in developing economic relations with the Soviet Union as an incentive for international cooperation. One important part of the economic relationship was grain sales. In 1972, due to internal shortages, the Soviet Union made a substantial purchase of US grain at below-market prices. When the US harvest proved unreliable, this had the effect of increasing the cost of food for many in America.[24] Opponents of détente seized on the event to claim that the Soviets were intentionally manipulating the price of US grain, calling it "the Great Grain Robbery."[25]

Two years later, the Soviets signed a contract with Continental to purchase 1 million tons of corn and 2.5 million tons of wheat. The timing was unfortunate because the US corn crop was damaged by drought and early cold weather. In a memo to Henry Kissinger, an administration official remarked that "in view of the poisonous residue of the 1972 Soviet purchase, *news of this purchase would almost certainly result in immediate Congressional action to prohibit exports to the USSR, if not to all foreign countries.*"[26] Political concerns led Kissinger to negotiate with the Soviet ambassador to reduce their purchases of corn and grain, and in the end he cancelled the Soviet contracts.[27] This alienated the Soviet leadership, who saw the cancellation as discriminatory in a period when other US clients, such as Iran and China, continued to receive grain shipments.[28]

Broader cooperation over trade was also soured by détente's critics. Shortly after the Moscow summit, the superpowers agreed to a trade deal that called for the extension of most-favored-nation status to the Soviet Union. This deal was important because trade with the United States was an important incentive for Soviet participation in arms control.[29] Even before Nixon introduced the trade bill in the Senate in early 1973, it came under attack. The Soviet Union had recently placed an "education tax" on Jewish emigrants who sought to move to Israel and elsewhere.[30] Jackson used the Soviet restriction on Jewish emigration to form a coalition of liberal and conservative opponents to Nixon, rallying them behind the Jackson-Vanik amendment to the 1974 trade bill that curtailed trade with the Soviet Union until the restriction was relaxed.[31]

The White House response to concerns about Jewish emigration from the Soviet Union had been to reach a deal in 1973 that stipulated that the

Soviets would not interfere with Jewish emigration except for national security purposes.[32] Conservative senators responded that this was not enough. Jackson and his allies argued that there were at least three hundred thousand potential Soviet émigrés whose applications were denied, and that those who wanted to emigrate were subject to widespread harassment. To ensure they were afforded the opportunity to leave, Jackson wanted a specific quota, citing forty-five thousand or sixty thousand as reasonable figures. In addition, he wanted annual congressional review of Soviet most-favored-nation status. The White House opposed both of these provisions. The former would kill the trade deal because the Soviets would reject it the quotas as interference in their sovereign affairs. The congressional review would create inevitable political problems for the White House as it would have to face controversial legislation before the 1976 election. Despite several efforts by the White House to compromise (and a lack of support by the Senate leadership), antidétente legislators prevailed. The Soviet Union pulled out of its trade negotiations with the United States, refusing to accept restrictions on its internal policies.[33]

The economic debate has three important theoretical implications. First, it complicates the claim that détente was caused by high expectations for international trade and that declining expectations reduced the impetus for cooperation. The economic explanation for cooperation gets the story—at least on the US side—backward. Elites who preferred cooperation with the Soviet Union, such as Kissinger and Ford, favored a trade deal with the Soviet Union, and elites who did not want cooperation, such as Jackson, opposed the deal. In other words, general preferences about cooperation determined elites' stance on trade; their stance on trade did not influence their preferences about cooperation. Moreover, the Soviet Union expressed interest in arms control long after the trade deal was dead. By the end of 1974, the Soviet Union did not expect most-favored-nation status with the United States; but throughout the 1970s, the Soviets expressed more interest in arms control than their American counterparts did. Therefore, economic incentives were not necessary for cooperation because cooperation continued for an extended period after the main economic levers of influence no longer existed.

The second implication of the economic debate is that misperceptions rooted in détente did not cause the decline of economic cooperation. The misperception argument—discussed by Garthoff and others—suggests that one cause of confrontation was that misperceptions about détente were revealed over time, increasing distrust. The fate of trade and grain, however, tells a different story. US conservatives caused a confrontation without any precipitating Soviet action. As Kissinger explained in a White House meeting, the pressure over grain and trade was "economic warfare and they haven't done a thing."[34] Misperception and mistrust were not the cause of the decline of cooperation; US conservatives were.

The third and most important development resulting from the economic debate was the organization of an antidétente alliance. The trade issue enabled Jackson to form an alliance with organized labor, pro-Israeli groups, liberal human rights advocates, and conservatives to halt détente. Media commentators, as well as many in the White House, saw the trade debate as drawing a battle line between conservatives and the Ford administration over the control of US foreign policy.[35]

At about the same time, the superpower conflict in the Third World became increasingly difficult to manage, most noticeably in Angola. After the collapse of the Portuguese government in Angola in 1974, three factions began to compete for control of the country. In 1975, Cuba began sending troops to assist the Popular Movement for the Liberation of Angola (MPLA) against a South African intervention. When the United States, concerned about growing Cuban involvement in Africa and the fate of its Angolan allies, convinced Barbados to retract landing rights from Cuban airplanes headed to Angola, Cuba requested Soviet assistance to transport arms and soldiers.[36]

During the Angola crisis, the stakes for each superpower were low. In early 1976, Brezhnev and Kissinger joked while pointing at a map that "showed" the Soviet invasion of the United States would begin in southwest Africa.[37] Unlike the Middle East, there were few long-standing superpower commitments; southern Africa was an unimportant Cold War battleground, and the region did not have sufficient economic resources to justify hard-nosed competition.[38] For the politburo, supporting the MPLA was not worth jeopardizing détente.[39] Soviet diplomats communicated to the White House the seeming unimportance of the conflict on several occasions, and White House officials acknowledged that real Soviet interest was low.[40]

The low-stakes nature of the crisis in some ways meant it was more of a challenge for US policymakers. Congress opposed funding for the conflict because there was little strategic interest and little prospect for success. The result was that Kissinger had few foreign policy tools to use to reduce Soviet involvement.[41] Moreover, because the stakes were low and the level of Soviet support comparable to US support, the Brezhnev leadership did not believe the conflict could undermine détente. When South Africa intervened in 1975, Brezhnev agreed to increase Soviet aid to Angola. As noted in chapter 2, part of the Soviet conception of détente was that military parity meant the Soviet Union could be an active player in supporting national liberation movements; resisting a South African intervention was germane to that understanding.[42]

The real difficulty emerged in the United States. In 1976, Congress passed the Clark amendment to the Arms Export Control Act, which prohibited the US from funding private groups in the Angolan conflict. This hampered Kissinger's détente policy because he could not compete in Angola to minimize Soviet influence. Using his normal dire tone, Kissinger remarked, "We are being deprived of both the carrot and the stick. We will lose Angola and then they will want us to cut off grain to the Soviet Union. We are losing all flexibility and we will soon be in a position of nuclear war or nothing." Ford, absurdly, said, "I couldn't agree more."[43]

The challenge for Kissinger was that he was running low on issues he could use to bargain with the Soviet Union. First, the Right cut off economic sweeteners for cooperation, and then the Left cut off his ability to compete in the Third World. The only remaining issue area he could bargain with was SALT. Kissinger half-heartedly tried to use SALT as leverage to reduce Soviet influence in Angola, but he did not push. He worried that SALT, the centerpiece of Nixon's Soviet policy, would fail if linked to Angola.[44] He favored cooperation in arms control to competition in Africa.

One lasting legacy of the conflict in Angola was another emerging issue that antidétente groups could rally around. In his memoirs, Ford recounts that he needed to paint the Soviets as a threat to get a reluctant Congress to obtain funds for his Angola policy. He explained that the Left's position required that "the Soviet Union can operate with impunity many thousands of miles away with Cuban troops and massive amounts of military equipment, while we refuse any assistance to the majority of the local people who ask only for military equipment to defend themselves."[45] Even more dangerous for détente, Soviet involvement in Angola became an issue in the Republican primary. Ronald Reagan increasingly sought to depict Ford as weak on Angola and to show the inability of détente to contain increased Soviet power.[46] As Ford explained, "the public quite understandably found it hard to comprehend why we should have any dealings with the Russians when they were stealing a march on us in Africa."[47] As a result, Ford stopped using the term "détente" and delayed arms control negotiations until after the election.[48]

The same hawkish turn may also have occurred in the Soviet Union. The limited available evidence indicates that Soviet hawks gained influence over decision making in Angola, preventing Brezhnev from asserting his peace program.[49] One reason is likely the rise of conservatives in the Soviet Union: as Brezhnev's health declined, hawks were well placed to assert influence over foreign policy. The Ford administration's position, however, also likely led the Soviets to take a harder line in Angola. Odd Arne Westad's analysis of Soviet archival material reveals that the Soviets initially limited supplies to Angola that were requested by Cuba because they worried it would risk détente.[50] As the conflict continued, however, the Soviets thought that the United States was using a double standard, claiming that the Soviets broke the spirit of détente in Angola by providing aid when the United States was providing similar support.[51]

Tensions over Angola underscore the insufficiency of structural explanations. Concerns about the balance of power do not explain confrontation and cooperation in Angola because policymakers realized that the balance of power did not hinge on Angola's fate. Moreover, these structural explanations fail to explain the limited nature of competition over Angola and why Kissinger did not use arms control as leverage to reduce Soviet influence there. Structural explanations, in other words, are too broadly cast to explain mixed patterns of cooperation and conflict. In addition, the false intersubjective beliefs formed during détente did not contribute to its demise. The central reason is that those who favored competition—conservatives in the United States, especially Ronald Reagan—never shared the beliefs of those in the Nixon administration about détente. They may have had a different set of misperceptions, such as overstating Soviet involvement in and the importance of southern Africa, but these were far removed from the set of misperceptions that contributed to cooperation.

Despite the failure of economic cooperation and increased Third World confrontation, the Ford administration continued to cooperate on arms control. In November 1974, only a few months after Nixon left office,

Ford traveled to Vladivostok to meet with Brezhnev. The final product of the meeting was the sketch of an agreement to serve as the basis for SALT II. It contained equal aggregate amounts of US and Soviet weaponry, consistent with the Jackson amendment to SALT I, and improved on the 1972 interim agreement by limiting multiple independently targetable reentry vehicles (MIRVs). Conservative critics of détente tried to mount pressure on Ford against another arms control agreement but failed get him to change course. When Ford went to Vladivostok, however, he knew—because of the conservative pressure on the 1972 agreements—that any new pact would be attacked by the Right, and therefore he needed to find a bargain attractive to them.[52]

When Ford returned from Vladivostok, the first significant criticism came from within his administration. Shortly after returning, Paul Nitze, who was a delegate to SALT and proponent of SALT I, resigned from the administration and became SALT II's most outspoken critic. He published a series of high-profile articles criticizing the arms control deal; these were so influential that one arms control observer noted, "If the [SALT II] treaty is killed in the Senate, Nitze will be entitled to much of the blame and the credit sure to be passed around."[53] At the same time, many in the Senate, especially Jackson, argued that Vladivostok risked sparking an arms race.[54] Because Vladivostok provided only a numeric cap on missiles, conservative critics argued that this provided a "throw-weight" advantage to the Soviet Union and that the United States would need to engage in a military modernization program to counter that advantage. Finally, in late 1975, Jackson, Nixon's former secretary of defense Melvin Laird, and Ford's own secretary of defense, James Schlesinger, began to publicly accuse the Soviet Union of violating the provisions of SALT I.[55] These charges were not new, but Laird popularized the claims in *Reader's Digest*.[56]

In addition to critics from within the administration, a group of conservative defense intellectuals began to contend that the estimates of Soviet strength that Nixon's foreign policy was premised on drastically understated Soviet power.[57] Albert Wohlsetter, an influential academic, led the charge by arguing that the Soviet Union intended to achieve superiority.[58] Within the Ford White House, the President's Foreign Intelligence Advisory Board picked up these concerns. Its members were skeptical of détente and in particular were concerned that evaluations of Soviet power, especially those produced by the CIA, underestimated the Soviet threat.

These critics of détente within the administration developed the controversial Team B exercises at the CIA. Team B's job, in theory, was to evaluate the accuracy of CIA estimates of Soviet strength. Using the same figures and same sources as the CIA's normal analysis units, they were to make sure the conclusions followed from the raw intelligence. In reality, Team B went much further. The team was led by Richard Pipes—a strident opponent of détente who referred to it as a "tragedy of errors"—and included other critics of Nixon and Ford's foreign policy such as Nitze.[59] In their final report, they argued that previous estimates of Soviet power drastically underestimated Soviet capabilities.[60] Using slightly different estimates of Soviet capabilities, they portrayed a growing Soviet military that was intent on developing a war-winning capability. By developing a more hawkish estimate of Soviet capabilities, Team B was able to offer a revised understanding of Soviet intentions: Team B claimed that, rather than playing by the rules of détente and limiting the arms race, the Soviets were intent on winning an arms race.

The final Team B report substantiated the conservative case against arms control. The report was leaked to the press in October 1976 and created a sensation as George H. W. Bush, then director of the Central Intelligence Agency, promoted Team B's findings.[61] Members of Team B formed the Committee on the Present Danger. As Anne Hessing Cahn explains, "the panel members were well placed to keep the report's conclusions before the public for the next four years. Through op-ed pieces, radio and television interviews, and the large outreach program of the Committee on the Present Danger, the mantra of the United States falling behind the Soviet Union in military might was repeated over and over again."[62]

The conservative attack on the Vladivostok accords has two important implications. First, structural explanations related to power or economics do not explain the growth of anti-cooperation sentiment during the Ford years. The administration's critics, such as Jackson, Perle, and Pipes, had always opposed détente. Therefore, changes in the balance of power or economic interests did not cause changes in those individuals' beliefs because those beliefs simply did not change. Moreover, the analysis of the rise of anti-cooperation sentiments shows that the misperceptions that led to détente—about the meaning of equality or the status of the Third World—did not contribute to détente's decline. If misperception contributed to the decline of détente, then we should expect to see Soviet

behaviors described as cheating in the United States because of misinter-
pretations about what counted as cheating. The Soviets, however, did not
cheat. Simply put, the Soviets did not violate either the interim agreement
or build an ABM system. The main tactic of conservatives was to show that
the Soviets' arms program was a threat and therefore the United States
should not cooperate. The central argument was that the deals we made
were bad, not that the Soviets had failed to follow through on them. Allegations of cheating were always secondary to the main aim, which was to
depict a growing Soviet nuclear arsenal.

In the end, cooperation was reduced, but it did not end. What began
in the early 1970s as an ambitious agenda to enhance trade; cultural
exchanges; and scientific, technical, and agricultural cooperation was
reduced to just arms control. In the United States, a coalition of conservative and liberal critics of the Ford administration began to make inroads
on that issue as well. The Brezhnev leadership remained committed to
détente, although the leadership that was emerging as his health declined
increasingly protested his arms control policies. SALT II, especially the
Vladivostok accords, was the last "thin reed" on which relations could be
built.[63]

The Opposition in Power

When Carter was elected president in 1976, antidétente forces came to
occupy substantial positions of influence in the White House for the first
time. Cooperation collapsed as a result. During Carter's term the Soviets
realized that the United States no longer valued détente, which contributed to problems cooperating over arms control and in Afghanistan. Even
before Reagan's election, cooperation was replaced by competition because
elites in both superpowers held very different beliefs from those held by
elites in 1972.

During the 1976 presidential election campaign, Carter promised to
improve US-Soviet relations but not at the expense of human rights.[64] He
repeatedly stressed the failure of the Kissinger-Nixon-Ford foreign policy
to include human rights as a priority.[65] Echoing hawkish sentiments from
earlier in the decade, Carter stated in his inaugural address, "Because we
are free, we can never be indifferent to the fate of freedom elsewhere. Our
moral sense dictates a clear-cut preference for those societies which share

with us an abiding respect for individual human rights."[66] Consistent with his human rights policy, Carter appointed Zbigniew Brzezinski as national security adviser. Brzezinski was a Polish émigré, author of *The Permanent Purge* and an outspoken critic of Soviet human rights policies, who sought to use US foreign policy to restore freedom to Eastern Europe and to protect dissidents in the Soviet Union.[67] Carter's appointments and policies placed critics of détente into the highest positions of power, and, for the first time since 1972, administration policy dictated confrontation.[68]

Carter's election strongly affected Soviet beliefs about the future conduct of superpower relations. The Soviet leadership was circumspect about Carter before he entered office, identifying him with antidétente forces.[69] They thought Carter's human rights campaign was an attempt to embarrass them, encourage dissident movements in Russia and Eastern Europe, and that it violated the principle of noninterference in their internal affairs enshrined in the Basic Principles agreement.[70] Brezhnev would later write to Carter that he would not "allow interference in our internal affairs, whatever pseudo-humanitarian slogans are used to present it."[71]

If Carter's human rights platform risked souring relations, his election-year position on arms control was worse. Carter campaigned, in part, against the Vladivostok accords, arguing that the agreement enabled the superpowers to increase their nuclear arsenals. He promised to pursue a new agreement that would require "deep reductions." For Brezhnev, this shift in arms control policy was disturbing. He had invested heavily in the accord and fought for its approval.[72] In the words of one insider, he "spilled political blood" to gain agreement on Vladivostok at the risk of alienating politburo conservatives.[73]

Carter understood the risks of campaigning against Vladivostok and attempted to show the Soviets that this was an election tactic. During the campaign, Carter asked Gov. Averill Harriman, as a former ambassador to the Soviet Union, to assure the Soviet leadership that Carter was committed to completing the Vladivostok accord. Harriman was successful. Brezhnev believed that Carter agreed that the accord was sacrosanct and would be pursued before negotiation of deep cuts.[74]

Carter's promise not to pursue deep cuts was short lived. Early in his term, Senate conservatives blocked the nomination of Theodore Sorenson to head the CIA and won a symbolic victory by casting forty votes against Paul Warnke, Carter's dovish arms control negotiator. The latter was considered a victory because fewer than forty votes were needed to block ratification of SALT II.[75] Conservatives and the Joint Chiefs also prodded Carter to pursue deep cuts rather than Vladivostok's limited cuts, secretly hoping that this might create an unrealistic proposal the Soviets would reject, thereby ending arms control.[76] Ignoring his promise to Brezhnev, Carter returned to the deep-cuts line promised during his campaign; contrary to the conservative position, he naively thought Soviet acceptance was possible. He sent his secretary of state, Cyrus Vance, to Moscow with instructions to first try to find agreement on deep reductions while relying on Vladivostok as a fallback position.[77] As a negotiating tactic, he ordered Vance to bargain hard by initially making an unbalanced offer that favored the US position.

Carter's strategy proved a disaster. The Soviets were outraged, not only that Carter was reneging on his explicit commitment to Vladivostok, but also that he was presenting a new and unfair proposal. The Soviets immediately ended the negotiations, preventing Vance from presenting Vladivostok as a fallback position.[78] To make matters (much) worse, the Carter administration decided to make all diplomacy public. Vance publicly explained that Carter had offered deep reductions and the Soviets had refused. Brezhnev was appalled and went public with the full details of the one-sided American offer. The episode led the Soviets to suspect that Carter was more interested in publicity than diplomacy.[79]

The delays caused by the hope to get deep cuts had consequences that were not apparent at the time. Garthoff explains, "By the time the negotiation of SALT II was back on track, the roadbed undergirding that track was being weakened and would soon be disrupted by new American-Soviet confrontations."[80] The delays in SALT II caused by Carter's errors meant the ratification debate would take place after US-Soviet relations were rocked by events in Cuba and Africa. Whereas quick success on SALT II might have disarmed critics, proved Carter's sincerity to the Soviets, and maintained momentum in cooperation, failure meant SALT did not provide the needed impetus to maintain détente.

Arms control was not the only area where confrontation replaced cooperation. In 1977, a war between Somalia and Ethiopia threatened to pull in the superpowers.[81] The conflict sparked a debate in the White House. Key figures, such as Vance, found the Ogaden War unimportant and undeserving of a military response. In contrast, Brzezinski believed the Horn

of Africa was a pressing national security concern; it is near important
Middle Eastern states and inaction risked encouraging Algerian, Libyan,
and Cuban adventurism.[82] While Carter administration doves blocked US
intervention, hawks prevented superpower cooperation. The Brezhnev
politburo offered to jointly mediate the conflict, as the superpowers had
done in the Middle East in 1973. Rather than cooperate, Brzezinski convinced Carter to do nothing.[83]

Competition in Africa, problems with SALT, and the Soviets' strong
rejection of Carter's human rights rhetoric led Carter to take increasingly strong public stands against Soviet conduct. Throughout the summer of 1978, Carter began to pepper his comments on US-Soviet relations
with terminology favored by détente's critics. He no longer used the
term "détente," instead describing the Soviet buildup as "aggressive" and
"beyond a level necessary for defense." He also started discussing new US
military programs.[84] Criticism of Carter's "appeasement" of Soviet aggression in the Horn was so severe that the Carter team strongly and publicly
reacted to all future provocations.[85] This pattern of overreaction led Brzezinski to say, "SALT lies buried in the sands of the Ogaden."[86]

Even more damaging to the prospects for SALT ratification was the
"Cuban brigade." That summer, Soviet combat forces, in Cuba for more
than a decade, were "discovered."[87] The brigade's existence was leaked to
the press by Sen. Frank Church, a liberal supporter of arms control, and
led to a significant public outcry.[88] Vance and Brzezinski publicly argued
that the Cuban brigade was unacceptable Soviet adventurism and threatened SALT II; Carter wrote to Brezhnev, pressuring him to withdraw
the troops.[89] Carter and Brzezinski issued a presidential directive stating
the US goal was to end Soviet support for Cuba and requiring the State
Department to take every opportunity to link superpower relations to
Soviet-Cuban ties.[90]

The Cuban brigade posed a significant threat to arms control. Dan
Caldwell argues that even without the Soviet invasion of Afghanistan,
ratification of SALT II was dead because of the publicity of the Cuban
brigade.[91] Even supporters of SALT II threatened to refuse to ratify it if
the Soviets did not remove the brigade.[92] Brezhnev refused to remove the
troops, writing to Carter that there was a training center in Cuba that did
not violate the agreements made after the missile crisis and added that "it

appears to us that the only result of exaggerating this artificially contrived campaign is to render noticeable damage to relations between our countries and to the cause of strengthening peace."[93]

The decline of détente during the Carter administration has important implications. First, structural explanations are insufficient to explain the breakdown of cooperation over arms control. During the Nixon and Ford administrations, cooperation was crippled by concerns about human rights, especially related to Jewish emigration. With Carter's election, the White House, in addition to the Senate, treated human rights as a centerpiece of foreign policy. Moreover, détente's critics—such as Brzezinski—obtained key positions of influence in the White House, providing them with power through which to challenge cooperation. The coming to power of antidétente policymakers—not a change in the balance of power or economic pressure—collapsed détente, showing how precarious it had always been.

Second, the antidétente beliefs of these administration officials did not stem from supposed Soviet cheating on détente: misperceptions did not fuel conflict. The agreement under dispute concerning Cuba pre-existed détente, and no new Soviet position was taken in Cuba during the period (the brigade had long been there). Similarly, Soviet conduct in the Horn of Africa crisis was similar to its conduct during the 1973 Arab-Israeli War. The key difference was that Kissinger found a route to cooperation in the former while Brzezinski sought confrontation in the latter. Political elites' attitude toward cooperation, not the nature of the misperceptions that had gotten states to cooperate, led to the end of cooperation.

The same trend is evidenced in Soviet decision making. Between 1973 and 1979, the Soviet Union limited its conduct in the Third World because of concerns about US conservatives. In high-stakes situations, Brezhnev offered to cooperate in managing crises. As discussed in chapter 2, the politburo actively considered détente during the 1973 Arab-Israeli War, and they offered to allow the United States to participate in mediation of the crisis in the Horn. In low-stakes situations, like Angola, Brezhnev tried to prevent conflicts from escalating.[94]

The Soviet Union continued to press for cooperation, believing, even as late as 1979, that the United States valued détente and was serious about cooperating on arms control. In March 1979, the politburo met to consider intervening in Afghanistan and considered its implications for détente. Gromyko remarked:

> Sending out troops would mean our occupation of Afghanistan. This would place us in a very difficult position in the international arena. We would ruin everything that we have constructed with such great difficulty, détente above all. The SALT II talks would be ruined. And this is the overriding issue for us now. There would be no meeting between Leonid Ilyich and Carter. . . . This is why, despite the difficult situation, we cannot send troops.[95]

Détente, especially the upcoming summit, exercised a restraining influence on the Soviet decision to intervene.

However, once the Soviets realized the United States was no longer willing to cooperate, there was a shift toward confrontation. In 1979, the Senate Armed Services Committee rejected SALT II, and NATO decided to deploy intermediate-range missiles in Europe. From the Soviet perspective, détente was dead. Not only was trade declining and arms control no longer promising, but a series of "phony" issues, such as the Cuban brigade, and growing anti-Soviet sentiment showed that relations would likely not improve. There was no longer a geopolitical reason not to intervene in Afghanistan.[96] Georgy Kornienko, the Soviet first deputy prime minister, later wrote, "All of the arguments previously made about the negative impact in the West suddenly became irrelevant. People felt that relations were already spoiled, so there was nothing left to lose."[97]

The Soviet invasion of Afghanistan that winter, coming so close to a US election, destroyed any remaining chance for SALT II ratification. In January, Carter requested that the Senate not debate SALT II and began a series of sanctions against the Soviet Union, explaining that "détente was dead."[98] American public opinion, which had become increasingly opposed to détente since Nixon left office, began to strongly favor a return to confrontation.[99] When Reagan entered office, Team B, the group of conservative defense intellectuals who sounded alarms at Soviet military programs, "became Team A," occupying most positions of influence in the new administration.[100]

Did Misperception End Détente?

One conventional view of détente—described in the beginning of this chapter—is that détente was inevitable because of structural factors and the decline of détente was driven by misperceptions. My analysis of the decline of détente undermines both arguments. Many diplomatic historians and some political scientists argue that one reason détente failed is that it was premised on a misperception. Because the two sides wrongly believed that there was a mutual understanding about the terms of cooperation (a false intersubjective belief), behavior that did not conform to expectations about the terms of cooperation appeared to be cheating. This claim—if true—would undermine my argument that FIBs promoted cooperation by allowing the parties to overlook important conflicts. Chapter 2 traced the process through which FIBs positively contributed to cooperation during the 1973 Arab-Israeli War and the arriving at the Basic Principles agreement. The analysis of the decline of détente shows that these misunderstandings are not what led to a long-term threat to cooperation.

There are two key observable implications of the claim that misperceptions led to a decline in cooperation. The first is whether some group changed its beliefs about cooperation between 1972 and 1979. If a group did not change its beliefs after these misperceptions arose, then the misperceptions themselves do not explain the decline of cooperation. The second is whether the other superpower's behavior caused decision makers' beliefs to change by creating the impression that it was cheating on the deal. Both claims have been shown to be dubious.

The first observable phenomenon—that some group changed its beliefs—is not well supported. The most strident opponents of cooperation, such as Henry Jackson, Richard Perle, Paul Nitze, Zbigniew Brzezinski, Ronald Reagan, and their supporters, had opposed détente from the beginning. What changed during the 1970s was not their position on cooperation but their influence. Their rise was not the result of a misperception; it was primarily caused by the weakness of the post-Watergate Republican Party. The confrontational turn undertaken by Congressional liberals—most noticeably during the Cuba brigade crisis—was an election ploy to defuse conservative attacks on Carter's foreign policy. It was not driven by a real belief that the Soviets were cheating on détente.

The second observable implication—that Soviet conduct looked like cheating on the deal—has even less evidence in support of it. Economic cooperation was damaged by attaching restrictions to trade related to Jewish emigration and cancelling Soviet grain contracts. Misperceptions about détente had little to do with these events. No one believed the Soviets had committed to allowing Jewish emigration as part of détente and then had somehow backed out of the agreement; it was an altogether new issue, introduced in part to reduce US-Soviet cooperation. The decline in cooperation in the Third World—especially in Angola and the Horn of Africa—also had less to do with misperceptions related to détente and more to do with the rise of conservatives who wanted to compete with the Soviet Union. The decline of the arms control agenda, similarly, was not due to concerns about the Soviets cheating on détente. Hawks—in public and in the administration—attacked Vladivostok and later arms control pacts by trying to show that they would weaken the United States. The deals were said to be unfair, regardless of whether the Soviets cheated on them. In other words, détente was in sum a set of bad deals that left the United States badly off, plus the Soviets might be cheating.

A critic might agree that conservative groups had always opposed détente but argue that these groups obtained power because misperceptions led to a decline in détente's popularity. Conservatives could seize on allegations of Soviet adventurism to win elections and leadership positions. There is little evidence for this claim. Neither the 1976, 1978, nor 1980 election saw voters going to the ballot box focused on détente. As in more recent elections, the economy was the central issue.[101] Moreover, changes in administrative personnel, such as the dismissal of doves in the Nixon administration and the introduction of Team B into the CIA, came before rather than after Soviet behavior that might have revealed US misperceptions.[102]

Misperceptions therefore may have contributed to the decline of détente. Conservatives were wrong that Soviet power would overtake US power and that the Soviets were using Angola are part of a strategy to conquer Africa. The existence of these illusions, however, does not mean there the specific illusions that were necessary for cooperation—the imagined intersubjectivity described in chapters 2 and 3—were any less important.

Was Détente Inevitable?

Structural explanations of détente—often taken to mean that it was inevitable—also are far from sufficient to explain the growth of cooperation. The argument from process tracing explored earlier looked at specific evidence related to the balance of power, institutions, and trade. These explanations do not explain the decline of détente because there is little evidence of the specific causal mechanisms highlighted by the theories.

In addition, examining the same evidence through the lens of an interrupted time series design of a single case shows the evidence more starkly. Specifically, if structural, institutional, or economic pressures were sufficient to explain cooperation, then these structural pressures should exist before cooperation begins and disappear before cooperation declines. This basic correlation is a hoops test for any argument that FIBs were not necessary because détente was inevitable.[103] The strategy, therefore, is to see if variation on the independent variables highlighted by these theories correlates with the rise and decline of cooperation.

The results, discussed more extensively below, are summarized in table 4.1. Cooperation varied during the period.[104] This variation, however, does not correlate with changes in levels of power, institutionalization, or trade predicted by mainstream IR theories. This provides indirect evidence for the argument in chapters 2 and 3 in two ways. First, alternative explanations that make détente seem inevitable are not persuasive, making the theory of FIBs more than plausible. Second, that beliefs seem to matter so much provides indirect—perhaps decisive—evidence that the specific misperceptions that Nixon, Kissinger, and to a lesser extent Ford shared mattered for cooperation. This does not demonstrate the causal logic—chapters 2 and 3 detail the role of false intersubjective beliefs in the pathway to cooperation—but it eliminates rival explanations that tend to discount beliefs.

Power

In the beginning of this chapter, I outlined two power-based explanations for cooperation. On the one hand, some structural realists argue that when

TABLE 4.1. Summary of the Decline of Détente

Period	Level of cooperation	Military parity	Level of institutionalization	Trade	Administration beliefs
1972–73	High	Yes	Low	Low	Prodétente
1973–75	Intermediate	Yes	Medium	Low	Mixed
1976–79	Low	Yes	Medium	Low	Antidétente

states reach parity, cooperation becomes possible because security fears are muted by a stable balance of power; others argue that as states near parity, conflict becomes more likely as states are worried about a transition in the balance of power. These opposing views are summarized in Hypotheses 4.1 and 4.2:

> H4.1: The shifting balance of power is sufficient for explaining détente. As the superpowers approached parity, cooperation became possible, especially in areas that did not implicate their relative security. When parity ended, cooperation was reduced.
> H4.2: The perceived power transition between the United States and the Soviet Union is sufficient for explaining the decline of détente. As the superpowers approached parity, cooperation became impossible because of mutual security fears.

There is some evidence for both hypotheses. In many ways, the shifting balance of power in Europe during the 1920s was similar to the way policymakers in Washington and Moscow understood the shifting superpower balance of power in the 1970s. Inspecting the measure of national power in the Correlates of War, a leading measure of relative state power, shows that the United States was more powerful than the Soviet Union before the 1970s, they reached parity in exactly 1972 when the ABM Treaty was signed and détente reached its height, and the Soviet Union continued to rise thereafter. This measure, as I explain below, is enormously inaccurate, but it does reflect the kind of thinking that influenced US policy. Figure 4.1 shows the estimated rise of Soviet power over time. Balance-of-power theory can explain why agreements were not reached before 1972 (the United States did not fear the Soviet Union enough), why they were reached in 1972 (mutual fear), and why détente deteriorated (the growth of Soviet power meant the Soviets did not fear the United States).[105] Similarly, power-transition theory can explain the decline of détente. As the United States and the Soviet Union reached parity, a period of tense relations began. American conservatives become increasingly concerned about growing Soviet power.

Despite this evidence, however, there are a number of reasons why shifts in power cannot explain the growth and decline of cooperation. Each theory is only able to explain half of the story. Power-transition theories cannot explain the emergence of cooperation. Whereas the power-transition

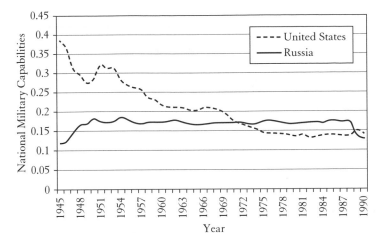

Figure 4.1. Estimated rise of Soviet power over time relative to the United States. *Source:* Generated from the CINC score in the Correlates of War project's National Military Capabilities database (v 3.0). Singer, Bremer, and Stuckey 1972.

hypothesis indicates that parity leads to conflict, during détente the advent of parity led to one of the most significant periods of cooperation during the Cold War. Therefore, parity does not *necessarily* lead to conflict, an argument conceded by many power-transition theorists who agree that there is no perfect relationship between power transitions and war. Conversely, balance-of-power theory cannot explain the decline of détente. After the Soviets reached parity in the late 1960s and early 1970s, there was no sudden shift that would account for the end of cooperation later in the decade. To show that balance of power explains the end of cooperation, the Soviets would have to break out of parity, emerging as a stronger power than the United States. This shift never occurred. Despite the evidence cited by conservative policymakers, the Soviet Union never actually obtained dominance. As Wohlforth explains, "The picture requiring the most creative genius to paint would be 'Dynamic Soviet Union Challenges America in Decline.' Yet that was how power trends were perceived in the 1970s."[106]

Why was the evidence of a power transition so misleading? First, the data presented in figure 4.1 is estimated in dollars. This creates the well-known index-number problem, which inflates the size of Soviet military expenditures.[107] If one removes the inflated military expenditures and relies on other elements of the Correlates of War index—total population, energy, iron and steel production, urban population, and military personnel—the United States and the Soviet Union did not achieve parity in the 1970s. In fact, the Soviet Union never achieved parity in terms of its war-fighting potential, a statistic that few today are likely to question. Moreover, the decisive US technological edge also substantially increased its material power over the Soviet Union.[108]

Further, neither the conventional nor the nuclear balance ever favored the Soviet Union. Despite antagonistic debates over relative strategic power during the 1970s,[109] recent materials from the Soviet archives show that the Soviet Union neither intended to nor obtained strategic dominance. Pavel Podvig's 2008 definitive analysis of the Soviet nuclear arms program finds that the Soviet effort to improve accuracy and harden silos was significantly less effective than détente's critics claimed.[110] The conventional balance is more obscure, but there is little evidence that, in the event of a conventional great power war, the Soviet Union would have had a decisive edge over the United States.

Therefore, while the emergence of nuclear parity with the United States may have been new in the 1970s, it is clear that the Soviet Union never achieved nuclear or conventional supremacy and did not have the capability to outproduce the United States in the event of a war. Therefore, variation in international cooperation between 1972 and 1979 cannot be explained by actual power because actual power remained roughly constant.

Moreover, even if evidence supported the assertion that shifts in power might support cooperation, neither the power-transition hypothesis nor the balance-of-power hypothesis is specific enough to prove that the shift in the balance of power directly caused the ABM Treaty, the Basic Principles agreement, or cooperation during the 1973 Arab-Israeli War. Structural variables tend to predict general outcomes but not specific agreements.

Another more specific realist explanation for the growth of détente relates to US triangular diplomacy. This theory—most noticeably advanced by former members of Nixon's administration—contends that the United States enhanced its leverage over the Soviet Union by opening diplomatic relations with China.[111] This forced the Soviet Union to the bargaining table because Soviet policymakers feared a US-China alliance aimed at reducing Soviet influence.[112] The historical record suggests that forcing the Soviet hand was an aim of US policy.[113] Did triangular diplomacy lead then to détente?

To show that US policy toward China was crucial for cooperation relies on four claims, only one of which is true. If triangular diplomacy pushed the Soviets to cooperate, then (1) the Johnson and Nixon administrations wanted to cooperate with the Soviets but could not because (2) the Soviets showed no interest in cooperation. Nixon's overtures to China (3) created fear in the Soviet politburo, and this fear dominated Soviet decision making. Fears of encirclement (4) led the Soviets to make suboptimal deals that they would not otherwise have made.

There is little evidence for any claim besides the third one. The Soviets were interested in cooperation before Nixon began making overtures to China. Chapter 3 showed Soviet interest in an arms deal during the Johnson administration; Americans, not the Soviets, slowed progress. The Soviets also had already expressed interest in an agreement on basic principles, a trade deal, and cooperation in other issue areas before Nixon's visit to Beijing. Moreover, the Soviets never made a deal they considered suboptimal. Chapter 2 shows that the Soviets thought that their strategic strength had led them finally to get a fair shake from direct negotiations with Washington, and chapter 3 highlights the importance of parity to the SALT process. If the US had enhanced its power, driving the Soviets into a corner, there was little to be seen of it at the negotiating table.

Finally, while the Soviets were worried about US-Chinese collaboration, this was not an overriding factor driving their decision making. In the early 1970s, the Soviets rejected a trade deal because of human rights conditions; and in the mid-1970s, the Soviets increased their influence by aiding national liberation movements throughout the developing world. Soviet behavior is inconsistent with the claim that China dominated Soviet decision making: the Soviet emphases on human rights or promoting revolution are not the likely emphases of a power that so feared encirclement it was willing to trade away programs it considered important for its security in order to satisfy the United States.

Institutional Explanations

Liberal scholars tend to emphasize democracy, institutions, and trade as drivers of cooperation. Democratic peace theory is not relevant to détente because one of the parties was not a democracy. Students of institutions and trade, however, might argue that the growth of security institutions or rising expectations for trade drove cooperation.

The institutionalist argument for cooperation is summarized by Hypothesis 4.3:

> H4.3: Détente and the ABM Treaty developed because of the establishment of a security regime. The security regime provided information, established reputations, enabled issue linkages, and ensured reciprocity. The development of the regime was sufficient for the improvement in relations and the treaty.

Despite the intuitive appeal of liberal institutionalism, in the case of détente, the causal arrows run in the wrong direction. In order for an institutionalist explanation to sufficiently explain détente, the conditions that explain cooperation should be present before cooperation begins and absent before cooperation fails. During the 1970s, however, institutionalist conditions for cooperation only emerged *after* cooperation began and were present *before* cooperation failed. Therefore, institutional arguments have difficulty explaining détente.

Before cooperation began, institutionalist variables were only weakly present. Before 1972, the United States and the Soviet Union had only a thinly institutionalized relationship, did not realize the extent of possible issue linkages, and reputations were unclear. Only after the Basic Principles agreement, interim agreement, and ABM Treaty were signed, for example, were many standing commissions created in other issue areas to resolve trade, environmental, and technological problems. Those that did exist earlier, such as the arms talks, were not central to explaining cooperation because key players including Kissinger and Dobrynin did not attend the talks and key proposals were not offered there.[114] Similarly, concerns about reputation cannot explain cooperation. Brezhnev and Nixon established reputations for reliability as a result of cooperation. Reputation did not cause cooperation.

More important, institutionalist conditions for cooperation were strongly present at the time of détente's decline. By the end of the Nixon administration, as noted in chapter 2, the United States and the Soviet Union had institutionalized a pattern of cooperation and developed reputations as cooperative rivals. They signed more than 150 agreements, met at a series of summits, and credibly committed to each other by attempting to shift domestic opinion toward favoring continued cooperation. By the time Nixon left office, there were sunk costs in détente, reputations were on the line, and the superpower relationship was more institutionalized than at any other point during the Cold War. At the moment when institutionalist theories would expect the regime to have its strongest effect, cooperation declined. Therefore, institutionalist variables are neither able to explain the emergence of cooperation in 1972 nor its failure later in the decade.

There is one additional liberal institutionalist theory that I deal with separately, in part because of its sophistication, but also because of its specificity to the case. Steve Weber explains the origins of the ABM Treaty through liberal institutional factors. He argues that arms control was a prisoner's dilemma: each party preferred mutual cooperation and arms control over mutual defection and no arms control. However, each would be better off if their opponent did not build arms (cooperate) while they continued to do so (defect). To escape the prisoner's dilemma, Weber argues, Nixon pursued a strategy of enhanced contingent restraint, threatening the Soviet Union with an American ABM system if the Soviets did not cooperate on ABMs. In the meantime, the Nixon administration enhanced the credibility of this threat by taking steps to demonstrate its resolve by expanding production of ABMs. This enabled the Nixon administration to extend the shadow of the future by encouraging the Soviet Union to evaluate possible future negative payoffs that would emerge from US retaliation if the Soviets reneged on their arms control commitments in the present. Thus, reciprocity enabled cooperation by increasing the costs of Soviet defection.[115]

There are two problems with Weber's argument. Empirically, I have shown that Nixon did not prefer cooperation to mutual defection.[116] In chapter 3, I showed that Kissinger and Nixon wanted the Soviet Union to *reject* the offer to negotiate ABM limitations so that they could win support in the Senate for building ABMs. Nixon pursued a policy of restraint to win domestic support, not Soviet support. In other words, Weber is right to argue that the Soviets thought of arms control as a prisoner's dilemma because they did prefer mutual cooperation to mutual defection. Nixon and Kissinger, however, thought of arms control as a game of chicken: whichever side refused an ABM deal first would pay a political cost at home and abroad, while the side that defected second would pay no political cost and still get to build an ABM system.

Even if Weber is empirically correct and Nixon designed a strategy to force the Soviets to accept a treaty, this explanation does not undermine the argument of chapter 3. Several additional misunderstandings arose during the process that contributed to cooperation (e.g., misperceptions in reaching the May 20 agreement and over Vietnam). Enhanced restraint only would get the Soviets to negotiate ABMs; it would not solve the internal White House political problems concerning the substance or timing of the treaty.

The second liberal theory considered in this chapter is that high expectations for trade drove US-Soviet cooperation. This hypothesis is summarized in Hypothesis 4.4:

> H4.4: Cooperation during détente was caused by high Soviet expectations for trade with the United States. These expectations were sufficient to explain cooperation, and when expectations declined, cooperation ended.

There may be an important measure of truth in the trade argument. Trade may have been a sweetener for Soviet cooperation. And when US conservatives undermined trade deals, cooperation may have become less rewarding for Soviet officials.

On balance, however, expectations for trade are not sufficient to explain cooperation. The reason relates to the timing of the attack on trade in the United States. The trade hypothesis presumes that interests in trade create interests in cooperation. In the United States, however, an interest in opposing cooperation drove opposition to trade, such as the debates over the grain deal and linking trade to Jewish emigration. Therefore, at least on the US side, the underlying cause of the decline of security cooperation and economic cooperation was the same: US conservatives who had always opposed cooperation with the Soviet Union.

Cooperation is always a tricky process. Structural accounts that focus on macrolevel causes—the balance of power or the state of economic interdependence—posit that cooperation is determined by the structure of the international system and not by leaders' beliefs. There is indirect (but

decisive) evidence that cooperation was much more personality dependent than structural arguments suggest. Structural theories related to
power cannot paint détente as inevitable because the same structure that
supposedly drove cooperation in 1972 remained in place when cooperation was replaced by conflict later in the decade. Furthermore, there is
little evidence that policymakers changed their minds about the value of
cooperation as a result of structural changes in the international system.
Conversely, institutionalist theories cannot explain cooperation because
institutions were weak when cooperation began and robust when cooperation declined. And the causal mechanism posited by the claim that trade
drives peace is unsupported: beliefs about the value of trade appeared to
result from, not cause beliefs about, the value of cooperation.

There is indirect evidence that an illusion was a necessary condition
for the emergence of détente. If détente were inevitable because of structural pressures, then the beliefs of decision makers are just noise in the
system, speed bumps and not barriers to cooperation. Since cooperation
was not inevitable because of structural pressures, it becomes apparent
that the beliefs of decision makers—the noisy way that cooperation was
reached—was crucial to the process. Moreover, the misperception that
underlay détente did not contribute to the decline of détente. The central
driver of confrontation was the introduction of new political elites, first in
the United States and later in the Soviet Union, who held different beliefs
about how to conduct the Cold War.

Conclusion

The conventional wisdom in International Relations is that mutual understanding—common knowledge, intersubjectivity, or shared ideas—is crucial for international cooperation. Specifically, the conventional wisdom in political science is that détente occurred in part because of reduced misperception between the superpowers. I have argued, in contrast, that cooperation is often best secured because of misperception. When actors hold false intersubjective beliefs—in which agents wrongly believe that their understanding of a relationship is shared—cooperation may be much more likely, especially if there are principled differences or conflicts of interest. In the case of détente, there were significant principled differences and conflicts of interest. Misperception, however, led the Nixon and Kissinger in particular to make concessions to the Soviets that they did not prefer and allowed both sides to overlook differences that may have undermined cooperation. The intersubjective consensus—the supposed mutual understanding between the superpowers—was more imagined than real. But, even though it was imagined, its effects on cooperation were tangible.

Détente is not an isolated case. Some of the most fundamental rules of international society do not require common agreements in order to be successful. For example, the 1961 United Nations Conference on Diplomatic Intercourse and Immunities was charged with deciding the protocols for diplomats and immunities for diplomats abroad. For many legal commentators, these protocols are the foundational law governing diplomatic relations and one of the most widely used and effective multilateral instruments in the international system.[1] In asking for the conference, the representative from Yugoslavia argued that violations of customary diplomatic immunities had become common and "the time [has] come to find a general legal solution for the problem."[2] After the conference, many commentators found the conference to be a complete success: "The Vienna Conference was successful, in that it was able to reach agreement on the totality of its subject matter."[3]

One of the most important issues at the conference was the definition of "members of the household." Delegates agreed that members of the household should receive diplomatic immunity. But who is a member of a household? The United States proposed that a household include spouses, minor children, children who are full-time students, and other members of the immediate family living in the residence. The Soviet legal tradition is less expansive, and the Soviet representative sought to exclude full-time students. Mexico demanded that by custom dependents not living in the residence also be mentioned. Vietnamese tradition required that only persons dependent on the person in residence be listed. Indian law includes a legal obligation to support aged parents.[4] In the end, the conference decided not to make a decision, and no definition is offered in the 1975 Vienna Convention on Diplomatic Relations or the Vienna Convention on Representations of States in their Relations with International Organizations of a Universal Character. Because these issues rarely led to disputes, why make the conference fail by insisting that "members of the household" be clarified? Failure to obtain common knowledge or an intersubjective consensus concerning the meaning of "family" was unimportant; the effort to obtain agreement made a simple issue difficult. The effort to make the rule clear stood in the way of cooperation.

During the US-Soviet détente, the rules were also ambiguous. Would détente authorize Soviet military intervention in the Third World? Would the United States continue to seek political dominance over the

Soviet Union? Would the parties continue to rely on nuclear threats to obtain short-term gains? The leadership in both states thought a deal had been reached that had fundamentally changed the nature of the superpower relationship, providing clear answers to all these questions. Unlike the parties to the Vienna Conference, the parties to détente were unaware of their complex differences. This was a laudatory oversight; in contrast to the Vienna Conference, if US-Soviet differences over high politics had become apparent, they could not have been ignored and would have damaged chances for cooperation in the Middle East, on the arms race, on the ground rules for peaceful competition, and in other issue areas. Because of imagined intersubjectivity, cooperation blossomed.

A Theory of Cooperation

A consensus among most students of IR is that misperception leads to conflict while mutual understanding makes cooperation and peace more likely. Undoubtedly, in many cases this is true. Misperceptions of the offense-defense balance contributed to the First World War, misperceptions of Germany's intentions in part led to the failure to deter Germany before the Second World War, and the mistaken belief that Iraq possessed weapons of mass destruction contributed to the Iraq War. Is misperception, however, always a cause of conflict and never a cause of cooperation?

In this book I have argued that misperceptions can play a central role in creating international cooperation. Actors can choose cooperation over conflict if there are false intersubjective beliefs that lead to cooperation. Specifically, détente—the most robust period of cooperation between the superpowers—was only possible because of FIBs. The United States and the Soviets had different expectations for their political relations. The Brezhnev politburo thought that their achievement of military parity had compelled the Nixon administration to accept it as a political equal. Détente to the Soviets meant that they could safely support national liberation movements without US meddling, have a legitimate sphere of influence in Eastern Europe, and that superpower negotiations would take place without the United States trying to obtain positions of strength. The Nixon administration, in contrast, thought that Soviet strategic parity meant that military competition had been replaced by political competition. Far from accepting Soviet political equality, Kissinger intended to rely on linkages and threats—"containment by web"—to improve the US position over the Soviets and prevent the Soviet Union from translating strategic equality into political power. The parties unknowingly disagreed about the principles underlying détente—political equality or competition for political dominance—and, as a result, unknowingly expected different behaviors during negotiations over arms control and conflict in the periphery. These differences in principles and expectations for behavior make détente a paradigmatic example of imagined intersubjectivity.

The Basic Principles agreement codified the differences in political principles (equality or competition) into international law. The Soviets thought the Nixon administration agreed that the BPA implied that the White House would treat the Soviets as political equals. The Nixon administration, in contrast, thought the Soviets agreed that the BPA did not acknowledge political equality but instead sought to create ground rules for competition in the Third World. Neither side paid sufficient attention to the details of the language added by the other. If they had, the negotiation of the ground rules likely would have quickly ended or resulted in a shallower agreement. Moreover, imagined intersubjectivity aided crisis management during the 1973 Arab-Israeli War. During negotiation of the ceasefire, the United States and the Soviet Union reached a critical "understanding" in which each believed the agreement was in their own long-term interests. For the United States, the Understanding implied US dominance in the region and Soviet influence limited to a seat at a future peace conference. For the Soviet Union, the Understanding implied a continuing Soviet role in Egypt and equality with the United States in negotiating the war's settlement.

The same dynamic occurred during the ABM negotiations, which saw three instances of imagined intersubjectivity that contributed to cooperation. Kissinger offered to negotiate an ABM treaty because he thought the Soviets would refuse. Kissinger, who favored at least partial ABM deployment, believed a Soviet refusal would be opportune: he could safely make an offer, have the Soviets reject it, and then take the Soviet rejection to the Senate as evidence for why the United States needed an ABM system. When the Soviets accepted his offer, Kissinger was disappointed and later referred to his decision to cooperate as a "first-class blunder."

Critical concessions were also reached because of imagined intersubjectivity. During the negotiation of the May 20 agreement in 1971, both parties thought the other made a critical first concession concerning the sequence of negotiations. Neither was right, but both reciprocated this phantom concession with counterconcessions, leading each party to bend on important issues. These ambiguities, which were premised on misreading the behavior of the other and misunderstanding the principles that guided the behavior of the other, led to the form and substance of the ABM Treaty.

Even after the treaty was prepared and ready for signature, imagined intersubjectivity overcame a final hurdle to its conclusion. In early 1972, a North Vietnamese offensive led Nixon to contemplate cancelling the summit and the signing of the ABM Treaty; Nixon even ordered Kissinger to begin the cancellation process. Nixon thought meeting with Brezhnev was politically impossible while Soviet tanks were overrunning US troops and US bombs were falling on a Soviet ally. Nixon changed his mind because he discovered the summit was popular. He decided on a new strategy. If Brezhnev canceled, he would not have to meet the Soviets during the North Vietnamese offensive, and Nixon would not pay the political price of cancelling. This belief led Nixon to ignore concerns about the summit, enabling him to escalate in Vietnam without worrying about the political optics of meeting with Brezhnev. This was a case of imagined intersubjectivity. Nixon assumed that he knew what Brezhnev would do (cancel) because he thought he understood what Brezhnev valued (reputation). Nixon was wrong. Brezhnev never intended to cancel. In all of these cases, the US and Soviet leadership projected their beliefs onto the other party, which led to an unlikely episode of cooperation.

Imagined intersubjectivity was necessary for the broad improvement of US-Soviet relations, crisis management of the 1973 Arab-Israeli War, the Basics Principles agreement, and the ABM Treaty. Without imagined intersubjectivity, cooperation likely would not have occurred or would have been fatefully delayed.[5]

Rethinking the Origins of Cooperation

Understanding the role of misperception during détente leads to three larger lessons. The first broad lesson is that we should be careful when we ascribe cases of cooperation to shared ideas. Policymakers and IR scholars often postulate that beliefs, identities, or norms are generally shared. When scholars look to key international institutions—the origins of NATO, the United Nations, or multilateral trade institutions—they often suggest that common knowledge or shared ideas explain cooperation. *Ideas* might matter, but there is remarkably little empirical evidence that *shared* ideas are important.

The assertion that cooperation implies shared ideas has gotten in the way of careful empirical work. Many researchers only investigate the beliefs of one individual or one state without making a comparative assessment of beliefs across populations.[6] Indeed, methodological texts on social constructivism—the area that places the largest emphasis on shared ideas—do not mention the importance of comparative analysis, despite their claim to laying the foundation for the study of intersubjectivity.[7] To show that a belief is intersubjective, researchers need to compare the beliefs of group members. Careful comparison may lead to the discovery that the international system is characterized by high levels of difference rather than high levels of shared ideas. Moreover, even less attention has been paid to showing why *shared* ideas promote cooperation. To cooperate, agents must believe that cooperation is in their interests, but this does not imply that they must understand their interests or the goals of cooperation in similar ways. Scholars too often assume, instead of demonstrate, that shared ideas exist and that they are related to cooperation. This has created a bias toward mutual understanding in policy and academic discussions with little appreciation of the dangers of mutual understanding.

The second lesson relates to theories of international regimes and institutions. Liberal institutionalists often argue that international regimes form to serve important functions such as providing information, creating enforcement mechanisms, and establishing trust.[8] Studying détente, however, shows that misperception, rather than shared information, may lead to better and deeper cooperation. The important theoretical point is that much of the literature on regimes and institutions pays attention to the ways that information promotes cooperation without considering the conditions under which more information might be counterproductive. Regimes, however, may only be successful in some cases when they are selective in the kinds of information they disseminate. For example, the Strategic Arms Limitation Talks enabled the diffusion of technical knowledge, which promoted cooperation, but they did not provide information about the principled orientation of US and Soviet foreign policy. Had

SALT led to such a diffusion of information, cooperation likely would have ended. When we consider how to design future regimes, it is crucial to think through what kinds of information might be important for cooperation and what types of information might lead to conflict. More information is not necessarily better for cooperation.

FIBs further provide a second route to the evolution of cooperation often unnoticed in discussions of regime design. One perennial problem in explaining how actors reach cooperative outcomes is discerning why an actor will make the first concession if it does not expect the other to reciprocate. However, if one actor engages in a behavior that another wrongly interprets as a concession (e.g., Kissinger's offer to delink offense from defense interpreted as a concession), the second actor, believing that a concession has been made, might make a counterconcession (e.g., dropping demands on missiles in Europe). The first actor, believing the second actor's concession was the first, responds in kind. FIBs might jumpstart a cycle of reciprocity that will evolve into cooperation. Given the difficulties involved in cooperating first in situations of mistrust, close attention to how misperception gets cooperation started is important.[9]

The third broad lesson relates to practical politics in the twenty-first century. Today the United States may be headed into a new "era of negotiations" with rivals and enemies, such as Iran and North Korea. Perhaps, this new era will not be too dissimilar from the era that confronted Nixon and Kissinger as they chose to negotiate with long-standing enemies and reluctant allies. What can we learn from them? Nixon and Kissinger, because of either ego or fate, never understood the Soviet Union's position and thus were able to cooperate. We cannot rely on chance mistakes today; but, we can learn that cooperation is more important than mutual understanding. If a pressing global problem is on the agenda, understanding the future aspirations or long-term plans of others may be less important than cooperating on the issue at hand, and understanding may be in tension with cooperation. If global warming, war, and global poverty are eliminated because we do not understand one another, so be it.

International Social Theory

Beyond a theory of cooperation, there is a much broader and deeper theoretical consequence of the likely prevalence and importance of FIBs.

The theory presented in Chapter 1 provides an alternative account of cooperation from theories that rely on analogies to sociological literature, which concentrates on local politics. In so doing, it undermines the argument from abduction and creates promising avenues for future research.

Many of the most significant approaches to social theory discuss the importance of intersubjectivity for the production of social order. An important consequence of a theory of FIBs is the undermining of the argument for shared ideas through abduction. Many IR scholars, such as Alexander Wendt, posit that shared ideas must exist because, otherwise, there would be no cooperation. This is an abductive argument because it infers the premise from the consequent, claiming it is the best explanation for the existence of the consequent. There is cooperation, therefore there are shared ideas. The problem with this argument is that FIBs provide a second route to cooperation. Misperceptions, not common knowledge, can promote cooperation. The existence of cooperation can no longer be considered prima facie evidence that the international system contains a thick level of intersubjectivity.

By undermining the argument from abduction, we can rethink the intuition that the international order is established in similar ways to the founding of domestic orders. I suspect that we intuitively think that mutual understanding is important for cooperation in international politics because it seems so important to the way in which we think about domestic politics. A theory of FIBs, however, shows that the study of international social life may require different assumptions than studies of local politics. In brief, it points away from a "social theory of international politics" that draws on the assumptions of a sociology that emphasizes joint socialization, face-to-face interaction, dense societies, shared cultures and languages, and rich intersubjective backdrops for social reality, and toward an "international social theory" that starts from assumptions more likely to hold true at the international level. These assumptions—that the international system as a social system contains agents with different educational, linguistic, and cultural backgrounds who rarely directly interact for extended periods of time in high-quality ways—are likely more productive for thinking about the role of mutual understanding in international society. An international social theory, starting from these more reasonable assumptions, cautions against "rummaging in the 'graveyard' of sociological studies" and urges the creation of novel arguments rooted in the diversity that characterizes international life.[10]

An international social theory cannot be fully fleshed out in this book. Such a theory would, however, have certain central features. It would highlight barriers to the sharing of ideas in international politics, focusing on the consequences of having an international system populated by agents who speak different languages, come from different types of families, hold different religious beliefs, and perhaps have different hopes for the future. In short, it would hold that *pluralism* is a fact of international life, today and in the foreseeable future. Starting with pluralism or difference as a fundamental assumption, an international social theory would spotlight differences in kind between domestic and international life, and perhaps thereby help us understand domestic politics better as well.

Captain Cook and the Cold War

In concluding, I return to Captain Cook's visit to Hawaii. When Cook arrived at the Island of Hawaii, a series of accidents led him to be mistaken for Lono, the Hawaiian god of peace and fertility. During Cook's stay, Hawaiian ritual beliefs went unchallenged, preventing a cosmological crisis and outbreaks of violence (as happened during his stay on Kauai). Cook's men were resupplied and their ships outfitted. Cooperation blossomed because of false intersubjective beliefs. When Cook left the island in accordance with the Hawaiian myth, his departure was celebrated. Unfortunately for Cook, a ship's mast broke and he was forced to return to the island. Marshall Sahlins tells the story of Cook's end, "Unlike his arrival, his return was generally unintelligible and unwanted, especially by the king and chiefs. And things fell apart."[11] Cook's return created a cosmological crisis on Hawaii, as it constituted a challenge to the sovereignty of the Hawaiian king. In the end, Cook was killed and offered as a sacrifice. Cooperation based on FIBs does not always end well for everyone.

One might suspect that the story of Cook's death means that FIBs cannot provide a reliable route to cooperation. Beyond Captain Cook, the other examples of cooperation cited in this book eventually failed. US cooperation with Vietnam was followed by war, US cooperation with Stalin was followed by the Cold War, détente was followed by a return to enmity, and the Anti-Ballistic Missile Treaty no longer exists. The discovery of FIBs, while they might not always lead to cosmological crises, may occasion resentment and overreaction if actors are not prepared to interact with a real, rather than an imagined, other.

On the other hand, few cases of cooperation are long lasting. Cooperation between European powers, throughout history, until recently has always been followed by war. Yet, even if cooperation lasts only a short time, it may be useful. Cook died, but his men were fed, they obtained a new mast, and the voyage continued. The Cold War began, but Hitler had been defeated. The ABM Treaty no longer exists, but the defensive arms race was delayed. Delaying war, creating years of peace, and encouraging cooperation, even if short-lived, is not bad. It may be the best one can hope for.

Notes

.

Introduction

1. Sahlins 1995. Sahlins's account is the subject of significant controversy. See Obeyesekere 1992. Many independent observers agree with Sahlins for evidentiary reasons. See Hacking 1999, 207–26. The details of this controversy are not important for my argument because, on balance, Obeyesekere posits the same role for misperceptions as does Sahlins. For Obeyesekere, Europeans' misperceptions of Hawaiian culture—their desire to be considered gods by Hawaiians and an inaccurate belief that this deification occurred—led to a successful period of cooperation.

2. Sahlins 1995, 33.

3. Cook's return and subsequent death are discussed in the final chapter of this book. He was killed by the Hawaiians, but not for the reasons that Cook's men believed.

4. On misperceptions and war, see Jervis 1968, 1976, and 1988; Levy 1983; A. Stein 1982; and J. Stein 1988. Compare Garfinkel and Skaperdas 2000; and Kim and Bueno de Mesquita 1995.

5. On misperceptions in the First World War, see Jervis 1976 and 1978; Glaser 1992, 1994/5, and 1997; and van Evera 1999. The literature describing the Cold War is discussed in chapters 1 and 2.

6. On common knowledge in liberal institutionalism, see Keohane 1984; and Morrow 2002. The argument was introduced by Thomas Schelling. Schelling 1960 and 1966. On realism and misperception, see Blainey 1973; Jervis 1976; and van Evera 1999. On norms, culture, and cooperation, see Wendt 1999; and Finnemore 1996a. Alexander Wendt argues that shared ideas explain cooperation *and* conflict, an important alternative view.

7. Hearings before the Committee on Foreign Relations, US Senate, "Memorandum from Captain Herbert J. Bluechel to CO OSS Detachment 404," September 30, 1945, 284.

8. Warner 1972, 381. See also, Spector 1982.

9. Halberstam 2007, 223.

10. Lynn-Jones 1986.

11. Jervis 1988, 68.

12. Quoted in Carter 1982, 118.

13. Murray, Holmes, and Griffin 1996.

14. Social psychologists root this observation in evidence that most individuals believe that their beliefs are shared by a majority of people in a society, even if they are in fact only shared by a minority. See Krueger 1998; Krueger and Clement 1997.

15. This literature is reviewed extensively in chapters 3 and 4.

16. Osgood 1962.

17. Kydd 2005.

18. On reciprocity and cooperation, see Axelrod 1984.

19. Fearon 1994.

20. Mitzen 2011.

21. Bull 1977; Wendt 1999.

22. This literature is discussed in chapter 1.

23. Katzenstein 1996, 1.

24. This account of pluralism is distinct from that of the English school. See Wheeler and Dunne 1996.

25. The literature on international socialization, for example, often cites the classic works of sociologists such as George H. Mead or Peter Berger and Thomas Luckmann, who studied socialization within the state and especially in local communities or families. Wendt 1995, 76. In some cases, Berger and Luckmann's influence in IR scholarship is shrouded in the references. Jeffrey Checkel's view of complex learning is elaborated with reference to Alderson, who in turn cites Berger and Luckmann 1966. Checkel 2005; Alderson 2001.

26. This does not mean that the influence of ideas on policy is not important.

27. Carlson 2005.

28. An abductive argument infers the antecedent of a condition from its consequence if and only if there is no better explanation of the consequence than the antecedent. Its logical form may be simplified as: if A then B, B therefore A (assuming there is no better explanation than A). See Wendt 1999, 62–67.

29. Durkheim 1984. See also Hume 1978, 3.2.2; and Parsons 1937, 308–24.

30. Wendt 2006, 211.

1. Common Knowledge, Intersubjectivity, and False Intersubjective Beliefs

1. This is distinct from the problem of common knowledge in economics. Economists often discuss cases in which actors are unsure of the state of the world and describe how they develop common knowledge. The discussion here focuses on cases in which actors believe they know the state of the world, believe that this is common knowledge, and are incorrect. Aumann 1976; and Geanakoplos 1992.

2. Fearon 1995. See also Kirshner 2000, who shows that differences in perceptions of events can lead to different beliefs.

3. Morrow 2002.

4. Morrow 1994, 55. Also see Aumann 1976; and D. Lewis 1969.

5. Morrow 1994, 61.

6. Morrow 1994, 97–98; Osborne and Rubenstein 1994.

7. Hume 1978, 3.2.2. On conventions in IR, see Kratochwil 1978.

8. Von Neumann and Morgenstern 1944.

9. See, for example, Fearon 1998; Kahler 1998, and Weingast 1995.

10. See, for example, canonical coordination problems—such as the "coordinated attack" or "byzantine agreement problem"—in which a reliable communication system is necessary for cooperation. Fagin, Hapern, Moses, and Vardi 1995.

11. Jervis 1970.

12. Talbott 1979.

13. MacMillan 2007, 311.

14. Acheson 1969, 391.

15. Schelling 1960. Also see Chayes and Chayes 1993; Goldstein and Keohane 1993; and Morrow 2002.

16. Wendt 1999, 159–60.

17. See, for example, Blainey 1973; Kydd 2005; and Mearsheimer 2001. For an overview, see Rathbun 2007.

18. Giddens 1991; see also McSweeney 1999; and Mitzen 2006.

19. Wendt 2006, 210–12.

20. Hayek 1944 and 1960. Douglass North's treatment of ideology is similar in some respects. See North 1981.

21. Kratochwil and Ruggie 1986. On nonuse of weapons, see Price 1995; and Tannenwald 2007. On the Red Cross and human rights, respectively, see Finnemore 1996a; and Risse and Sikkink 1999. On economic policy, see Judith Goldstein 1989; and Widmaier 2003 and 2004.

22. Wendt 1999, 1.

23. Farrell 2001; see also Hopf 1998.

24. Christiansen, Jorgensen, and Wiener 1999.

25. Habermas 1984; Stolorow and Atwood 1996. For alternative accounts, see Coelho and Figueiredo 2003; de Quincey 2000; Markova 2003; and Zahavi 2001.

26. Durkheim, 1907; Searle 1995.

27. Wendt 1999, 159–60.

28. Aumann 1976; Lewis 1969.

29. Kratochwil 1989, 72–83.

30. Cox 1986, 218.

31. Wendt 1999, 161. See also Keohane 2000.

32. Checkel 1999 and 2001; Cortell and Davis 1996; Finnemore and Sikkink 1998. See also Nye 1987.

33. See Kratochwil 1989; Onuf 1989.

34. Wendt 1999.

35. Hasenclever, Mayer, and Rittberger 1997, 137–39.

36. Often, this research does not intend to explain the sources of international cooperation. For example, research that attempts to demonstrate the existence of the state as an actor, the role of emotions, or even the diffusion of human rights practices to new groups does not require intersubjective understanding to exist between states and does not necessarily attempt to explain cooperation. See, for example, Finnemore 1996a; Risse and Sikkink 1999; and Wendt 2004.

37. Finnemore 1996a, 5–8; Price 1995; Wendt 2003.

38. Barnett 1996, 415.

39. Katzenstein 1996, 5. This definition has become standard and is relied on, for example, by Risse and Sikkink 1999. Other definitions are very similar. See Finnemore 1996a, 22.

40. Finnemore 2003, 24–51.

41. Kratochwil 1989, 7.

42. Ibid., 70.

43. Adler and Barnett 1998a.

44. See Adler 1997; Adler and Barnett 1998b; and Waever 1998.

45. Goldstein and Keohane 1993; Finnemore 1996a; Jervis 2006.

46. Chwe 2001.

47. Burdick and Wheeler 1964, 75.

48. Price 1995. Many empirical studies on the roles of norms do not confirm the importance of public beliefs. For example, during fighting between Austria and Prussia in 1866 and China and Japan in 1894, one state complied with the Geneva Convention, despite the failure of its enemy to do the same. This implies that common expectations for compliance may not be necessary in all cases for cooperation to be successful. Finnemore 1996a, 82.

49. Laclau 2005.

50. Tom Baldwin, "Obama's Army Is United in Desire for Change, but Less Sure What It Means," *The Times* (U.K.), March 4, 2008, 6.

51. Parsons 1937, 44.

52. Habermas1984, 96.

53. Ibid., 98; Hopf 2010.

54. Arrow 1963, 17; Frieden 1991.

55. Frieden 1991, 45.

56. Sunstein 1994/5, 1996, and 2000.

57. Sunstein 1994/5, 1735.

58. I am restricting the use of the term "functional incompletely theorized agreements" to cases in which agreement on principles is lacking. Sunstein also argues that cases in which constitution makers agree on an abstract principle but disagree on how to decide specific cases may be incompletely theorized agreements, but in the interests of precision I use the term "functional overlapping principles" to refer to cases of the latter. See Sunstein 2000, 122.

59. See Byers 2004.

60. Gaddis 2000, chap. 5.

61. Spector 1982, 23–50; Warner 1972, 379–94.

62. Rawls 1993, 15.

63. On shared values and the creation of NATO, see, for example, P. Jackson 2003; Kaplan 2007; and Milloy 2006.

64. Kaplan 2004, 5.

65. B. Anderson 1983, 53.

66. Ibid., 154.

67. Keohane 1984, 51–52.

68. On this distinction, see Downs, Rocke, and Barsoom 1996.

69. Garthoff 1994, 24.

70. Gerring 2007a and 2007b.

71. Gerard Smith 1985; Garthoff 1994.

72. Brezhnev 1979, 74.

73. Levy 2008, 10.

74. Gerring 2007a.

75. See, for example, Schelling and Halperin 1961; and Osgood 1962.

76. Larson 1997.

77. Farrell 2005.

78. Bially Mattern 2005.

79. Downs and Rocke 1990; Guzman 2008, 29–48; Rice 1988.

80. Blacker 1983, 135.
81. Garthoff 1994, 1163.
82. See Bennett 2010; and George and Bennett 2005. By necessary, I mean that cooperation would not have arisen unless there was a FIB. This is similar to an INUS cause, because there were circumstances in the Cold War, such as a conflict of interest between the parties, that created a situation in which FIBs were a necessary cause. See Mahoney 2008.
83. Collier 2011.
84. Bennett and Elman 2007.
85. Collier 2011; George and Bennett 2005, 188–89.
86. On the use of counterfactuals to demonstrate causation, see Fearon 1991; Grynaviski forthcoming; Lebow 2000; and Tetlock and Belkin 1996.
87. See Weingast 1996.
88. See Breslauer 1996.
89. See Lebow 2010, chap. 2; and Tetlock and Belkin 1996.
90. Cook and Campbell 1979, chap. 5.
91. Campbell and Stanley 1963, chap. 5; King, Keohane, and Verba 1994.
92. Campbell and Stanley 1963, chap. 5; George and Bennett 2005, 166–67.
93. Mahoney 2010, 128.
94. Bennett 2010.

2. Détente

1. Wendt 1999, 251.
2. Superpower relations have received surprisingly little attention from constructivists. While specific elements, especially the role of nuclear weapons, have been extensively treated, discussion of the relationship as a whole is often only mentioned in passing. See Bially Mattern 2005, 22–23; Farrell 2005; Tannenwald 2007; and Wendt 1999, 36. Cf. Ringmar 2002. Most work is dedicated to understanding the end of the Cold War rather than its conduct. See, for example, Evangelista 2001. This does not mean the period has escaped attention; scholars have focused instead on specific relationships between states within a single bloc or shown the importance of a single superpower's culture. See Bially Mattern 2005; Hopf 2002; and Risse-Kappen 1996. The lack of a systematic attempt to determine whether the superpower rivalry was mitigated by shared ideas is odd: it is clearly a paradigmatic case, crucial for understanding US foreign policy, and an important case in the sense that if constructivism cannot contribute to understanding the Cold War—if the balance of power is sufficient—then one may question the utility of the paradigm as a whole.
3. For a small selection of these works, see Dobrynin 1995; Garthoff 1994; George 1983; Kissinger 1979, 1982, and 1994; Israelyan 1995; Lebow and Stein 1994; Nixon 1990; and Saivetz 1997, 73–76.
4. Wendt 1999. The selection of Wendt's theory is appropriate for three reasons. First, there are few explicit empirical considerations of Wendt's theory, and thus an empirical test is useful. Second, unlike many constructivist theorists, Wendt is explicitly interested in the cultural preconditions for international cooperation, whereas many others are interested in why specific policies change. Third, there are few constructivist theories of superpower cooperation and therefore few off-the-shelf constructivist explanations for détente.
5. Ibid., 251.
6. Ibid., 260–62.
7. There are few systematic tests of Wendt's theory and even fewer attempts relating to the Cold War. See McLeod 2008; Thies 2008; and Widmaier 2003 and 2004. In the context of the Cold War, see Sala, Scott, and Spriggs 2007.

8. Wendt 1999, 279.

9. Ibid., 282.

10. Garthoff 1994, 24.

11. Ibid., 326.

12. Philip Shabecoff, "Talk by Brezhnev," *New York Times,* June 23, 1973, 65; "Brezhnev: Mankind Has Outgrown Rigid 'Cold War' Armor," *Washington Post,* June 25, 1973, A10.

13. Nixon-Agnew Campaign Committee, "Nixon on the Issues," 1968, *Foreign Relations of the United States, 1969–1976,* vol. 1, *Foundations of US Foreign Policy, 1969–1972* (Washington, DC: Government Printing Office, 2003), 49 (hereafter cited as *FRUS: 1969–1972* with appropriate page numbers). Nixon repeated this sentiment a few months later at the request of the Soviet Union as a signal of his intentions to negotiate. Nixon, "Inaugural Address," 1969, *FRUS: 1969–1972,* 53; and on the use of the inaugural address as a signal, see Nixon 1990, 346–47. Also see Memorandum of Conversation (MEMCON): Sedov and Kissinger, January 2, 1969, *Foreign Relations of the United States, 1969–1976,* vol. 12, *Soviet Union, January 1969–October 1970* (Washington, DC: Government Printing Office, 2006), 3 (hereafter cited as *FRUS: Soviet Union, 1969–1970* with appropriate page numbers).

14. Russett and Deluca 1981, 389–91; Smith 1983. The period also saw public support for a reduction in support for military spending, an issue of significance for relations. See Russett 1974 and 1975.

15. Volten 1982.

16. Stewart, Warhola, and Blough 1984.

17. Husband 1979.

18. Richard Nixon Library, "Address by Richard M. Nixon to the Bohemian Club," July 28, 1967, *FRUS: 1969–1972,* 8. There were early signs of this shift. See Nixon 1967; and Nixon-Agnew Campaign Committee, "Nixon on the Issues," 1968, *FRUS: 1969–1972,* 48–49.

19. "Letter from President Nixon to Secretary of Defense Laird," February 4, 1969, *FRUS: Soviet Union, 1969–1970,* 56.

20. The Nixon administration was often explicit about turning the corner from enmity. See "Paper Prepared for the National Security Council by the Interdepartmental Group for Europe," February 18, 1969, *FRUS: Soviet Union, 1969–1970,* 53–55.

21. Wendt 1999, 249.

22. The role of material factors is explored in chapter 4.

23. A similar dynamic may occur in romantic relationships. The most satisfying relationships are those where lovers idealize their imperfect partners. Murray, Holmes, and Griffin 1996.

24. Wendt 1999, 283.

25. Ibid.

26. Bluhm 1967, 1–3; Edmonds 1983, 137–39; Garthoff 1994, 27.

27. Leffler 2007, 238.

28. Ibid. See also Podvig 2008; Schilling 1981; and Steinberg 1990.

29. The perception of parity was not accurate; the United States in fact remained dominant. See chapter 5.

30. Zubok 2007, 202.

31. Dobrynin 1995, 192–93; Gromyko 1989, 278.

32. Garthoff 1994, 42–73.

33. Ibid., 66. Garthoff shows that this view prevailed in leading military journals, political speeches, and deliberations.

34. Ibid., 64.

35. See "Defense Officials Tell Senators Soviet Nears Nuclear Equality," *New York Times,* July 19, 1968, 5; "Missiles: Russia Works Hard to Close the Gap," *New York Times,* February 25, 1968, E2; and "Westmoreland Says Soviet All But Closes Missile Gap," *New York Times,* February 1, 1970, 46.

36. "Nixon Queries Stand on Missile Parity," *New York Times,* February 22, 1968, 26; Max Frankel, "Humphrey Scores Nixon on Defense: Terms Rival 'Irresponsible' for His Attack on the Concept of Parity with Soviet," *New York Times,* October 28, 1968, 1.

37. For example, *Foreign Affairs* included articles related to parity in every issue. Brzezinski 1972 and 1973; Buchan 1972; Kennan 1972; Schulman 1971; Stone 1970.

38. James Reston, "The Word War: A 'Sufficiency' of Arms," *New York Times,* January 31, 1969, 38; " 'Sufficiency' vs. 'Superiority,' " *New York Times,* February 2, 1969, E12; Thomas P. Ronan, "Expert Finds US and Soviet in Arms Sufficiency," *New York Times,* January 30, 1969, 6. For the defense debate, see Garthoff 1994, 61; and Moulton 1973.

39. Kissinger 1979, 317. See also Burr 2005, 52–56; and Dallek 2007, 136–37.

40. "Memorandum from Director of Central Intelligence Helms to Secretary of State Rogers: Gromyko's Review of Current Soviet Policy," July 14, 1969, *FRUS: Soviet Union, 1969–1970,* 200.

41. In many ways, this is similar to the argument that rising powers demand prestige. See Gilpin 1981, 30–32. I use political parity, prestige, and influence interchangeably.

42. Fursenko and Naftali 1997, 354–55.

43. Leffler 2007, 238.

44. Dobrynin 1995, 184; Lerner 2008; Loth 2002, 101; Ouimet 2003, 32–37.

45. Leffler 2007, 240. See also Lerner 2008.

46. Husband 1979.

47. Garthoff 1994, 42.

48. Ibid., 45; Herring 2008, 772; Litwak 1984.

49. Husband 1979.

50. Kissinger 1979, 69. Kissinger's emphasis on the virtues of multipolarity stands in contrast to many other realist thinkers who suggest that bipolarity produces stability by rendering conflict on the periphery less important. See Waltz 1979, chap. 8.

51. Ibid. For Kissinger, independent French and German foreign policies and an independent China evidenced an emerging multipolarity. See Chang 1990; Costigliola 1992; Hofmann 2007; and Sarotte 2001.

52. Goh 2005; Isaacson 2005, 335–36.

53. Kissinger 1954, 2. On the influence of this thesis on Nixon, see Gaddis 1982, 278.

54. Kissinger 1954, 141.

55. Gaddis 1982, 287.

56. Garthoff 1994, 1164.

57. By maximum gains, I mean a Pareto-optimal outcome where any change in the bargain would leave at least one superpower worse off.

58. A similar theory of bargaining power to Kissinger's is in Gruber 2000; and Krasner 1991.

59. Hedrick Smith, "Nixon Would Link Political Issues to Missile Talks," *New York Times,* January 28, 1969, 1; "Linkage—the New Thing in Foreign Policy," *Washington Post,* February 12, 1969, A20; "President Nixon on Foreign Policy," *Washington Post,* January 28, 1969, A14; "State Insists: No Strings to Arms Talks," *Washington Post,* November 7, 1969, A17.

60. Nixon 1990, 346.

61. Nixon considered linkages as a shift from the Johnson administration policy of attempting to isolate issues from one another. See "Letter from President Nixon to Secretary of State Rogers," February 4, 1969, *FRUS: Soviet Union, 1969–1970,* 26–28.

62. Kissinger also suggests a third benefit: linkages enable a grand strategy to relate different areas of foreign policy. Kissinger 1979, 139.

63. This logic is familiar to IR. See Krasner 1991; Lipson 1984; Powell 1991; Snidal 1991; and Waltz 1979. On issue linkage, see Haas 1958 and 1980; Keohane 1984, 91–92; and Tollison and Willett 1979.

64. Garthoff 1994, 33.

65. Ibid., 37.
66. Larson 1997, 185.
67. See also Gaddis 1982, 290–92.
68. Burr and Kimball 2003; Sagan and Suri 2003.
69. Blechman and Hart 1982.
70. Garthoff 1994, 52–53; Husband 1979, 504.
71. Garthoff 1994, 52; Herring 2008, 772.
72. See Ovinnikov 1980; and Winkel and Winkel 1987 for representative examples.
73. Herrmann 1985, 80.
74. "Memorandum from the President's Special Assistant (Buchanan) to President Nixon," *FRUS: 1969–1972*, 59–61.
75. Garthoff 1994, 41.
76. Light 1991, 264. Also see Golan 1988, 261–342; and Limberg 1990.
77. On Soviet beliefs about escalation and détente, see MacFarlane 1990, 35–48.
78. Kaiser 1980, 501. Also see Kohler et al. 1973, 76–78.
79. Garthoff 1994, 56. Also see Westad 1997, 18.
80. MEMCON "Meeting with Leonid Brezhnev and Soviet Officials," January 21, 1976, Digital National Security Archives (DNSA), Kissinger Transcripts (KT) 01876.
81. The Agreement on the Prevention of Nuclear War had a similar dynamic. See Garthoff 1994, 376–86.
82. Kissinger 1979, 1132.
83. Allison and Williams 1990, 6–7.
84. MEMCON (Kissinger) "Meeting between President Nixon and General Secretary Brezhnev," May 22, 1972, *Soviet American Relations: Détente Years, 1969–1972*, (Washington, DC: Government Printing Office, 2007), 835 (hereafter cited as *Soviet-American Relations*).
85. MEMCON (Dobrynin), February 7, 1972, *Soviet-American Relations*, 584; MEMCON (Kissinger), February 7, 1972, *Soviet-American Relations*, 582. This anecdote is the epigraph to chapter 3 of this book.
86. "Text of the Basic Principles," Department of State Bulletin, 1972, vol. 66, 898–99.
87. George 1988, 589.
88. Ibid.; MacFarlane 1985, 303.
89. Garthoff 1994, 46–47.
90. "Text of the Basic Principles," *Department of State Bulletin,* 1972, vol. 66, 898–99.
91. Garthoff 1994, 335.
92. MEMCON "Meeting between President Nixon and General Secretary Brezhnev," May 22, 1972, *Soviet-American Relations*, 835.
93. Holloway 1983, 89; Ringmar 2002.
94. Garthoff 1994, 331–33; see also Larson 1997, 185.
95. Garthoff 1994, 328.
96. MEMCON (Dobrynin), February 7, 1972, *Soviet-American Relations*, 584; MEMCON (Kissinger), February 7, 1972, *Soviet-American Relations*, 582.
97. In Garthoff 1994, 328. Only a few years later Kissinger did wave the piece of paper at the Soviets on several occasions. See "Department of State Cable: Kissinger to Graham Martin," April 23, 1975, Declassified Documents Reference Service (hereafter cited as DDRS), CK3100498927.
98. George 1983, 110.
99. Larson 1997, 185.
100. The following account of the superpower perceptions draws on Garthoff 1994, 404–57; Kissinger 1982, 450–613; and Quandt 1977a and 1977b.

101. Kissinger 1982, 486.

102. Israelyan 1995, 17–18.

103. On Brezhnev's control of the crisis, see Israelyan 1995, 25–31. For Kissinger's influence, see Isaacson 2005, 514; and Siniver 2008, 217–23. On the importance of the crisis to détente, see Hanhimäki 2004, 303; and Israelyan 1995.

104. Memoirs include Dinitz 2000; Dobrynin 1995; Haig 1992; Israelyan 1995; Kissinger 1982; and Sadat 1978. Historical literature includes Garthoff 1994; Golan 1977; Isaacson 1992; Lebow and Stein 1994; and Parker 2001. Relying on secondary sources is appropriate given their convergence. The main disagreements do not concern whether détente was a central factor in decision making. See Britton 1990, 300–304.

105. Siniver 2008.

106. Haig 1992, 409–10; Kissinger 1982, 454. See also US Interests Section Egypt, Cable 3243 to State Department, "Soviet View on Causes and Timing of Egyptian Decision to Resume Hostilities," October 26, 1973, NPMP, NSCF, box 1175, 1973 War (Middle East), file 21, NSA website; and Memorandum from William B. Quandt to Brent Scowcroft, "Arab-Israeli Tensions," October 6, 1973, NPMP, NSCF, box 1173, 1973 War (Middle East), file 1 of 2, NSA website.

107. For example, Murrey Marder, "Mideast Fighting Threatens US-Soviet Aims in Détente," *Washington Post,* October 7, 1973, A1; Joseph Kraft, "US-Soviet Détente and the Mideast," *Washington Post,* October 11,1973, A31; and Bernard Gwertzman, "Détente and Mideast," *New York Times*, October 18, 1973, 19.

108. Kissinger 1982, 600.

109. See, for example, "Memorandum from Sonnefeldt to Kissinger," October 10, 1973, *Foreign Relations of the United States,* vol. 25, *Arab-Israeli Crisis and War, 1973,* 306), 416–18 (hereafter cited as *FRUS: Arab-Israeli War* with appropriate page numbers).

110. MEMCON "Kissinger and Huang Zhen," October 6, 1973, *FRUS: Arab-Israeli War*, 338–39. See also Kissinger's remark about wanting to keep the Soviet Union out of the Middle East in MEMCON "Nixon, Kissinger, Scowcroft, and the Congressional Leadership," October 10, 1973, *FRUS: Arab-Israeli War*, 420–22.

111. Memorandum of Telephone Conversation (TELCON) Nixon and Kissinger, October 6, 1973, *FRUS: Arab-Israeli War,* 306.

112. TELCON Kissinger and Haig, October 6, 1973, *FRUS: Arab-Israeli War*, 311. Reports that the Soviets were prodding Jordan to get involved increased Kissinger's suspicions. See MEMCON Washington Special Actions Group (Principals Only), October 9, 1973, *FRUS: Arab-Israeli War*, 398–401.

113. TELCON Scowcroft and Dobrynin, October 6, 1973, *FRUS: Arab-Israeli War*, 317–18.

114. Kissinger knew that a ceasefire position calling on the parties to return to the status quo ex ante would be rejected by the Soviet Union, which could not ask its Arab clients to relinquish lands regained from the 1967 war. TELCON Kissinger and Dobrynin, October 6, 1973, *FRUS: Arab-Israeli War*, 317–23.

115. "Minutes of Washington Special Actions Group Meeting," October 6, 1973, *FRUS: Arab-Israeli War*, 332. See also TELCON Kissinger and Dinitz, October 8, 1973, *FRUS: Arab-Israeli War*, 371; MEMCON Nixon, Kissinger, Haig, Zeigler, and Scowcroft, October 9, 1973, *FRUS: Arab-Israeli War*, 411; and MEMCON Nixon, Kissinger, Scowcroft, and the Congressional Leadership, October 10, 1973, *FRUS: Arab-Israeli War*, 420–22.The next morning, Kissinger had rethought offering a ceasefire. The United States could not offer a ceasefire that Israel would likely reject because of "incalculable domestic consequences." TELCON Kissinger and Haig, October 7, 1973, *FRUS: Arab-Israeli War*, 343.

116. TELCON Kissinger and Dobrynin, October 6, 1973, *FRUS: Arab-Israeli War*, 319.

117. Israelyan 1995. On the veracity of Israelyan's account, see Golan 2000, 147.

118. Israelyan 1995, 17. Brezhnev reminded Nixon and Kissinger of these warnings. See "Message from the Soviet Leadership to President Nixon and Secretary of State Kissinger," October 6, 1973, *FRUS: Arab-Israeli War*, 314–15.

119. Garthoff 1994, 207.

120. MEMCON "President's Meeting with General Secretary Leonid Brezhnev, June 23, 1973, San Clemente, California," HAKO, box 75, Brezhnev Visit, June 18–25 1973, NSA website.

121. Lebow and Stein 1994, 165–66.

122. TELCON Kissinger and Dobrynin, October 6, 1973, *FRUS: Arab-Israeli War*, 318–23.

123. Ceasefire negotiations began early, but at first neither side seriously attempted to end the fighting. By October 18, the negotiations began in earnest. Dobrynin called Kissinger with a draft proposal for a ceasefire resolution. Kissinger stalled; events on the battlefield favored Israel, and Kissinger wanted time for Israeli to make gains. The next day, Kissinger agreed to travel to Moscow after a message from Brezhnev warned of harm to US-Soviet relations if the crisis escalated. Kissinger 1982, 540; TELCON Kissinger and Dobrynin, October 18, 1973, *FRUS: Arab-Israeli War*, 591; TELCON Kissinger and Dobrynin, October 19, 1973, *FRUS: Arab-Israeli War*, 615–17; and Brezhnev to Nixon, October 19, 1973, handed to Kissinger 11:45 a.m., NPMP, HAKO, box 69, Dobrynin/Kissinger, vol. 20, October 12–November 27, 1973, NSA website. Kissinger was granted broad latitude to negotiate. Nixon to Brezhnev, October 20, 1973, NPMP, HAKO, box 69, Dobrynin/Kissinger, vol. 20, October 12–November 27, 1973, NSA website; and Message from Kissinger to Scowcroft, HAKTO, 06 October 20, 1973, NPMP, HAKO, box 39, HAK Trip—Moscow, Tel Aviv, London—October 20–23, 1973, HAKTO, SECTO, TOSEC, Misc. NSA website.

124. Israelyan 1995, 133–35.

125. Kissinger 1982, 553.

126. Ibid., 554.

127. TELCON Kissinger to Dinitz, October 19, 1973, DNSA, KA11321. Kissinger, for example, demanded a good night's sleep before the negotiations began. TELCON Kissinger and Dobrynin, October 19, 1973, *FRUS: Arab-Israeli War*, 615.

128. Telegram from Kissinger to Scowcroft, October 20, 1973, *FRUS: Arab-Israeli War*, 624.

129. The first two articles are also ambiguous. The first does not specify whether the ceasefire begins immediately or at the end of the twelve hours and whether the "positions they now occupy" means those before or after the twelve hours had elapsed. See TELCON Kissinger and Dinitz, October 23, 1973, *FRUS: Arab-Israeli War*, 678–79; and TELCON Kissinger and Vorontsov, October 19, 1973, *FRUS: Arab-Israeli War*, 679–81. In addition, "implementation" in the second article was left ambiguous to ensure that neither party rejected the inclusion of the contentious Resolution 242.

130. In Israelyan 1995, 137.

131. TELCON Kissinger and Dinitz, October 24, 1973, *FRUS: Arab-Israeli War*, 715. On Europe, MEMCON Secretary's Staff Meeting, October 23, 1973, DSNA, KT 00868; "Minutes of Secretary of State's Staff Meeting," October 23, 1973, *FRUS: Arab-Israeli War*, 692; Kissinger 1982, 555; MEMCON Kissinger, Schlesinger, Moorer, Colby, and Scowcroft. TELCON Kissinger and Dinitz, October 24, 1973, *FRUS: Arab-Israeli War*, 724. The importance of bilateralism (the exclusion of third parties) is explicitly discussed by the parties in MEMCON in Moscow, October 20, 1973, DSNA, KT 00861.

132. On the importance of not embarrassing the Soviets during the negotiations, see TELCON Kissinger and Dinitz, October 24, 1973, 9:22 a.m., *FRUS: Arab-Israeli War*, 704–5; TELCON Kissinger and Dinitz, October 24, 1973, 9:32 a.m., *FRUS: Arab-Israeli War*, 706–7; MEMCON Kissinger, Schlesinger, Colby, Moorer, and Scowcroft, October 19, 1973, DSNA, KT 00860. See also Secretary's Staff Meeting, October 23, 1973, DSNA, KT 00868.

133. Israelyan 1995.

134. Garthoff 1994, 419–20.

135. The misunderstanding was not limited to the superpowers. Many members of the United Nations decided that "under appropriate auspices" implied the Security Council or the UN Secretariat. Israelyan 1995, 141–42.

136. "Backchannel Message from Sadat to Nixon," October 23, 1973, *FRUS: Arab-Israeli War*, 687.

137. Kissinger 1982, 576.

138. "Message from Brezhnev to Nixon," October 24, 1973, *FRUS: Arab-Israeli War*, 734–35.

139. Israelyan 1995, 162, 169; Lebow and Stein 1994, 236–37.

140. Israelyan 1995, 160–62.

141. Ibid., 170.

142. TELCON Nixon and Haig, October 24, 1973, *FRUS: Arab-Israeli War*, 736–37; "Memorandum for the Record (CJCS Memo M-88–73)," October 24, 1973, *FRUS: Arab-Israeli War*, 737–42.

143. Lebow and Stein 1994, 246–47; and Siniver 2008, 212–16.

144. Schlesinger and William Quandt, an NSC staff member, agreed that the odds of a Soviet intervention were low. See Lebow and Stein 1994, 249; and Kissinger 2003, 212.

145. Lebow and Stein 1994, 249. The threat in Brezhnev's note was augmented by other information. First, Dobrynin's cold response in a discussion with Kissinger "dominated the deliberation that our government was about to start" because "he might have indicated in the hundred ways available to a seasoned professional that we were overreacting." Second, supplementary military information made the threat seem more menacing. William Colby, director of the CIA, believed that Soviet units were being readied to intervene. See Kissinger 1982, 585.

146. "Memorandum for the Record (CJCS Memo M-88–73)," October 24, 1973, *FRUS: Arab-Israeli War*, 737–42.

147. Kissinger 2003, 348.

148. "Memorandum for the Record (CJCS Memo M-88–73)," October 24, 1973, *FRUS: Arab-Israeli War*, 737–42.

149. Kissinger 1982, 594.

150. Ibid., 595.

151. Lebow and Stein 1994.

152. Kissinger 1982, 595.

153. Israelyan 1995, 179–83; Lebow and Stein 1994, 266–68.

154. Ibid.

155. Ibid., 183.

156. Nixon to Brezhnev, October 25, 1973, delivered to Soviet Embassy, 5:40 a.m., NPMP, HAKO, box 69, Dobrynin/Kissinger, vol. 20, October 12–November 27, 1973, NSA website.

157. Israelyan 1995, 188.

158. Scowcroft to Dobrynin, October 26, 1973, enclosing message from Nixon to Brezhnev, October 26, 1973, delivered at 1:00 p.m., MPMP, HAKO, box 69, Dobrynin/Kissinger, vol. 20, October 12–November 27, 1973, NSA website.

159. Garthoff 1994, 437.

160. Ibid., 437–40.

3. The Anti-Ballistic Missile Treaty

1. Schelling 1960 and 1966.

2. Abbott 1993; Downs and Rocke 1990; Guzman 2008.

3. Rice 1988. See also Weber 1991.

4. Adler 1992; Evangelista 1999.

5. "Minutes of a National Security Council Meeting," June 25, 1969, *Foreign Relations of the United States, 1969–1976*, vol. 32, *SALT I, 1969–1972* (Washington, DC: Government Printing Office, 2010), 83–85 (hereafter cited as *FRUS: SALT I* with appropriate page numbers).

6. Newhouse 1989, 154.

7. Spencer Rich, "ABM Wins Crucial Senate Test," *Washington Post*, August 7, 1969, A1; Warren Waever, "Nixon Missile Plan Wins in Senate by a 51–50 Vote; House Approval Likely," *New York Times*, August 7, 1969, 1.

8. Newhouse 1989, 83. The pressure that the Joint Chiefs put on Johnson is an intriguing element of the story. In the 1950s, the Joint Chiefs were divided over new weapons programs, with no branch wanting to concede a major new program to a rival. McNamara united the Joint Chiefs because they had to work together to counter McNamara's influence. See Halperin 1972, 77; and Korb 1974, 172–73.

9. Newhouse 1989, 132 and 152.

10. Garthoff 1994, 150.

11. Newhouse 1989, 51. It also enabled Nixon to argue that because the system was initially designed to only secure a second-strike capability it would not end the fledgling SALT process. He convinced Gerard Smith, the US chief negotiator during SALT I and an influential advocate of arms control, to testify to this effect before Congress, and this testimony carried enormous weight. John Finney, "Nixon Aide Denies Sentinel Imperils Atom Arms Talks," *New York Times*, March 7, 1969, 1.

12. Newhouse 1989, 89.

13. Dana Adams Schmidt, "Kosygin Is Cool to Missiles Curb," *New York Times*, February 10, 1967, 1; "Kosygin Sees Way Open to Peace Talks," *Washington Post*, February 10, 1967, A1. The following week, the Soviet Union shifted dramatically away from this statement. An article in *Pravda* suggested that the Soviet Union was willing to negotiate away these systems. "Soviet Hunts New Stand for US Missile Talks," *Washington Post*, February 16, 1967, A11. On the reliability of *Pravda* statements, see Axelrod and Zimmerman 1981.

14. Talensky 1964, 19.

15. Newhouse 1989, 81–82.

16. Bluth 1992, 213.

17. Savel'yev and Detinov 1995, 22. See also Evangelista 1999, 212–16; and Podvig 2004.

18. Bennett 2010.

19. Kissinger was the chief US SALT decision maker. On Kissinger's centralization of foreign policy decision making, see Hersh 1983, 25–45; Isaacson 2005, 151–56 and 183–211; and Kissinger 1979, 38–48. For his influence in other issue areas, see Isaacson 2005, 242–45; and MacMillan 2007, 182. On SALT, the back channel provided additional influence. As Gerard Smith recounts, "It was a one-man stand, a presidential aide against the resources of the Soviet leadership. . . . It was not a pleasing contrast—one American (presumably keeping the President informed) ranged against the top Soviet political and technical authorities." Smith 1985, 225.

20. Isaacson 2005, 321.

21. Garthoff 1994, 162–63; Smith 1985, 131.

22. The Limited Test Ban Treaty was less important and did not bring about a lasting détente. See Mastny 2008.

23. Garthoff 1994, 163.

24. Savel'yev and Detinov 1995, 22; Garthoff 1994, 163.

25. Nixon 1990, 414–18; Kissinger 1979, 204–10.

26. "Notes of a Verification Panel Meeting," June 24, 1970, *FRUS: SALT I*, 291–95; "Notes of Secretary of Defense Laird's Staff Meeting," August 24, 1970, *FRUS: SALT I*, 341–42; "Memorandum from Packard to Nixon," December 2 1970, *FRUS: SALT I*, 364–65.

27. "Conversation between Nixon, Kissinger, and Haldeman," April 17, 1971, *FRUS: SALT I*, 442–49.

28. "National Security Decision Memorandum 69," July 9, 1970, *FRUS: SALT I*, 310–13. The ban was considered impossible because it would either require intrusive inspection or the

destruction of radar sites in the Soviet Union—both impossibilities. See "Memorandum from Packard to Kissinger (Attachment)," June 20, 1970, *FRUS: SALT I*, 285–87. Interestingly, the leading advocates of anti-ballistic missiles were those who called for the ban (presumably because it would be rejected). See Packard's comments in "Notes of a Verification Panel Meeting," June 24, 1970, *FRUS: SALT I*, 291–95.

29. MEMCON, March 10, 1969, *Soviet-American Relations*, 134–38; TELCON, March 15, 1969, KA 00312, NSA website.

30. "Minutes of a National Security Council Meeting," November 10, 1969, *FRUS: SALT I*, 153–59. See Richard Nixon, "Statement on Deployment of the Antiballistic Missile System," *Public Papers of Richard Nixon*, March 16, 1969 (Washington, DC: Government Printing Office), 109 (hereafter cited as *PPRN* with appropriate date and page numbers). This argument was repeated often; see President's News Conference, *PPRN*, March 14, 1969, 108; President's News Conference, *PPRN*, April 18, 1969, 156; and President's News Conference, *PPRN*, June 19, 1969, 248. For Kissinger's views, see Kissinger 1979, 208–9; and Garthoff 1994, 165. This view was echoed by legislators. *New York Times*, February 23, 1969, 51. Papers prepared for the Washington SALT review panel echo these themes, and it was a common understanding throughout the administration; see "Paper Prepared by the Interagency SALT Steering Committee," n.d., *FRUS: SALT I*, 26–39; and "Memorandum from Packard to Richardson and Kissinger," December 8, 1969, *FRUS: SALT I*, 166–67.

31. "Conversation among Nixon, Rogers, Kissinger, Haig, and Ziegler," *FRUS: SALT I*, 800–801.

32. In his first book, which led to Kissinger's prestige and which Nixon praised, Kissinger argued that defense was necessary for deterrence. See Hersh 1983, 11–13; Isaacson 2005, 134–35; and Kissinger 1957.

33. Dallek 2007, 135–37.

34. "Memorandum from Kissinger to Nixon," January 22, 1970, *FRUS: SALT I*, 176–77. Nixon and Kissinger probably thought the Soviets would reject the offer because of an earlier Soviet stance at the Glassboro summit. See Evangelista 1999, 198–99.

35. Garthoff 1994, 163. Furthermore, Kissinger believed that the Soviet military would refuse to negotiate ABMs. See "Memorandum from Helmut Sonnenfeldt to Kissinger: Memorandum to the President on Soviet Developments—Comments on our Policy (tab A)," May 22, 1969, *FRUS: Soviet Union, 1969–1970*, 165.

36. Nixon 1990, 416.

37. The negotiating team in Helsinki was aware of this shift in the Soviet position. See "Letter from Smith to Nixon," December 9, 1969, *FRUS: SALT I*, 168–70.

38. In one conversation Kissinger questions whether the Soviets would be willing to negotiate because of Safeguard. However, Kissinger does not believe that is because of a genuine interest but because the Soviets might aim to reopen a divisive debate over Safeguard in the US Senate. He does not mention this argument again in the documents referring to SALT decision making, and there is no evidence that it played a role in offering a NCA-only deal. See "Memorandum from Kissinger to Nixon: Recent Soviet Policy Developments: SALT, China and Germany," December 23, 1969, *FRUS: Soviet Union, 1969–1970*, 327.

39. Garthoff 1994. 163. On the importance of the bargaining chip argument in persuading the Senate in the 1969 vote, see Bunn 1992, 125; and Schulzinger 1987, 91.

40. Smith 1985, 117–18; "Memorandum for the File by Smith," January 9, 1970, *FRUS: SALT I*, 172; "Letter from Smith to Nixon," March 23, 1970, *FRUS: SALT I*, 195–97. Paul Nitze agreed with this approach. Talbott 1988, 125.

41. Garthoff 1977, 20. On reverse bargaining, see Bresler and Gray 1977; and Garthoff 1977, 20–21.

42. ABM advocates immediately worried that if the Soviet acceptance of the US offer were leaked it would undermine support for ABMs in the Senate. See "Memorandum from Laird to Kissinger," April 28, 1970, *FRUS: SALT I*, 259–60.

43. On the mirror-imaging of strategic cultures, see Booth 1979; Gray 1986; and Snyder 1977.

44. Adler 1992; Evangelista 1999.

45. Evangelista 1999, 230.

46. This was a long-standing US position and a critical security concern. See Garthoff 1994, 161; and Smith 1985, 11.

47. On the importance of FBS to the Soviet bargaining position, see Smith 1985, 179–98; MEMCON, June 10, 1970, *Soviet-American Relations,* 159–65. These frustrations are captured by Sonnefeldt, who wrote to Kissinger of the SALT process that "the shaker is running out." "Memorandum from Sonnefeldt to Kissinger," December 5, 1970, *FRUS: SALT I,* 366–72.

48. See NSC Meeting on SALT, March 8, 1971, DNSA, KT 00244. To make the issue more confusing, on recognizing his error in making the NCA-only offer, Kissinger attempted to rectify it by offering an ABM ban, which he was also sure the Soviets would reject. The presentation of this second alternative was not a sincere offer but was intended to move the United States off its NCA-only position and toward the position it maintained in the Senate. As noted earlier, when the Soviets hinted that they preferred an ABM ban, Kissinger told Smith to not push the ban further. Garthoff 1994, 173; Smith 1985, 256–63; Newhouse 1989, 229–30. Also see Verification Panel Meeting, January 16, 1971, DNSA, KT 00226.

49. MEMCON, October 22, 1970, *FRUS: SALT I,* 352–53; "Memorandum from Kissinger to Nixon," December 10, 1970, *FRUS: SALT I,* 373–74.

50. "Remarks Announcing an Agreement on Strategic Arms Limitation Talks," *PPRN,* May 20, 1970, 175.

51. The comprehensive offensive package would later become SALT II and was never ratified.

52. Kissinger 1979, 820–21; Smith 1985, 246. The vagueness of the limit on heavy missiles also enabled the Soviet Union to build larger missiles, such as the SS-9, and was considered a concession. Kissinger made a unilateral statement to attempt to settle the issue, but the Soviets never agreed. Garthoff 1994, 191–92.

53. Marilyn Berger, "Democrats Urge US-Soviet Agreement on ABMs," *Washington Post,* February 27, 1971, A12; "Muskie Asks Negotiations on ABM Ban," *Washington Post,* April 8, 1971, A19; "Soviets ABM Bid Attracts Symington," *Washington Post,* March 30, 1971, A5. The reason for the increased pressure was that the Soviet offer to limit ABM systems became public knowledge by January 1971. Chalmers Roberts, "Soviets Propose ABM Limit," *Washington Post,* January 9, 1971, A1; "Soviet ABM Plan Confirmed at Vienna," *New York Times,* May 1, 1971, 3.

54. "Summit Accord on SALT," *New York Times,* May 21, 1971, 38; Joseph Kraft, "Flexibility Gets Results," *Washington Post,* May 23, 1971, 35; John Finney, "Harvard-MIT Arms Experts Pleased by Nixon's Move on Talks," *New York Times,* May 27, 1971, 2. On Nixon's reaction, see Haldeman 1994, 289–90.

55. "Conversation between Nixon, Kissinger, and Haldeman," April 17, 1971, *FRUS: SALT I,* 442–49.

56. In Dallek 2007, 280.

57. This is similar to arguments for audient costs. See Fearon 1994. On going public, see Kernel 1993, 157–88.

58. Brezhnev 1971, 8–38; Volten 1982, 58–65.

59. Leffler 2007, 241.

60. On the implications of going public in the Brezhnev era, see Anderson 1993. On the connection of Brezhnev's power to détente, see Garthoff 1994, 117; and Gelman 1984, 129–30 and 156–60.

61. Smith 1985, 250.

62. Ibid.; Newhouse 1989, 219.

63. MEMCON, April 9, 1970, *Soviet-American Relations,* 144–45; MEMCON, June 10, 1970, *Soviet-American Relations,* 159–65.

64. AVP RF. MEMCON, January 9, 1971, *Soviet-American Relations,* 258–63.

65. AVP RF. MEMCON, February 10, 1971, *Soviet-American Relations,* 289–3.

66. TELCON Kissinger and Nixon, February 22, 1971, *Soviet-American Relations,* 301.

67. TELCON Kissinger and Dobrynin (4:23), March 26, 1971, *Soviet-American Relations,* 322; AVP RF. TELCON Kissinger and Dobrynin, March 26, 1971, *Soviet-American Relations,* 323.

68. AVP RF. MEMCON, March 12, 1971, *Soviet-American Relations,* 306–8.

69. TELCON Kissinger and Nixon, March 15, 1971, *Soviet-American Relations,* 308.

70. TELCON, March 26, 1971 (8:20 p.m.), *Soviet-American Relations,* 323–25.

71. TELCON, March 26, 1971 (4:23 p.m.), *Soviet-American Relations,* 322; AVP RF. TELCON, March 26, 1971, *Soviet-American Relations,* 323.

72. TELCON, March 26, 1971 (8:20 p.m.), *Soviet-American Relations,* 323–25. See also "Conversation between Nixon and Shultz," April 9, 1971, *FRUS: SALT I,* 439–40.

73. Amusingly, Kissinger was so convinced that the meaning of the conversation was clear that when the ambiguity was discovered later, he threatened to publish the "word for word" telephone conversations. Conversation between Nixon, Kissinger, and Haldeman, May 27, 1971, *FRUS: SALT I,* 505–7. When the media discovered the ambiguity, Kissinger told Nixon, "I really think that the Communists are beginning to dominate some of our media." "Conversation between Nixon, Kissinger, and Haldeman," May 29, 1971, *FRUS: SALT I,* 508–10.

74. In *Soviet-American Relations,* 327.

75. TELCON Nixon to Kissinger, May 12, 1971, *Soviet-American Relations,* 352.

76. Smith 1985, 250–25. See also Letter from President Nixon to Soviet General Secretary Brezhnev, October 19, 1971, *Foreign Relations of the United States, 1969–1976,* vol. 14, *Soviet Union, October 1971–May 1972* (Washington, DC: Government Printing Office, 2007), 18–20 (hereafter cited as *FRUS: Soviet Union, 1971–1972* with appropriate page numbers).

77. Memorandum for the President's Files, May 8, 1972, DNSA, KT 00480.

78. Hersh 1983, 503–8.

79. In Dallek 2007, 372.

80. Hersh 1983, 511.

81. Haldeman 1994, 452. Also see TELCON Kissinger and Nixon, April 15, 1972, *FRUS: Soviet Union, 1971–1972,* 341–43.

82. Haldeman1994, 444.

83. Ibid., 450.

84. Dallek 2007, 382–83.

85. "The President talked with Charles G. ('Bebe') Rebozo," White House telephone conversation no. 24–38, May 9, 1972, 11:07 a.m.–11:12 a.m., tape 24a. The Nixon tapes cited in this chapter are available at www.nixontapes.org.

86. Dallek 2007, 377.

87. "Conversation between Nixon and Haldeman," May 2, 1972, *FRUS: Soviet Union, 1971–1972,* 682–88. Nixon, however, would continue to vacillate through the coming week.

88. Haldeman 1994, 453. On Nixon's obsession with public opinion before the 1972 election, see Sandbrook, 2008; and Schwartz 2009.

89. TELCON Nixon and Kissinger, May 3, 1972, *FRUS: Soviet Union, 1971–1972,* 714–25.

90. Compare Haig and McCarry, 1992, 287–88. Haig suggests that Nixon wanted to go, but his account is generally suspect. For example, he claims that Nixon heard from Dobrynin the next day that the summit was on, which is not supported by the evidence. Sonnefeldt agreed with this position. See "Memo Sonnefeldt to Kissinger," *FRUS: Soviet Union, 1971–1972,* 729–32.

91. "The President talked with Charles G. ('Bebe') Rebozo," White House telephone conversation no. 24–38, May 9, 1972, 11:07 a.m.–11:12 a.m., tape 24a; "The President talked with John N. Mitchell," White House telephone conversation no. 24–45, May 9, 1972, 11:35 a.m.–11:39 a.m., tape 24a. There are many examples of Nixon and Kissinger attempting to play politics with the summit. See "Memorandum from Nixon to Kissinger," *FRUS: Soviet Union, 1971–1972,* 199–200.

92. "Conversation between Nixon and Kissinger," May 5, 1972, *FRUS: Soviet Union, 1971–1972*, 741–49.

93. "Memorandum for the President's Files," May 8, 1972, *FRUS: Soviet Union, 1971–1972*, 766–74.

94. See "Conversation between Nixon and Kissinger," May 5, 1972, *FRUS: Soviet Union, 1971–1972*, 741–49; and "Conversation between Nixon and Haldeman," May 3, 1972, *FRUS: Soviet Union, 1971–1972*, 710–13.

95. "Conversation between Nixon and Kissinger," May 4, 1972, *FRUS: Soviet Union, 1971–1972*, 732–37.

96. To be clear, the primary reason Nixon escalated was to win the war, not to cancel the summit. But, he welcomed the cancellation.

97. Robert Kaiser, "Tass Assails Nixon Steps; No Official Soviet Comment," *Washington Post*, May 10, 1972, A12; Robert Kaiser, "No Word on Visit," *Washington Post*, May 12, 1972, A1; Carroll Kirkpatrick, "Soviet Aides, Nixon Hold Affable Talk," *Washington Post*, May 12, 1972; Haig 1992, 287.

98. AVP RF. MEMCON, May 8, 1972, *Soviet-American Relations*, 801–2.

99. MEMCON, May 11, 1972, *Soviet-American Relations*, 806–7; AVP RF. MEMCON, May 11, 1972, *Soviet-American Relations*, 808–9.

100. TELCON Kissinger and Nixon, May 12, 1972, *Soviet-American Relations*, 808.

101. TELCON Kissinger and Nixon, 11:30, May 12, 1972, *Soviet-American Relations*, 813.

102. One reviewer helpfully suggested that these statements may have been rationalizations of the consequences of escalation in Vietnam: Nixon wanted to go to the summit but needed to justify scrapping of the summit to his administration. This argument is plausible but unlikely. First, Nixon clearly was concerned about the political costs of attending the summit. During the first week of May, he made this argument constantly. The moment when he changed his mind, however, is correlated with the new information that offering to go was popular, and therefore Brezhnev's cancellation would make Nixon look good. Rationalization cannot explain these shifts in Nixon's position.

103. Dallek 2007, 384.

104. One reason for this conventional interpretation is that it reflected Kissinger's view. Kissinger suggested canceling because he worried it would look bad if the Soviets canceled first, a view that Nixon did not share. See "Conversation among Nixon, Rogers, Kissinger, Haig, and Ziegler," May 1, 1972, *FRUS: SALT I*, 798–99.

105. "Conversation between Nixon and Haig," May 2, 1972, *FRUS: Soviet Union, 1971–1972*, 679–82.

106. "Conversation between Nixon and Haig," May 2, 1972, *FRUS: Soviet Union, 1971–1972*, 688–95. See also "Conversation between Nixon and Kissinger," May 3, 1972, *FRUS: Soviet Union, 1971–1972*, 695–708.

107. Arbatov 1992, 183.

108. Dobrynin 1995, 248.

109. Zubok 2007, 220–21.

110. A third relevant counterfactual question relates to the Senate, or at least the critical swing votes on which the fate of the ABM program turned. If the Senate had more information—if members knew that the Nixon administration was using negotiations with the Russians as leverage to build an ABM system—would cooperation still have occurred? If senators knew the administration attempted to use the SALT negotiations to increase support in the Senate, and senators knew that this was the case, more than likely they would have immediately canceled the ABM program, regardless of the Soviet position. Deception fails once its use becomes apparent. Moreover, if members of the Senate understood that the Soviets did not intend their ABM defenses as a part of a first-strike strategy and that they were slowly curtailing their ABM program, the Senate would most likely have cancelled the ABM program, regardless of whether Kissinger intended to

bargain it away. In that close 51–50 vote, fears of a Russian ABM system were a significant influence on some senators. The coalition would have faltered if it was common knowledge that the Soviets did not intend to develop its ABM system in the immediate future. Thus, the US ABM program would not have survived the summer of 1969.

111. A Soviet decision to accept a thin system was also a negative outcome, because an offer of a thin system, meaning a nationwide defense of population centers and Minutemen, was being explicitly rejected by the Senate, was unpopular, and the Senate would likely have considered it an insult and cut funds from the ABM program. Kissinger had to make an offer that the Soviets would reject to inspire support. Thus, Soviet acceptance of thin receives a -2.

112. This is a reasonable counterfactual change. The Soviets in fact preferred these options, and there were ample opportunities for Kissinger to learn the Soviet position. See Garthoff 1994, 173. My inference that the Soviets preferred NCA-only to an ABM ban is premised on evidence that Soviet hawks favored preserving the Galosh system that fell within the requirements of NCA-only. However, even if I am wrong, and the Soviets preferred the ban over NCA-only, or considered them equal, Kissinger's choice would remain the same and he would prefer not to negotiate.

113. "Conversation between Nixon and Kissinger," n.d., *FRUS: SALT I*, 477–83.

114. Nixon and Kissinger discussed agreements in these terms. They worried frequently over leaks that would leave them with tied hands, forced to agree to provisions they did not favor. See, for example, "The President talked with Henry A. Kissinger," White House telephone conversation no. 23–90, April 26, 1972, 7:07–7:10 p.m., tape 23b.

115. Garthoff 1994, 336.

116. Deborah Welch Larson (1997, 184) agrees with this assessment.

117. See, for example, Smith 1985, 401.

118. Ibid., 407–40; Garthoff 1994, 185–96.

119. Index of power-aperture product created clear guidelines for the power of radars that encouraged compliance. See Talbott 1988, 132.

4. The Decline of Détente

1. Garthoff 1994.

2. Ford and Brezhnev, November 24, 1974, DNSA, KT 01420.

3. Brooks and Wohlforth 2009, 53. See also Gilpin 1981; Grieco 1990; and Schweller and Priess 1997. Cf. Mearsheimer 1994/5.

4. Carr 1939, 105–6.

5. Schweller and Wohlforth 2000, 77.

6. See Waltz 1979.

7. See Gilpin 1981; Kugler and Lemki 1996; and Organski and Kugler 1980.

8. Oneal, Russett, and Berbaum 2003; Russett and Oneal 2001.

9. Keohane 1984, 87.

10. For a summary of these arguments, see Hasenclever, Mayer, and Rittberger 1997, 23–82.

11. Axelrod 1984; Keohane 1984; Oye 1985. For the Cold War, see Goldstein 1991; and Weber 1991.

12. On reciprocity in the Cold War, see Goldstein and Freeman 1990; Keohane 1986; and Patchen and Bogumil 1997.

13. For an early statement, see Angell 1933. Recent representative statements include Mansfield 1994; Mansfield and Pollins 2003; and Rosecrance 1986.

14. Copeland 1996; also see Bearce 2003.

15. Copeland 1999.

16. Garthoff 1994, 1128. Garthoff also suggests that these misperceptions led Nixon and Kissinger to oversell détente to the public, undermining public confidence in cooperation.

Kissinger in particular certainly oversold détente. But whether or not this undermined public confidence in cooperation is hard to assess because it would require careful analysis to determine (a) how aware the public was of the White House's sales message, (b) the effect this would have on public opinion several years later, and (c) how this affected public opinion during the Ford and Carter administrations. On balance, this causal chain likely would find little empirical support. Like many accounts of domestic politics from Washington insiders, it presumes that the public picks up on often nuances in foreign policy that voters outside the beltway understandably pay little attention to, and understates the importance of other factors—the economy or in this case the legacy of Watergate—that were more salient for voters.

17. Michael Getler, "Goldwater and Jackson Warn A-Pact Would Damage US," *Washington Post,* May 25, 1972, A1.

18. Carroll Kirkpatrick, "Nixon Urges Arms Buildup; SALT II Linked to Arms Plan," *Washington Post,* June 23, 1972, A1; and Spencer Rich, "Nixon Meets Hill Leaders on Arms Pact," *Washington Post,* June 3, 1972, A1.

19. Kaufman 2000, 249–51.

20. Gelb and Lake 1974.

21. Johnson 2006, 186; Kaufman 2000, 258.

22. Spencer Rich, "A-Pact Revision Softened; Jackson Wins White House's Full Support," *Washington Post*, August 8, 1972, A1.

23. Johnson 2006, 184; Kaufman 2000, 155–57; Talbott 1979, 24. This problem may not seem significant to IR scholars who do not study arms control, but the practical effect is nearly devastating. For example, arms control agreements could not limit "offensive weapons" at a certain level but rather different *categories* of offensive weapons. For example, any new arms control agreement would have to provide a set quota for bombers, missiles launched by submarines, and missiles launched from land, preventing trades (one side can have three missiles on submarines and the other will get three on land). This makes arms control agreements harder to reach because it means states must negotiate system by system, which is more complex than focusing on aggregate levels, and makes cooperation difficult if states have an interest in different mixes of weapons or have different abilities to produce types of weapons.

24. "The Soviet Grain Deal," *New York Times,* July 26, 1973, 36; *Los Angeles Times,* "The Soviet Grain Deal," August 4, 1975, A8.

25. Jack Anderson, "Did Soviets Manipulate US Market?," *Washington Post,* July 27, 1973, D19.

26. "Memorandum from Robert Hormats of the National Security Council Staff to Secretary of State Henry Kissinger," October 3, 1973, *Foreign Relations of the United States, 1969–1976,* vol. 15, *Soviet Union, 1972–1974,* 137–38 (hereafter cited as *FRUS: Soviet Union, 1972–1974* with appropriate page numbers). George Meany told the president the following year, "We got ripped off in 1972 and the American consumer had to pay for it. We don't want it to happen again." "Memorandum on Conversation," August 26, 1975, *Foreign Relations of the United States, 1969–1976,* vol. 16, *Soviet Union, 1974–1976,* 732–34 (hereafter cited as *FRUS: Soviet Union, 1974–1976* with appropriate page numbers).

27. TELCON Secretary of State Kissinger and the Soviet Ambassador, *FRUS: Soviet Union, 1972–1974,* October 4, 1973, 138–39; "Message from the President's Deputy Assistant for National Security Affairs to Secretary of State Kissinger," *FRUS: Soviet Union, 1974–1976,* October 14, 1973, 158–9.

28. MEMCON, October 24, 1973, *FRUS: Soviet Union, 1972–1974,* 176.

29. Copeland 1999; Garthoff 1994, 345–47. The Nixon administration explained its importance in these terms. See Philip Shabecoff, "President Warns Policy of Détente Bars Interference," *New York Times,* June 6, 1974, 77.

30. For the Soviet perspective, see Morozov 1999.

31. Stern 1979.

32. Kissinger frequently reiterated this position. See, for example, "Memorandum from the President's Assistant for National Security Affairs (Kissinger) to President Ford," *FRUS: Soviet Union, 1974–1976,* August 9, 1974, 7–8; and MEMCON, *FRUS: Soviet Union, 1974–1976,* 101–2.

33. "Letter from Soviet General Secretary Brezhnev to President Ford," December 25, 1974, *FRUS: Soviet Union, 1972–1974,* 405–6.

34. MEMCON, October 5, 1974, *FRUS: Soviet Union, 1974–1976,* 141–45.

35. "Text of Kissinger Statement on Accord Cancellation," *New York Times,* January 15, 1975, 4; Leslie Gelb, "Move by Moscow," *New York Times,* February 15, 1975, 1. Media commentaries described this as a power shift to détente's critics. See Leslie Gelb, "Détente and Politics," *New York Times,* January 16, 1975; and Leslie Gelb, "A Struggle Is Under Way over Foreign Policy, Too," *New York Times,* January 26, 1975, 251.

36. Gleijeses 1996/7.

37. MEMCON Brezhnev, Kissinger, et al., January 22, 1976, DNSA, KT 01878.

38. "Paper Prepared in the Department of State, Angola: Guidelines for Policy," September 1970, *Foreign Relations of the United States, 1969–1976,* vol. 28, *Southern Africa,* 213–17 (hereafter cited as *FRUS: Southern Africa* with appropriate page numbers).

39. Leffler 2007, 254–55; Westad 1996/7a, 27.

40. MEMCON Ford, Dobrynin, Kissinger and Scowcroft, December 9, 1975, *FRUS: Southern Africa,* 365–66; "Conversation among President Nixon, Vice President Agnew, and Secretary of State Rogers," August 5, 1971, *FRUS: Southern Africa,* 223–24.

41. Gleijeses 2002, 331–34.

42. Leffler 2007, 255. See also "Message from the Soviet Government to the United States Government," n.d., *FRUS: Southern Africa,* 422.

43. MEMCON Ford, Kissinger, and Scowcroft, December 17, 1975, *FRUS: Southern Africa,* 395–96.

44. Garthoff, 1994, 578–79.

45. Ford 1979, 346. See also Gleijeses 2002, 332.

46. Garthoff 1994, 592. See also Lou Cannon, "Ford Assails Cuba, Russia over Angola," *Washington Post,* December 21, 1975, 1; "Ford Says Angola Acts Hurt Détente, Cuba Tie," *New York Times,* December 21, 1975, 3; Clayton Fritchley, "Angola and US Politics," *Washington Post,* January 3, 1976, A19; and David Shipler, "Angolan War: Test for American-Soviet Détente," *New York Times,* January 8, 1976, 8.

47. Ford 1979, 346.

48. Gleijeses 2002, 390.

49. Haslam 2011, 292.

50. Westad 2007, 233.

51. Dobrynin 1995, 360–66; Gleijeses 2002, 371.

52. Leffler 2007, 245–46; MEMCON Ford and Brezhnev, November 23, 1974, DNSA, KT 01418; MEMCON Ford and Brezhnev, November 23, 1974, DNSA, KT 01419; and MEMCON Ford and Brezhnev, November 24, 1974, DNSA, KT 01420.

53. Tonelson 1979, 74. See Nitze 1974/5, 1976, 1978, and 1979. On Nitze's influence, see Talbott 1988.

54. Bernard Gwertzman, "Criticism Mounts on the Arms Pact," *New York Times,* November 28, 1974, 1; John Finney, "Missile Build-up Planned by US," *New York Times,* February 12, 1975, 5; and John Finney, "Pentagon Chief Sees Pact Leading to Arms Buildup," *New York Times,* December 7, 1974.

55. Nicholas Horrock, "1973 Arms Cover-Up is Laid to Kissinger," *New York Times,* December 18, 1975, 93.

56. Garthoff 1994, 504. On Ford's relationship with Schlesinger, see Ford 1979, 320–24. Even Schlesinger's resignation was cast as a criticism of Vladivostok. He publicly argued that the

reason for his dismissal was that he did not support agreeing for the sake of agreement. See Drew Middleton, "Schlesinger's View of Kissinger Described," *New York Times,* November 8, 1975, 2. Within the administration, these public disagreements were thought to be an important reason for Ford's unpopularity. Cahn 1998, 122; Ford 1979, 320.

57. Cahn 1998.

58. Wohlsetter 1974 and 1975. On Wohlsetter's influence on the administration, see Cahn 1998, 106–7.

59. Pipes 1981.

60. "Intelligence Community Experiment in Competitive Analysis: Soviet Strategic Objectives An Alternative View: Report of Team B," December 1976, DNSA, SE 00501.

61. William Beecher, "Special Unit Analyzing US Spy Data," *Boston Globe,* October 20, 1976, 1. Pipes continued to stress Team B's findings throughout that winter. See, for example, David Binder, "New CIA Estimate Finds Soviet Seeks Superiority in Arms, *New York Times,* December 26, 1976, 1; and Cahn 1998, 127–29.

62. Cahn 1998, 184. Also see Betts 1998.

63. Garthoff 1994, 525; Haslam 2011, 302.

64. Brzezinski 1983, 124–29; Carter 1982; Nichols 2002; Gaddis Smith 1986. On this commitment, see Clymer 2003.

65. Charles Mohr, "Carter Suggests That US Foster Rights Overseas," *New York Times,* September 9, 1976, 81; Leslie Gelb, "Human-Rights and Morality Issue Runs through Ford-Carter Debate," *New York Times,* October 8, 1976, 16; Joseph Kraft, "Morality in Foreign Policy, *Washington Post,* October 17, 1976, 35; Don Oberdorfer, "Carter Speaks on Human Rights," *Washington Post,* September 9, 1976, A8; and "Polish-Americans Cheer as Carter Vows to Back Freedom for Eastern Europe," *New York Times,* October 11, 1976, 41.

66. Jimmy Carter, "Inaugural Address," January 20, 1977, *Public Papers of Jimmy Carter,* Washington, DC: US Government Printing Office, 1977.

67. Garthoff 1994, 649.

68. Nichols 2002.

69. On the Soviet reception of Carter's human rights policies, see Talbott 1979, 38–39. On Carter's human rights commitments, see Hartmann 2001; and Gaddis Smith 1986, 49–55.

70. Dobrynin 1995, 382–92; Garthoff 1994, 632–34; Njølstad 1995, 227–56.

71. In Brzezinski 1983, 155.

72. Dobrynin 1995, 394.

73. Garthoff 1994, 889.

74. Talbott 1979, 39. Harriman suggested he might pursue deep cuts only after Vladivostok was complete.

75. Garthoff 1994, 627.

76. Brzezinski 1983, 157; Vance 1983, 51.

77. President Carter, Presidential Directive /NSC–Brzezinski 1983, DNSA, 159–61.

78. Carter 1982, 225.

79. Garthoff 1994; Talbott 1979.

80. Garthoff 1994, 898–99.

81. Carter's China policy also soured relations. Garthoff 1994, 758–85; Thornton 1991, 299–317.

82. Brzezinski 1983, 178–90.

83. Garthoff 1994, 718–19.

84. Ibid., 656. For Carter's public complaints about Ethiopia, see Bernard Gwertzman, "US Aides Frustrated over Soviet Gains in Ethiopia," *New York Times*, December 29, 1977, 3; Terence Smith, "Carter Assails Moscow on Ethiopia," *New York Times*, January 13, 1978; Craig Whitney, "View from Moscow: Relations with US Appear to Be Showing Downturn Again," *New York*

Times, January 23, 1978, A3; Graham Hovey, "US Reports Suggest Cubans and Bombing Targets in Somalia," *New York Times,* February 5, 1978, 1; Graham Hovey, "Brzezinski Asserts That Soviet General Leads Ethiopia Units," *New York Times,* February 25, 1978, 1; and Richard Burt, "If War in the Horn Is Over, Superpower Tension Is Not," *New York Times,* March 12, 1978, E3.

85. On the conservative criticism, see D. Jackson 2007, 715–16.

86. Brzezinski 1983, 189. Brzezinski argued that a stronger reaction to Ethiopia would have preserved détente by winning over hardliners. Talbott 1979, 291.

87. Caldwell 1991; Duffy 1983; Garrison 2001, 795–800; Garthoff 1994, 913–34. See Letter from Carter to Brezhnev, White House, September 25, 1979, DDRS, CK3100487737; and Memorandum: Brzezinski Relaying Carter's Instructions, White House, July 12, 1979, DDRS, CK3100511157.

88. "Senator Church Charges Moscow Has a Brigade of Troops in Cuba," *New York Times,* August 31, 1979, A2.

89. Brzezinski 1983, 344–53; Vance 1983, 358–64.

90. Zbigniew Brzezinski. Presidential Directive/NSC–52, October 4, 1979, DNSA, PR 01401.

91. Caldwell 1991.

92. Bernard Gwertzman, "Vance Tells Soviet Its Troops in Cuba Could Imperil Ties," *New York Times,* September 6, 1979, A1; Charles Mohr, "Some Liberals Balk at Pact Till Soviet Pulls Out Cuba Unit," *New York Times,* September 7,1979, A1.

93. Letter from Brezhnev to Carter, White House, September 27, 1979, DDRS, CK3100048854.

94. There are significant limitations to the evidence concerning Soviet decision making during this period. Therefore, this judgment is necessarily circumspect.

95. Quoted in Cordovez and Harrison 1995, 37.

96. Westad 1996/7b.

97. Quoted in Cordovez and Harrison 1995, 47.

98. Caldwell 1997, 111.

99. Mayer 1992, 61–62; Russett and Deluca 1981; Skidmore 1996, 101–2.

100. Cahn 1998, 189.

101. Kinder and Kiewiet 1979; Markus 1982.

102. By contrast, a case could be made that Vance's declining influence was linked to Soviet behavior in Africa. The balance of the evidence, however, indicates that conservative influence was growing regardless of Brzezinski's influence vis-à-vis Vance.

103. Bennett 2010.

104. The values for cooperation, institutionalization, and administration's beliefs—low, medium, and high—are relative to one another and do not represent absolute values. They key point is that the cooperation was "lower" when the level of institutionalization was "higher," for example.

105. Further, balance-of-power theory might also explain why agreement was reached in only some areas. Most agreements concerned technology, trade, the environment, and other issue areas that did not directly implicate security. See Lipson 1984. Even ABMs might not implicate relative gains if the superpowers thought that the balance of power was secured through offensive weapons. Matthews 1996. As such, balance-of-power theory may be able to explain the variation between cooperation over defensive weapons, trade, the environment, and technology with limited cooperation on offense.

106. Wohlforth 1993, 185.

107. On the index-number problem, see Holzman 1980, 1982, and 1989.

108. Brooks and Wohlforth 2000/1.

109. For example, see the differences between Gervasi 1986; and Lee and Staar 1986.

110. Podwig 2008.
111. Kissinger 1979.
112. Thornton 1991.
113. Dallek 2007, 146–47.
114. See chapter 3 for a more comprehensive discussion.
115. Weber 1991.
116. In fact, Soviet acceptance of NCA-only might have seemed to Kissinger like defection since he assumed that the Soviets understood that the offer was made to be rejected.

Conclusion

1. On the legal importance of the convention, see Denza 1998; and C. Lewis 1985.
2. In Liang 1953.
3. Kerley 1962. Also see "Accord Defines Consular Rights," *New York Times,* April 28, 1963, 35.
4. O'Keefe 1976; Thakore 1981.
5. This does not deny that common knowledge and intersubjective beliefs were also important to the improvement of relations. My claim is only that certain pieces of knowledge could not be shared if cooperation was to prove successful.
6. In certain cases this is appropriate if the aim is to show the importance of a changed belief on a specific outcome.
7. See, for example, Klotz and Lynch 2007.
8. Keohane 1984; Koremenos, Lipson, and Snidal 2001.
9. See Axelrod 1984; and Keohane 1986. Also see Downs and Rocke 1990 for a similar but more limited argument.
10. Katzenstein 1996, 1.
11. Sahlins 1995, 79.

References

Abbott, Kenneth. 1993. "Trust but Verify: The Production of Information in Arms Control Treaties and Other International Agreements." *Cornell International Law Journal* 26 (1): 1–58.

Acheson, Dean. 1969. *Present at the Creation: My Years in the State Department.* New York: W. W. Norton.

Adler, Emanuel. 1992. "The Emergence of Cooperation: National Epistemic Communities and the International Evolution of the Idea of Nuclear Arms Control." *International Organization* 46 (1): 101–45.

———. 1997. "Imagined (Security) Communities: Cognitive Regions in International Relations." *Millennium* 26 (2): 249–77.

Adler, Emanuel, and Michael Barnett. 1998a. "Security Communities in Theoretical Perspective." In *Security Communities*, ed. Emanuel Adler and Michael Barnett, 3–28. Cambridge: Cambridge University Press.

———. 1998b. "A Framework for the Study of Security Communities." In *Security Communities*, ed. Emanuel Adler and Michael Barnett, 29–66. Cambridge: Cambridge University Press.

Alderson, Kai. 2001. "Making Sense of State Socialization." *Review of International Studies* 27 (3): 415–33.

Allison, Roy, and Phil Williams. 1990. "Superpower Competition and Crisis Prevention in the Third World." In *Superpower Competition and Crisis Prevention in the Third World,* ed. Roy Allison and Phil Williams, 1–28. Cambridge: Cambridge University Press.

Anderson, Benedict. 1983. *Imagined Communities: Reflection on the Origin and Spread of Nationalism.* New York: Verso.

Anderson, Richard. 1993. *Public Politics in an Authoritarian State: Making Foreign Policy during the Brezhnev Years.* Ithaca: Cornell University Press.

Angell, Normal. 1933. *The Great Illusion.* New York: Putnam.

Arbatov, Georgi. 1992. *The System: An Insider's Life in Soviet Politics.* New York: Random House.

Arrow, Kenneth.1963. *Social Choice and Individual Values.* 2nd ed. New Haven: Yale University Press.

Athens, Lonnie. 2005. "Radical Interactionism: Going beyond Mead." *Journal of the Theory of Social Behavior* 37 (2): 137–65.

Aumann, Robert. 1976. "Agreeing to Disagree." *Annals of Statistics* 4 (6): 1236–39.

Avruck, Kevin, and Zheng Wang. 2005. "Culture, Apology, and International Negotiation: The Case of the Sino-US 'Spy Plane' Crisis." *International Negotiation* 10 (2): 337–53.

Axelrod, Robert. 1984. *The Evolution of Cooperation.* New York: Basic Books.

Axelrod, Robert, and William Zimmerman. 1981. "The Soviet Press on Soviet Foreign Policy: A Usually Reliable Source." *British Journal of Political Science* 11 (2): 183–200.

Bachrach, Peter, and Morton Baratz. 1962. "Two Faces of Power." *American Political Science Review* 56 (4): 947–52.

Ball, Donald. 1972. "'The Definition of Situation': Some Methodological Consequences of Taking W. I. Thomas Seriously." *Journal of the Theory of Social Behavior* 2 (1): 61–82.

Bar-Joseph, Uri. 2005. *The Watchman Fell Asleep: The Surprise of Yom Kippur and Its Sources.* Albany: State University of New York Press.

Barnett, Michael. 1996. "Identities and Alliances in the Middle East." In *The Culture of National Security: Norms and Identity in World Politics,* ed. Peter Katzenstein, 400–50. New York: Columbia University Press.

Bates, Robert, Avner Greif, Margaret Levi, Jean-Laurent Rosenthal, and Barry Weingast, eds. 1998. *Analytic Narratives.* Princeton: Princeton University Press.

——. 2000. "Analytic Narratives Revisited." *Social Science History* 24 (4): 685–96.

Bearce, David. 2003. "Grasping the Commercial Institutional Peace." *International Studies Quarterly* 47 (3): 347–70.

Bearce, David, and Stacy Bondanella. 2007. "Intergovernmental Organizations, Socialization, and Member-State Interest Convergence." *International Organization* 61 (4): 703–33.

Bennett, Andrew. 2010. "Process Tracing and Causal Inference" In *Rethinking Social Inquiry: Diverse Tools, Shared Standards.* 2nd ed., ed. Henry Brady and David Collier. Lanham, MD: Rowman and Littlefield, 207–20.

——. *Condemned to Repetition? The Rise, Fall, and Reprise of Soviet-Russian Military Intervention, 1973–1996.* Cambridge: MIT Press.

Bennett, Andrew, and Colin Elman. 2007. "Case Study Methods in the International Relations Subfield." *Comparative Political Studies* 40 (2): 170–95.

Berenskoetter, Felix Sebastian. 2005. "Mapping the Mind Gap: A Comparison of US and European Security Strategies." *Security Dialogue* 36 (1): 71–92.

Berger, Peter, and Thomas Luckmann. 1966. *The Social Construction of Reality: A Treatise in the Sociology of Knowledge.* New York: Anchor Books.

Bernstein, Steven, Richard Ned Lebow, and Janice Gross Stein. 2000. "God Gave Physics the Easy Problems: Adapting Social Science to an Unpredictable World." *European Journal of International Relations* 6 (1): 43–76.

Betts, Richard. 1998. *Enemies of Intelligence: Knowledge and Power in American National Security.* New York: Columbia University Press.

Beyers, Jan. 2005. "Multiple Embeddedness and Socialization in Europe: The Case of Council Officials." *International Organization* 59 (4): 899–936.

Bially Mattern, Janice. 2005. *Ordering International Politics: Identity, Crisis, and Representational Force.* New York: Routledge.

Bieler, Andreas, and Adam David Morton. 2001. "The Gordian Knot of Agency-Structure in International Relations: A Neo-Gramscian Perspective." *European Journal of International Relations* 7 (1): 5–35.

Blacker, Coit. 1983. "The Kremlin and Détente: Soviet Conceptions, Hopes, and Expectations." In *Managing US-Soviet Rivalry: Problems of Crisis Prevention,* ed. Alexander George, 119–37. Boulder, CO: Westview.

Blainey, Geoffrey. 1973. *The Causes of War.* New York: Free Press.

Blechman, Barry, and Douglas Hart. 1982. "The Political Utility of Nuclear Weapons: The 1973 Middle East Crisis." *International Security* 7 (1): 132–56.

Bluhm, George. 1967. *Détente and Military Relaxation in Europe: A German View.* Adelphi Papers 40. London: Institute for Strategic Studies.

Bluth, Christoph. 1992. *Soviet Strategic Arms Policy before SALT.* Cambridge: Cambridge University Press.

Boli, John, and George M. Thomas. 1997. "World Culture in the World Polity: A Century of International Non-Governmental Organization." *American Sociological Review* 62 (2): 171–90.

———. 1999. "INGOs and the Organization of World Culture." In *Constructing World Culture: International Nongovernmental Organizations since 1875,* ed. John Boli and George M. Thomas, 11–49. Stanford University Press.

Booth, Ken. 1979. *Strategy and Ethnocentrism.* London: Croom Helm.

Bottom, William. 2003. "Keynes' Attack on the Versailles Treaty: An Early Investigation of the Consequences of Bounded Rationality, Framing and Cognitive Illusions." *International Negotiation* 8 (2): 367–402.

Breslauer, George. 1996. "Counterfactual Reasoning in Western Studies of Soviet Politics and Foreign Relations." In *Counterfactual Thought Experiments in World Politics: Logical, Methodological, and Psychological Perspectives,* ed. Philip Tetlock and Aaron Belkin, 69–94. Princeton: Princeton University Press.

Bresler, Robert, and Robert Gray. 1977. "The Bargaining Chip and SALT." *Political Science Quarterly* 92 (1): 65–88.

Brezhnev, Leonid. 1971. *Report of the Central Committee of the Communist Party of the Soviet Union*. Moscow: Novosti Press Agency Publishing House.

———. 1979. *Peace, Détente, and Soviet-American Relations: Public Statements by Leonid Brezhnev*. New York: Harcourt Brace Jovanovich.

Britton, Stuart. 1990. "Competition or Collaboration? The Soviet Union, Détente, and the October 1973 War." *Comparative Strategy* 9 (3): 287–306.

Brooks, Stephen, and William Wohlforth. 2000/1. "Power, Globalization and the End of the Cold War: Reevaluating a Landmark Case for Ideas." *International Security* 25 (3): 5–53.

———. 2009. "Reshaping the World Order: How Washington Should Reform International Institutions." *Foreign Affairs* 88 (2): 49–63.

Brzezinski, Zbigniew. 1972. "How the Cold War Was Played." *Foreign Affairs* 51 (1): 181–209.

———. 1973. "US Foreign Policy: The Search for Focus." *Foreign Affairs* 51 (4): 708–27.

———. 1983. *Power and Principle: Memoirs of the National Security Adviser, 1977–1981*. New York: Farrar, Strauss, Giroux.

Buchan, Alastair. 1972. "A World Restored?" *Foreign Affairs* 50 (4): 644–59.

Bull, Hedley. 1977. *The Anarchical Society: A Study of Order in International Politics*. New York: Columbia University Press.

Bunn, George. 1992. *Arms Control by Committee: Managing Negotiations with the Russians*. Stanford: Stanford University Press.

Burdick, Eugene, and Harvey Wheeler. 1964. *Fail-Safe*. New York: Ecco.

Burr, William. 2005. "The Nixon Administration, the 'Horror Strategy,' and the Search for Limited Nuclear Options, 1969–1972: Prelude to the Schlesinger Doctrine." *Journal of Cold War Studies* 7 (3): 34–78.

Burr, William, and Jeffrey Kimball. 2003. "Nixon's Secret Nuclear Alert: Vietnam War Diplomacy and the Joint Chiefs of Staff Readiness Test, October 1969." *Cold War History* 3 (2): 113–56.

Byers, Michael. 2004. "Agreeing to Disagree: Security Council Resolution 1441 and Intentional Ambiguity." *Global Governance* 10 (2): 165–86.

Cahn, Anne Hessing. 1998. *Killing Détente: The Right Attacks the CIA*. University Park: Pennsylvania University Press.

Caldwell, Dan. 1997. "The Decline of Détente and US Domestic Politics." In *The Fall of Détente: Soviet American Relations during the Carter Years,* ed. Odd Arne Westad, 95–117. Oslo: Scandinavian University Press.

———. 2001. *The Dynamics of Domestic Politics and Arms Control: The Salt II Treaty Ratification Debate*. Columbia: University of South Carolina Press.

Campbell, Colin. 1998. *The Myth of Social Action*. Cambridge: Cambridge University Press.

Campbell, Donald, and Julian Stanley. 1963. *Experimental and Quasi-Experimental Design for Research*. Chicago: Rand McNally.

Carlsnaes, Walter. 1992. "The Agency-Structure Problem in Foreign Policy Analysis." *International Studies Quarterly* 36 (3): 245–70.

Carlson, Allen. 2005. *Unifying China, Integrating with the World: The Chinese Approach to Sovereignty during the Reform Era*. Stanford: Stanford University Press.

Carr, E. H. 1939. *The Twenty Years' Crisis, 1919–1939*. New York: Perennial.

Carter, Jimmy. 1982. *Keeping Faith: Memoirs of a President*. Fayetteville: University of Arkansas Press.

Chang, Gordon. 1990. *Friends and Enemies: The United States, China, and the Soviet Union, 1948–1972*. Stanford: Stanford University Press.

Chayes, Abram, and Antonia Handler Chayes. 1993. "On Compliance." *International Organization* 47 (2): 175–205.

Checkel, Jeffrey. 1999. "Norms, Institutions, and National Identity in Contemporary Europe." *International Studies Quarterly* 43 (1): 83–114.

———. 2001. "Why Comply? Social Learning and European Identity Change." *International Organization* 55 (3): 553–88.

———. 2005. "International Institutions and Socialization in Europe: Introduction and Framework." *International Organization* 59 (4): 801–26.

Christiansen, Thomas, Knud Erik Jorgensen, and Antje Wiener. 1999. "The Social Construction of Europe." *Journal of European Public Policy* 6 (4): 528–44.

Chwe, Michael Suk-Young. 2001. *Rational Ritual: Culture, Coordination, and Common Knowledge*. Princeton: Princeton University Press.

Clymer, Kenton. 2003. "Jimmy Carter, Human Rights, and Cambodia." *Diplomatic History* 27 (2): 245–78.

Coase, R. H. 1960. "The Problem of Social Cost." *Journal of Law and Economics* 3:1–44.

Coelho, Nelson Ernesto, Jr., and Luis Claudio Figueiredo. 2003. "Patterns of Intersubjectivity in the Constitution of Subjectivity: Dimensions of Otherness." *Culture and Psychology* 9 (3): 193–208.

Cohen, Raymond. 1991. *Negotiating across Cultures: Communication Obstacles in International Diplomacy*. Washington, DC: United States Institute of Peace.

———. 1996. "Cultural Aspects of International Mediation." In *Resolving International Conflicts: The Theory and Practice of Mediation*, ed. Jacob Bercovitch, 107–28. Boulder, CO: Lynne Rienner.

Collier, David. 2011. "Understanding Process Tracing." *PS: Political Science & Politics* 44 (4): 823–30.

Converse, Phillip. 1964. "The Nature of Belief Systems in Mass Publics." In *Ideology and Discontent*, ed. David Apter, 206–61. New York: Free Press of Glencoe.

Cook, Thomas, and Donald Campbell. 1979. *Quasi-Experimentation: Design and Analysis Issues for Field Settings*. Boston: Houghton Mifflin.

Coopersmith, Jonathan. 2006. "The Dog That Did Not Bark during the Night: The 'Normalcy' of Russian, Soviet, and Post-Soviet Science and Technology Studies." *Technology and Culture* 47 (3): 623–37.

Copeland, Dale. 1996. "Economic Interdependence and War: A Theory of Trade Expectations." *International Security* 20 (4): 5–41.

———. 1999. "Trade Expectations and the Outbreak of Peace: Détente 1970–74 and the End of the Cold War, 1985–91," *Security Studies* 9 (1): 15–58.

———. 2003. "Economic Interdependence and the Future of US-Chinese Relations." *International Relations Theory and the Asia-Pacific*, ed. John Ikenberry and Michael Mastanduno, 323–52. New York: Columbia University Press.

Cordovez, Diego, and Selig Harrison. 1995. *Out of Afghanistan: The Inside Story of Soviet Withdrawal*. New York: Oxford University Press.

Cortell, Andrew, and James Davis. 1996. "How Do International Institutions Matter? The Domestic Impact of International Rules and Norms." *International Studies Quarterly* 40 (4): 451–78.

Costigliola, Frank. 1992. *France and the United States: The Cold Alliance since World War II.* New York: Twain.

Cottam, Martha. 1986. *Foreign Policy Decision Making: The Influence of Cognition.* Boulder, CO: Westview.

Cox, Robert. 1986. "Social Forces, States, and World Orders: Beyond International Relations Theory." In *Neorealism and Its Critics*, ed. Robert Keohane, 204–54. New York: Columbia University Press.

Dahl, Robert. 1957. "The Concept of Power." *Behavioral Science* 2 (3): 201–15.

Dalgaard-Nielsen, Anja. 2005. "The Test of Strategic Culture: Germany, Pacifism and Pre-emptive Strikes." *Security Dialogue* (36) 3: 339–59.

Dallek, Robert. 2007. *Nixon and Kissinger: Partners in Power.* New York: Harper Collins.

Denza, Eileen. 1998. *Diplomatic Law: A Commentary on the Vienna Convention on Diplomatic Relations.* New York: Oxford University Press.

Dessler, David. 1989. "What's at Stake in the Agent-Structure Debate?" *International Organization* 43 (3): 441–73.

Dinitz, Simcha. 2000. "The Yom Kippur War: Diplomacy of War and Peace." In *Revisiting the Yom Kippur War*, ed. P. R. Kumaraswamy, 104–26. New York: Frank Cass.

Dobrynin, Anatoly. 1995. *In Confidence: Moscow's Ambassador to America's Six Cold War Presidents.* Seattle: University of Washington Press.

Doty, Roxanne Lynn. 1997. "Aporia: A Critical Exploration of the Agent-Structure Problematique in International Relations Theory." *European Journal of International Relations* 3 (3): 365–92.

Downs, George, and David Rocke. 1990. *Tacit Bargaining, Arms Races, and Arms Control.* Ann Arbor: University of Michigan Press.

Downs, George, David Rocke, and Peter Barsoom. 1996. "Is the Good News about Compliance Good News about Cooperation?" *International Organization* 50 (3): 379–406.

Duffy, Gloria. 1983. "Crisis Mangling and the Cuban Brigade." *International Security* 8 (1): 67–87.

Dunn, Keith. 1981. "Constraints on the USSR in Southwest Asia: A Military Analysis." *Orbis* 25 (3): 607–31.

Durkheim, Emile. 1919. *Les Regles de la Methode Sociologique.* Paris: F. Alcan.

———. 1984. *The Division of Labor in Society*, trans. W. D. Halls. New York: Free Press.

Edmonds, Robin. 1983. *Soviet Foreign Policy: The Brezhnev Years.* New York: Oxford University Press.

Eid, Michael, and Ed Diener. 2001. "Norms for Experiencing Emotions in Different Cultures: Inter- and Intranational Cultural Differences." *Journal of Personality and Social Psychology* 81 (5): 869–85.

Ember, Carol, and Melvin Ember. 1994. "War, Socialization, and Interpersonal Violence: A Cross-Cultural Study." *Journal of Conflict Resolution* 38 (4): 620–46.

Evangelista, Matthew. 1999. *Unmanned Forces: The Transnational Movement to End the Cold War.* Ithaca: Cornell University Press.

———. 2001. "Norms, Heresthetics, and the End of the Cold War." *Journal of Cold War Studies* 3 (1): 5–35.

Fagin, Ronald, Joseph Halpern, Yoram Moses, and Moshe Vardi. 1995. *Reasoning about Knowledge.* Cambridge: MIT Press.

Farrell, Theo. 1998. "Culture and Military Power." *Review of International Studies* 24 (3): 407–16.

———. 2001. "Transnational Norms and Military Development: Constructing Ireland's Professional Army." *European Journal of International Relations* 7 (1): 63–102.

———. 2005. *The Norms of War: Cultural Beliefs and Modern Conflict.* Boulder, CO: Lynne Rienner.

Fearon, James. 1991. "Counterfactuals and Hypothesis Testing in Political Science." *World Politics* 4 (3): 169–95.

———. 1994. "Domestic Political Audiences and the Escalation of International Disputes." *American Political Science Review* 88 (3): 577–92.

———. 1995. "Rationalist Explanations for War." *International Organization* 49 (3): 379–414.

———. 1998. "Bargaining, Enforcement, and International Cooperation." *International Organization* 52 (2): 269–305.

Finnemore, Martha. 1996a. *National Interests in International Society.* Ithaca: Cornell University Press.

———. 1996b. "Norms, Culture, and World Politics: Insights from Sociology's Institutionalism." *International Organization* 50 (2): 325–47.

———. 2003. *The Purpose of Intervention: Changing Beliefs about the Use of Force.* Ithaca: Cornell University Press.

Finnemore, Martha, and Kathryn Sikkink. 1998. "International Norm Dynamics and Political Change." *International Organization* 52 (4): 887–917.

Ford, Gerald. 1979. *A Time to Heal: The Autobiography of Gerald R. Ford.* New York: Harper and Row and Reader's Digest.

Frieden, Jeffrey. 1991. "Actors and Preferences in International Relations," In *Strategic Choice in International Relations,* ed. David Lake and Robert Powell, 39–76. Princeton: Princeton University Press.

Friedberg, Aaron. 1987/8. "Review: The Assessment of Military Power: A Review Essay." *International Security* 12 (3): 190–202.

Fudenberg, Drew, and David M. Kreps. 2005. "Learning in Extensive-Form Games: 1. Self-Confirming Equilibria." *Games and Economic Behavior* 8:20–55.

Fudenberg, Drew, and David K. Levine. 1993. "Self-Confirming Equilibrium." *Econometrica* 61 (3): 523–45.

Fursenko, Alexsandr, and Timothy Naftali. 1997. *"One Hell of a Gamble": Khrushchev, Castro, and Kennedy, 1958–1964.* New York: W. W. Norton.

Gaddis, John Lewis. 1982. *Strategies of Containment: A Critical Appraisal of Postwar American National Security Policy.* New York: Oxford University Press.

———. 1997. *We Now Know: Rethinking Cold War History.* New York: Oxford University Press.

———. 2000. *The United States and the Origins of the Cold War.* New York: Columbia University Press.

Garfinkel, Michelle, and Stergios Skaperdas. 2000. "Conflict without Misperceptions or Incomplete Information." *Journal of Conflict Resolution* 44 (6): 793–807.

Garrison, Jean. 2001. "Framing Foreign Policy Alternatives in the Inner Circle: President Carter, His Advisors, and the Struggle for the Arms Control Agenda." *Political Psychology* 22 (4): 775–807.

Garthoff, Raymond. 1977. "Negotiating with the Russians: Some Lessons from SALT." *International Security* 1 (4): 3–24.

———. 1979. "Soviet Views on the Interrelation of Diplomacy and Military Strategy." *Political Science Quarterly* 94 (3): 391–405.

———. 1994. *Détente and Confrontation: American-Soviet Relations from Nixon to Reagan.* Washington, DC: Brookings Institution.

Geanakoplos, John. 1992. "Common Knowledge." *Journal of Economic Perspectives* 6 (4): 53–82.

Gelb, Leslie H., and Anthony Lake. 1974. "Washington Dateline: The Age of Jackson?" *Foreign Policy* (14): 178–88.

Gelman, Harry. 1984. *The Brezhnev Politburo and the Decline of Détente.* Ithaca: Cornell University Press.

George, Alexander. 1983. "The Basic Principles Agreement of 1972: Origins and Expectations." In *Managing US-Soviet Rivalry: Problems of Crisis Prevention*, ed. Alexander George, 107–17. Boulder, CO: Westview.

———. 1988. "US-Soviet Efforts to Cooperate in Crisis Management and Crisis Avoidance." In *US-Soviet Security Cooperation: Achievements, Failures, Lessons,* ed. Alexander George, Philip Farley, and Alexander Dallin, 581–99. New York: Oxford University Press.

George, Alexander, and Andrew Bennett. 2005. *Case Studies and Theory Development in the Social Sciences.* Cambridge: MIT Press.

Gerring, John. 2007. *Case Study Research: Principles and Practices.* Cambridge: Cambridge University Press.

———. 2007. "Is There a (Viable) Crucial-Case Method?" *Comparative Political Studies* 40 (3): 231–53.

Gervasi, Tom. 1986. *The Myth of Soviet Military Supremacy.* New York: Harper and Row.

Gheciu, Alexandra. 2005. "Security Institutions as Agents of Socialization? NATO and the 'New Europe.'" *International Organization* 59 (4): 973–1012.

Giddens, Anthony. 1991. *Modernity and Self-Identity: Self and Society in the Late Modern Age.* Stanford: Stanford University Press.

Gilpin. Robert. 1981. *War and Change in World Politics.* Cambridge: Cambridge University Press.

Glaser, Charles. 1992. "Political Consequences of Military Strategy: Expanding and Refining the Spiral and Deterrence Models." *World Politics* 44 (4): 108–46.

———. 1994/5. "Realists as Optimists: Cooperation as Self-Help." *International Security* 19 (3): 50–90.

———. 1997. "The Security Dilemma Revisited." *World Politics* 50 (1): 171–201.

Gleijeses, Piero. 1996/7. "Havana's Policy in Africa, 1959–76: New Evidence from Cuban Archives." *Cold War International History Project Bulletin* (8/9): 5–18.

——. 2002. *Conflicting Missions: Havana, Washington, and Africa, 1959–1976.* Chapel Hill: University of North Carolina Press.

Goh, Evelyn. 2005. "Nixon, Kissinger, and the 'Soviet Card' in the US Opening to China." *Diplomatic History* 29 (3): 475–502.

Golan. Galia. 1977. *Yom Kippur and After: The Soviet Union and the Middle East Crisis.* Cambridge: Cambridge University Press.

——. 1988. *The Soviet Union and National Liberation Movements in the Third World.* Boston: Unwin Hyman.

——. 2000. "The Soviet Union and the Yom Kippur War." In *Revisiting the Yom Kippur War*, ed. P. R. Kumaraswamy, 127–52. New York: Frank Cass.

Goldstein, Joshua. 1991. "Reciprocity in Superpower Relations: An Empirical Analysis." *International Studies Quarterly* 35 (92): 195–209.

Goldstein, Joshua, and John Freeman. 1990. *Three-Way Street: Strategic Reciprocity in World Politics.* Chicago: University of Chicago Press.

Goldstein, Judith. 1989. "The Impact of Ideas on Trade Policy: The Origins of US Agricultural and Manufacturing Policies." *International Organization* 32 (1): 31–71.

Goldstein, Judith, and Robert Keohane. 1993. "Ideas and Foreign Policy: An Analytical Framework." In *Ideas and Foreign Policy,* ed. Judith Goldstein and Robert Keohane, 3–30. Ithaca: Cornell University Press.

Gray, Colin. 1986. *Nuclear Strategy and National Style.* Lanham, MD: Hamilton Press.

——. 1999. "Strategic Culture as Context: The First Generation of Theory Strikes Back." *Review of International Studies* 25 (1): 49–69.

Grieco, Joseph. 1990. *Cooperation among Nations: Europe, America, and Non-Tariff Barriers to Trade.* Ithaca: Cornell University Press.

Gromyko, Andrei. 1989. *Memoirs.* New York: Doubleday.

Gruber, Lloyd. 2000. *Ruling the World: Power Politics and the Rise of Supranational Institutions.* Princeton: Princeton University Press.

Guzman, Andrew. 2008. *How International Law Works: A Rational Choice Approach.* Oxford: Oxford University Press.

Haas, Ernst. 1958. *The Uniting of Europe.* Stanford University Press.

——. 1980. "Why Collaborate? Issue-Linkage and International Regimes." *World Politics* 32 (3): 357–405.

Habermas, Jurgen. 1984. *The Theory of Communicative Action.* Vol. 1, *Reason and the Rationalization of Society,* trans. Thomas McCarthy. Boston: Beacon.

Haig, Alexander, with Charles McCarry. 1992. *Inner Circles: How American Changed the World: A Memoir.* New York: Warner.

Halberstam, David. 2007. *The Coldest Winter: American and the Korean War.* New York: Hyperion.

Haldeman, H. R. 1994. *The Haldeman Diaries: Inside the Nixon White House.* New York: G. P. Putnam and Sons.

Halperin, Morton. 1972. "The Decision to Deploy the ABM: Bureaucratic and Domestic Politics in the Johnson Administration." *World Politics* 25 (1): 62–95.

Hanhimäki, Jussi. 2004. *The Flawed Architect: Henry Kissinger and American Foreign Policy.* New York: Oxford University Press.

Hardin, Garrett. 1968. "The Tragedy of the Commons." *Science* 162 (3859): 1243–48.

Hartmann, Hauke. 2001. "US Human Rights Policy under Carter and Reagan, 1977–1981." *Human Rights Quarterly* 23 (2): 402–30.

Hasenclever, Andreas, Peter Mayer, and Volker Rittberger. 1997. *Theories of International Regimes.* Cambridge: Cambridge University Press.

Haslam, Jonathan. 2011. *Russia's Cold War: From the October Revolution to the Fall of the Wall.* New Haven: Yale University Press.

Hayek, F. A. 1944. *The Road to Serfdom.* Chicago: University of Chicago Press.

———. 1960. *The Constitution of Liberty.* New York: Routledge.

Herrmann, Richard. 1985. *Perceptions and Behavior in Soviet Foreign* Policy. Pittsburgh, PA: University of Pittsburgh Press.

Herring, George. 2008. *From Colony to Superpower.* Oxford: Oxford University Press.

Hersh, Seymour. 1983. *The Price of Power: Kissinger in the Nixon White House.* New York: Summit Books.

Hofmann, Arne. 2007. *The Emergence of Détente in Europe: Brandt, Kennedy, and the Formation of Ostpolitik.* New York: Routledge.

Holloway, David. 1983. *The Soviet Union and the Arms Race.* New Haven: Yale University Press.

Holmes, Kim. 2003. "The United Nations and American Multilateral Diplomacy." *US Foreign Policy Agenda* 8 (1): 8–11.

Holzman, Franklyn. 1980. "Are the Soviets Really Outspending the US on Defense?" *International Security* 4 (4): 86–104.

———. 1982. "Soviet Military Spending: Assessing the Numbers Game." *International Security* 6 (4): 78–101.

———. 1989. "Politics and Guesswork: CIA and DIA Estimates of Soviet Military Spending." *International Security* 14 (2): 101–31.

Hooghe, Liesbet. 2005. "Several Roads Lead to International Norms, but Few via International Socialization: A Case Study of the European Commission." *International Organization* 59 (4): 861–98.

Hopf, Ted. 1998. "The Promise of Constructivism in IR Theory." *International Security* 23 (1): 171–200.

———. 2002. *Social Construction of International Politics: Identities and Foreign Policies, Moscow, 1955 and 1999.* Ithaca: Cornell University Press.

———. 2010. "The Logic of Habit in International Relations." *European Journal of International Relations* 16 (4): 539–61.

Hume, David. 1978 [1739–40]. *A Treatise of Human Nature*, ed. L. A. Selby-Bigge. Oxford: Clarendon Press.

Husband, William. 1979. "Soviet Perception of US 'Positions-of-Strength' Diplomacy in the 1970s." *World Politics* 31 (4): 495–517.

Ikenberry, G. John. 2001. *After Victory: Institutions, Strategic Restraint, and the Rebuilding of Order after Major Wars.* Princeton: Princeton University Press.

Isaacson, Walter. 2005. *Kissinger: A Biography.* New York: Simon and Schuster.

Israelyan, Victor. 1995. *Inside the Kremlin during the Yom Kippur War.* University Park: Pennsylvania State University Press.

Jackson, Donna. 2007. "The Carter Administration and Somalia." *Diplomatic History* 31 (4): 703–21.

Jackson, Patrick T. 2003. "Defending the West: Occidentalism and the Formation of NATO." *Journal of Political Philosophy* 11 (3): 223–52.

Jackson, Todd, Hong Chen, Cheng Guo, and Xiao Gao. 2006. "Stories We Love By: Conceptions of Love among Couples from the People's Republic of China and the United States." *Journal of Cross-Cultural Psychology* 37 (4): 446–64.

Jervis, Robert. 1968. "Hypotheses on Misperception." *World Politics* 20 (3): 454–79.

——. 1970. *The Logic of Images in International Relations*. New York: Columbia University Press.

——. 1976. *Perception and Misperception in International Politics*. Princeton: Princeton University Press.

——. 1978. "Cooperation under the Security Dilemma." *World Politics* 30 (2): 317–49.

——. 1988. "War and Misperception." *Journal of Interdisciplinary History* 18 (4): 675–700.

——. 2006. "Understanding Beliefs." *Political Psychology* 27 (5): 641–63.

Johnson, Robert David. 2003. "The Unintended Consequences of Congressional Reform: The Clark and Tunney Amendments and US Policy toward Angola." *Diplomatic History* 27 (2): 215–43.

——. 2006. *Congress and the Cold War*. Cambridge: Cambridge University Press.

Johnston, Alastair Iain. 1995. *Cultural Realism: Strategic Culture and Grand Strategy in Chinese History*. Princeton: Princeton University Press.

——. 1999. "Strategic Cultures Revisited: Reply to Colin Gray." *Review of International Studies* 25 (3): 519–23.

Kahler, Miles. 1998. "Rationality in International Relations." *International Organization* 52 (4): 919–41.

Kalai, Ehud, and Ehud Lehrer. 1993. "Subjective Equilibrium in Repeated Games." *Econometrica* 61 (5): 1231–40.

Kaiser, Robert. 1980. "US-Soviet Relations: Goodbye to Détente." *Foreign Affairs* 59 (3): 500–521.

Kaplan, Lawrence S. 2007. *NATO 1948: The Birth of the Transatlantic Alliance*. Lanham, MD: Rowman and Littlefield.

——. 2004. *NATO Divided, NATO United: The Evolution of an Alliance*. Westport, CN: Praeger.

Katzenstein, Peter. 1996. "Introduction: Alternative Perspectives on National Security." In *The Culture of National Security: Norms and Identity in World Politics,* ed. Peter J. Katzenstein, 1–32. New York: Columbia University Press.

Kaufman, Robert. 2000. *Henry M. Jackson: A Life in Politics*. Seattle: University of Washington Press.

Kennan, George. 1960. "Peaceful Coexistence: A Western View." *Foreign Affairs* 38 (2): 171–90.

——. 1967. *Memoirs: 1925–1950*. Boston: Little, Brown and Company.

——. 1972. "After the Cold War: American Foreign Policy in the 1970s." *Foreign Affairs* 51 (1): 210–27.

Keohane, Robert. 1984. *After Hegemony*. Princeton: Princeton University Press.

——. 1986. "Reciprocity in International Relations." *International Organization* 40 (1): 1–28.

——. 2000. "Ideas Part-Way Down." *Review of International Studies* 26 (1): 125–30.

Kerley, Ernest. 1962. "Some Aspects of the Vienna Conference on Diplomatic Intercourse and Immunities." *American Journal of International Law* 56 (1): 88–129.

Kernel, Samuel. 1993. *Going Public: New Strategies of Presidential Leadership.* 2nd ed. Washington: CQ Press.

Khong, Yuen Foong. 1992. *Analogies at War.* Princeton: Princeton University Press.

Khrushchev, Nikita. 1959. "On Peaceful Coexistence." *Foreign Affairs* 38 (1): 1–18.

Kier, Elizabeth. 1999. *Imagining War: French and British Military Doctrine between the Wars.* Princeton: Princeton University Press.

Kim, Woosang, and Bruce Bueno de Mesquita. 1995. "How Perceptions Influence the Risk of War." *International Studies Quarterly* 39 (1): 51–65.

Kinder, Donald, and D. Roderick Kiewiet. 1979. "Economic Discontent and Political Behavior: The Role of Personal Grievances and Collective Economic Judgments in Congressional Voting." *American Journal of Political Science* 23 (3): 495–527.

King, Gary, Robert Keohane, and Sidney Verba. 1994. *Designing Social Inquiry: Scientific Inference in Qualitative Research.* Princeton: Princeton University Press.

Kirshner, Jonathan. 2000. "Rationalist Explanations for War?" *Security Studies* 10 (1): 143–50.

Kissinger, Henry. 1954. *A World Restored.* New York: Grosset and Dunlap.

——. 1957. *Nuclear Weapons and Foreign Policy.* New York: Council on Foreign Relations (Harper and Brothers).

——. 1974. *American Foreign Policy.* Expanded ed. New York: W. W. Norton.

——. 1979. *White House Years.* Boston: Little Brown and Company.

——. 1982. *Years of Upheaval.* London: Phoenix Press.

——. 1994. *Diplomacy.* New York: Simon and Schuster.

——. 2003. *Crisis: The Anatomy of Two Major Foreign Policy Crises.* New York: Simon and Schuster.

Klotz, Audie, and Celia Lynch. 2007. *Strategies for Research in Constructivist International Relations.* Armonk, NY: M. E. Sharp.

Kochavi, Noam. 2005. "Insights Abandoned, Flexibility Lost: Kissinger, Soviet Jewish Emigrations, and the Demise of Détente." *Diplomatic History* 29 (3): 503–30.

Kohler, Foy, Mose Harvet, Leon Goure, and Richard Soll. 1973. *Soviet Strategy for the Seventies: From Cold War to Peaceful Coexistence.* Miami, FL: Center for Advanced International Studies.

Korb, Lawrence. 1974. "The Joint Chiefs of Staff: Access and Impact in Foreign Policy." *Policy Studies Journal* 3 (2): 170–73.

——. 1976. *The Joint Chiefs of Staff: The First Twenty-Five Years.* Bloomington: University of Indiana Press.

Koremenos, Barbara, Charles Lipson, and Duncan Snidal. 2001. "The Rational Design of International Institutions." *International Organization* 55 (4): 761–99.

Krasner, Stephen. 1991. "Global Communications and National Power: Life on the Pareto Frontier." *World Politics* 43 (3): 336–66.

Kratochwil, Friedrich. 1978. *International Order and Foreign Policy.* Boulder, CO: Westview.

——. 1989. *Rules, Norms and Decisions: On the Conditions of Practical and Legal Reasoning in International Relations and Domestic Society.* Cambridge: Cambridge University Press.

Kratochwil, Friedrich, and John Gerard Ruggie. 1986. "International Organization: A State of the Art or an Art of the State." *International Organization* 40 (4): 753–75.

Krueger, Joachim. 1998. "On the Perception of Social Consensus." In vol. 30 of *Advances in Experimental Social Psychology*, ed. Mark P. Zanna, 163–240. San Diego: Academic Press.

Krueger, Joachim, and Russell Clement. 1997. "Estimates of Social Consensus by Majorities and Minorities: The Case for Social Projection." *Personality and Social Psychology Review* 1 (4): 299–313.

Kugler, Jacek, and Douglas Lemke, eds. 1996. *Parity and War: Evaluations and Extensions of the War Ledger.* Ann Arbor: University of Michigan Press.

Kydd, Andrew. 2005. *Trust and Mistrust in International Relations.* Princeton: Princeton University Press.

Laclau, Ernesto. 2005. *On Populist Reason.* Verso: New York.

Larson, Deborah Welch. 1997. *Anatomy of Mistrust: US Soviet Relations during the Cold War.* Ithaca: Cornell University Press.

Lebow, Richard Ned. 2000. "What's So Different about a Counterfactual?" *World Politics* 52 (4): 550–85.

——. 2010. *Forbidden Fruit: Counterfactuals and International Relations.* Princeton: Princeton University Press.

Lebow, Richard Ned, and Janice Gross Stein. 1994. *We All Lost the Cold War.* Princeton: Princeton University Press.

Lee, William, and Richard Staar. 1986. *Soviet Military Policy since World War II.* Stanford: Hoover Institution Press.

Leffler, Melvyn. 2007. *For the Soul of Mankind: The United States, the Soviet Union, and the Cold War.* New York: Hill and Wang.

Lerner, Mitchell. 2008. " 'Trying to Find the Guy Who Invited Them': Lyndon Johnson, Bridge Building, and the End of the Prague Spring." *Diplomatic History* 32 (1): 77–103.

Levy, Jack. 1983. "Misperception and the Causes of War: Theoretical Linkages and Analytical Problems." *World Politics* 36 (1): 76–99.

——. 2003. "Political Psychology and Foreign Policy." In *Oxford Handbook of Political Psychology*, ed. David O. Sears, Leonie Huddy, and Robert Jervis, 253–84. New York: Oxford University Press.

——. 2008. "Counterfactuals and Case Studies." In *Oxford Handbook of Political Methodology*, ed. Janet Box-Steffensmeier, Henry Brady, and David Collier, 627–44. New York: Oxford University Press.

Lewis, Charles. 1985. *State and Diplomatic Immunity.* London: Lloyd's of London Press.

Lewis, David. 1969. *Convention: A Philosophical Study.* Cambridge: Harvard University Press.

Liang, Yuen-Li. 1953. "Diplomatic Intercourse and Immunities as a Subject for Codification." *American Journal of International Law* 47 (3): 439–49.

Light, Margot. 1991. "Soviet Policy in the Third World." *International Affairs* 67 (2): 263–80.

Limberg, Wayne. 1990. "Soviet Military Support for Third-World Marxist Regimes." In *The USSR and Marxist Revolutions in the Third World,* ed. Mark Katz, 51–118. Cambridge: Woodrow Wilson International Center for Scholars and Cambridge University Press.

Lippmann, Walter. 1997. *Public Opinion*. New York: Free Press.

Lipson, Charles. 1984. "International Cooperation in Security and Economic Affairs." *World Politics* 37 (1): 1–23.

Litwak, Robert. 1984. *Détente and the Nixon Doctrine: American Foreign Policy and the Pursuit of Stability, 1969–1976*. Cambridge: Cambridge University Press.

Loth, William. 2002. *Overcoming the Cold War: A History of Détente, 1950–1991*, trans. Robert Hogg. New York: Palgrave.

Lynn-Jones, Sean. 1986. "Detente and Deterrence: Anglo-German Relations, 1911–1914." *International Security* 11 (2): 121–50.

MacFarlane, S. Neil. 1985. "The Soviet Conception of Regional Security." *World Politics* 37 (3): 295–316.

———. 1990. "Success and Failures in Soviet Policy toward Marxist Revolutions in the Third World, 1917–1985." In *The USSR and Marxist Revolutions in the Third World*, ed. Mark Katz, 6–50. Cambridge: Woodrow Wilson International Center for Scholars and Cambridge University Press.

MacMillan, Margaret. 2007. *Nixon and Mao: The Week that Changed the World*. New York: Random House.

Mahoney, James. 2008. "Toward a Unified Theory of Causality." *Comparative Political Studies* 41 (4–5): 412.

———. 2010. "After KKV: The New Methodology of Qualitative Research," *World Politics* 62 (1): 120–47.

Mansfield, Edward. 1994. *Power, Trade, and War*. Princeton: Princeton University Press.

Mansfield, Edward, and Brian Pollins, eds. 2003. *Economic Interdependence and International Conflict: New Perspectives on an Enduring Debate*. Ann Arbor: University of Michigan Press.

Markova, Ivana. 2003. "Constitution of the Self: Intersubjectivity and Dialogicality." *Culture and Psychology* 9 (3): 249–59.

Markus, Gregory. 1982. "Political Attitudes during an Election Year: A Report on the 1980 NES Study." *American Political Science Review* 76 (3): 538–60.

Mastny, Vojtech. 2008. "The 1963 Nuclear Test Ban Treaty: A Missed Opportunity for Détente?" *Journal of Cold War Studies* 10 (1): 3–25.

Matthews, John. 1996. "Current Gains and Future Outcomes: When Cumulative Relative Gains Matter." *International Security* 21 (1): 112–46.

Mayer, William. 1992. *The Changing American Mind: How and Why American Public Opinion Changed between 1960 and 1988*. Ann Arbor: University of Michigan Press.

McLeod, Duncan. 2008. *India and Pakistan: Friends, Rivals, or Enemies?* Burlington, VT: Ashgate.

McNamara, Robert. 1968. *The Essence of Security: Reflections in Office*. New York: Harper and Row.

McSweeney, Bill. 1999. *Security, Identity, and Interests: A Sociology of International Relations*. Cambridge: Cambridge University Press.

Mead, George Herbert. 1936. *Mind, Self and Society*. Chicago: University of Chicago Press.

Mearsheimer, John. 1994/5. "The False Promise of International Institutions." *International Security* 19 (3): 5–49.

———. 2001. *The Tragedy of Great Power Politics*. New York: W. W. Norton.

Milloy, John. 2006. *The North Atlantic Treaty Organization, 1948–1957: Community or Alliance?* Montreal: McGill-Queen's University Press.

Mitzen, Jennifer. 2006. "Ontological Security in World Politics." *European Journal of International Relations* 12 (3): 341–70.

———. 2011. "Governing Together: Global Governance as Collective Intention" In *Arguing Global Governance: Agency, Lifeworld, and Shared Reasoning,* ed. Cornelio Bjola and Markus Kornprobst, 52–66. New York: Routledge.

Morozov, Boris. 1999. *Documents on Jewish Soviet Emigration*. London: Frank Cass.

Morrow, James. 1994. *Game Theory for Political Scientists*. Princeton: Princeton University Press.

———. 2002. "The Laws of War, Common Conjectures, and Legal Systems in International Politics." *Journal of Legal Studies* 31 (1): 41–60.

Moulton, Harland. 1973. *From Superiority to Parity: The United States and the Strategic Arms Race, 1961–1971*. Westport, CT: Greenwood.

Murray, Sandra, John Holmes, and Dale Griffin. 1996. "The Self-Fulfilling Nature of Positive Illusions in Romantic Relationships: Love Is Not Blind, but Prescient." *Journal of Personality and Social Psychology* 71 (6): 1155–80.

Newhouse, John. 1989. *Cold Dawn: The Story of SALT.* Washington, DC: Pergamon-Brassey.

Nichols, T. M. 2002. "Carter and the Soviets: The Origins of the US Return to a Strategy of Confrontation." *Diplomacy and Statecraft* 13 (2): 21–42.

Nitze, Paul. 1974/5. "The Strategic Balance between Hope and Skepticism." *Foreign Policy* (17): 136–56.

———. 1976. "Assuring Strategic Stability in an Era of Détente." *Foreign Affairs* 54 (2): 207–32.

———. 1978. "The Global Military Balance." *Proceedings if the Academy of Political Science* 33 (1): 4–14.

———. 1979. "The Merits and Demerits of a SALT II Agreement." In *The Fateful Ends and Shades of SALT: Past . . . Present . . . and Yet to Come?*, ed. Paul Nitze, James Dougherty, and Francis Kane, 37–89. New York: Crane, Russak, and Company.

Nixon, Richard. 1967. "Asia after Vietnam." *Foreign Affairs* 46 (1): 113–25.

———. 1990. *RN: The Memoirs of Richard Nixon*. New York: Simon and Schuster.

Njølstad, Olav. 1995. *Peacekeeper and Troublemaker: The Containment Policy of Jimmy Carter, 1977–1978*. Oslo: Norwegian Institute for Defense Studies.

North, Douglass. 1981. *Structure and Change in Economic History*. New York: W. W. Norton.

Nye, Joseph. 1987. "Nuclear Learning and the US-Soviet Security Regimes." *International Organization* 41 (3): 371–402.

Obeyesekere, Gananath. 1992. *The Apotheosis of Captain Cook*. Princeton: Princeton University Press.

O'Keefe, Patrick. 1976. "Privileges and Immunities of the Diplomatic Family." *International and Comparative Law Quarterly* 23 (2): 329–50.

Oneal, John, Bruce Russett, and Michael Berbaum. 2003. "Causes of Peace: Democracy, Interdependence, and International Organizations, 1885–1992." *International Studies Quarterly* 43 (3): 271–393.

Onuf, Nicholas. 1989. *World of Our Making: Rules and Rule in Social Theory and International Relations.* Columbia: University of South Carolina Press.

Organski, A. F. K., and Jacek Kugler. 1980. *The War Ledger.* Chicago: University of Chicago Press.

Osborne, Martin, and Ariel Rubinstein. 1994. *A Course in Game Theory.* Cambridge: MIT Press.

Osgood, Charles. 1962. *An Alternative to War or Surrender.* Urbana: University of Illinois Press.

Ouimet, Matthew. 2003. *The Rise and Fall of the Brezhnev Doctrine in Soviet Foreign Policy.* Chapel Hill: University of North Carolina Press.

Ovinnikov, R. 1980. "How the USA Orchestrated the Attack on Detente." *International Affairs* 26 (6): 92–100.

Oye, Kenneth. 1985. "Explaining Cooperation under Anarchy: Hypotheses and Strategies." *World Politics* 38 (1): 1–24.

Parker, Robert, ed. 2001. *The October War: A Retrospective.* Gainesville: University Press of Florida.

Parsons, Talcott. 1937. *The Structure of Social Action: A Study in Social Theory with Special Reference to a Group of Recent European Writers.* Vol. 1, *Marshall, Pareto, Durkheim.* Free Press: New York.

Patchen, Martin, and David Bogumil. 1997. "Comparative Reciprocity during the Cold War." *Peace and Conflict: Journal of Peace Psychology* 3 (1): 37–58.

Pipes, Richard. 1976. "Détente: Moscow's View." In *Soviet Strategy in Europe*, ed. Richard Pipes, 3–44. New York: Crane, Russak and Company.

——. 1981. *US-Soviet Relations in the Era of Detente: A Tragedy of Errors.* Boulder, CO: Westview.

Plokhy, S. M. 2010. *Yalta: The Price of Peace.* New York: Viking.

Podvig, Pavel, ed. 2004. *Russian Strategic Nuclear Forces.* Cambridge: MIT Press.

——. 2008. "The Window of Vulnerability That Wasn't: Soviet Military Buildup in the 1970s—a Research Note." *International Security* 33 (1): 118–38.

Powell, Robert. 1991. "Absolute and Relative Gains in International Relations Theory." *American Political Science Review* 85 (4): 1303–20.

Price, Richard. 1995. "A Genealogy of the Chemical Weapons Taboo." *International Organization* 49 (1): 73–103.

Quandt, William. 1977a. "Soviet Policy in the October Middle East War, Part 1." *International Affairs* 53 (3): 377–89.

——. 1977b. "Soviet Policy in the October Middle East War, Part 2." *International Affairs* 53 (4): 587–603.

Rathbun, Brian. 2007. "Uncertain about Uncertainty: Clarifying a Crucial Concept for International Relations Theory." *International Studies Quarterly* 51 (3): 271–99.

Rawls, John. 1993. *Political Liberalism.* New York: Columbia University Press.

Rice, Condoleezza. 1988. "SALT and the Search for a Security Regime." In *US-Soviet Security Cooperation*, ed. Alexander George, Philip Farley and Alexander Dallin, 293–306. New York: Oxford University Press.

Ringmar, Erik. 2002. "The Recognition Game: Soviet Russia against the West." *Cooperation and Conflict* 37 (2): 115–36.

Risse, Thomas, and Kathryn Sikkink. 1999. "The Socialization of International Human Rights Norms into Domestic Practices." In *The Power of Human Rights,* ed. Thomas Risse, Stephen Ropp, and Kathryn Sikkink, 1–38. Cambridge: Cambridge University Press.

Risse, Thomas, Stephen Ropp, and Kathryn Sikkink, eds. 1999. *The Power of Human Rights: International Norms and Domestic Change.* Cambridge: Cambridge University Press.

Risse-Kappen, Thomas. 1996. "Collective Identity in a Democratic Community: The Case of NATO." In *The Culture of National Security: Norms and Identities in World Politics,* ed. Peter Katzenstein, 357–99. New York: Columbia University Press.

Russett, Bruce. 1974. "The Revolt of the Masses: Public Opinion on Military Expenditures." In *New Civil-Military Relations: The Agonies of Adjustment to Post-Vietnam Realities,* ed. John Lovell and Philip Kronenberg, New Brunswick, NJ: Transaction.

——. 1975. "The Americans' Retreat from World Power." *Political Science Quarterly* 90 (1): 1–21.

Russett, Bruce, and Donald R. Deluca. 1981. " 'Don't Tread on Me': Public Opinion and Foreign Policy in the Eighties." *Political Science Quarterly* 96 (3): 381–99.

Russett, Bruce, and John Oneal. 2001. *Triangulating Peace: Democracy, Interdependence, and International Organizations.* New York: W. W. Norton.

Sadat, Anwar. 1978. *In Search of Identity: An Autobiography.* New York: Harper and Row.

Sagan, Scott, and Jeremi Suri. 2003. "The Madman Nuclear Alert: Secrecy, Signaling, and Safety in October 1969." *International Security* 27 (4): 150–83.

Sahlins, Marshall. 1995. *How "Natives" Think: About Captain Cook, for Example.* Chicago: University of Chicago Press.

Saivetz, Carol. 1997. "Superpower Competition in the Middle East and the Collapse of Détente." In *The Fall of Détente: Soviet American Relations during the Carter Years,* ed. Odd Arne Westad, 72–94. Oslo: Scandinavian University Press.

Sala, Brian, John Scott, and James Spriggs II. 2007. "The Cold War on Ice: Constructivism and the Politics of Olympic Figure Skating Judging." *Perspectives on Politics* 5 (1): 17–29.

Sandbrook, Dominic. 2008. "Salesmanship and Substance: The Influence of Domestic Policy and Watergate." In *Nixon in the World: American Foreign Relations, 1969–1977,* ed. Fredrik Logevall and Andrew Preston, 86–106. Oxford: Oxford University Press.

Sarotte, Mary. 2001. *Dealing with the Devil: East Germany, Détente, and Ostpolitik, 1969–1973.* Chapel Hill: University of North Carolina Press.

Savel'yev, Aleksandr, and Nikolay N. Detinov. 1995. *The Big Five: Arms Control Decision-Making in the Soviet Union.* Westport, CT: Greenwood.

Schelling, Thomas. 1960. *The Strategy of Conflict.* Cambridge: Harvard University Press.

——. 1966. *Arms and Influence.* New Haven: Yale University Press

Schelling, Thomas, and Morton Halperin. 1961. *Strategy and Arms Control.* Twentieth Century Fund.

Schilling, Warner. 1981. "US Strategic Nuclear Concepts in the 1970s: The Search for Sufficiently Equivalent Countervailing Parity." *International Security* 6 (2): 48–79.

Schulzinger, Robert. 1987. "The Senate, Detente, and SALT I." In *Congress and United States Foreign Policy: Controlling the Use of Force in the Nuclear Age*, ed. Michael Barnhart, 90–97. New York: State University of New York Press.

Schulman, Marshall. 1971. "What Does Security Mean Today? *Foreign Affairs* 49 (4): 607–18.

Schwartz, Thomas Alan. 2009. "'Henry, . . . Winning an Election Is Terribly Important': Partisan Politics in the History of US Foreign Relations." *Diplomatic History* (33) 2: 173–90.

Schweller, Randall, and David Priess. 1997. A Tale of Two Realisms: Expanding the Institutions Debate." *International Studies Review* 41 (1): 1–32.

Schweller, Randall, and William Wohlforth. 2000. "Power Test: Evaluating Realism in Response to the End of the Cold War." *Security Studies* 9 (3): 60–107.

Searle, John. 1995. *The Construction of Social Reality.* New York: Free Press.

Singer, J. David, Stuart Bremer, and John Stuckey. 1972. "Capability Distribution, Uncertainty, and Major Power War, 1820–1965." In *Peace, War, and Numbers*, ed., Bruce Russett, 19–48. Beverly Hills, CA: Sage.

Siniver, Asaf. 2008. *Nixon, Kissinger and US Foreign Policy Making: The Machinery of Crisis.* Cambridge: Cambridge University Press.

Skidmore, David. 1996. *Reversing Course: Carter's Foreign Policy, Domestic Politics, and the Failure of Reform.* Nashville: Vanderbilt University Press.

Smith, Gaddis. 1986. *Morality, Reason, and Power: American Diplomacy in the Carter Years.* New York: Hill and Wang.

Smith, Gerard. 1985. *Doubletalk: The Story of SALT I.* Lanham, MD: University Press of America.

Smith, Tom. 1983. "The Polls: American Attitudes toward the Soviet Union and Communism." *Public Opinion Quarterly* 47 (2): 277–92.

Smolinski, Remigiusz. 2008. "How Was the Fifth European Union Enlargement Actually Negotiated? A Comparative Analysis of Selected Traits." *International Negotiation* 13 (2): 247–83.

Snidal, Duncan. 1985. "Coordination versus Prisoners' Dilemma: Implications for International Cooperation and Regimes." *American Political Science Review* 79 (4): 923–42.

———. 1991. "Relative Gains and the Pattern of International Cooperation." *American Review of Political Science* 85 (3): 701–26.

Snyder, Jack. 1977. *The Soviet Strategic Culture: Implications for Limited Nuclear Operations.* Santa Monica, CA: RAND Corp.

Spector, Ronald. 1982. "Allied Intelligence and Indochina, 1943–1945." *Pacific Historical Review* 51 (1): 23–50.

Stein, Arthur. 1982. "When Misperception Matters." *World Politics* 34 (4): 505–26.

Stein, Janice Gross. 1985. "Calculation, Miscalculation, and Conventional Deterrence I: The View from Cairo." In *Psychology and Deterrence,* ed. Robert Jervis, Richard Ned Lebow, and Janice Gross Stein, 34–59. Baltimore: Johns Hopkins University Press.

———. 1988. "Building Politics into Psychology: The Misperception of Threat." *Political Psychology* 9 (2): 245–71.

Steinberg, Dmitri. 1990. "Trends in Soviet Military Expenditure." *Soviet Studies* 42 (4): 675–99.

Stern, Paula. 1979. *Water's Edge: Domestic Politics and the Making of American Foreign Policy.* Westport, CT: Greenwood.

Stewart, Philip, James Warhola, and Roger Blough. 1984. "Issue Salience and Foreign Policy Role Specialization in the Soviet Politburo of the 1970s." *American Journal of Political Science* 28 (1): 1–22.

Stolorow, Robert, and George Atwood. 1996. "The Intersubjective Perspective." *Psychoanalytic Review* 83 (2): 181–94.

Stone, Jeremy. 1970. "When and How to Use 'SALT.'" *Foreign Affair* 48 (2): 262–73.

Sunstein, Cass. 1994/5. "Incompletely Theorized Agreements." *Harvard Law Review* 108:1733–72.

———. 1996. *Legal Reasoning and Political Conflict.* New York: Oxford University Press.

———. 2000. "Constitutional Agreements without Constitutional Theories." *Ratio Juris* 13 (1): 117–30.

Talbott, Strobe. 1979. *Endgame: The Inside Story of SALT II.* New York: Harper Colophon Books.

———. 1988. *The Master of the Game: Paul Nitze and the Nuclear Peace.* New York: Vintage.

Talensky, N. 1964. "Anti-Missile Systems and Disarmament." *International Affairs* (Moscow) 10: 15–19.

Tannenwald, Nina. 2007. *The Nuclear Taboo: The United States and the Non-Use of Nuclear Weapons since 1945.* New York: Cambridge University Press.

Tetlock, Philip, and Aaron Belkin. 1996. "Counterfactual Thought Experiments in World Politics." In *Counterfactual Thought Experiments in World Politics: Logical, Methodological, and Psychological Perspectives,* ed. Philip Tetlock and Aaron Belkin, 3–38. Princeton: Princeton University Press.

Thakore, K. 1981. "Some Recent International Codification Conferences and Cultural Interactions." In *Cultural Factors in International Relations,* ed. R. P. Anand, 129–48. Honolulu: Abhinav Publications.

Thatcher, Ian. 2002. "Brezhnev as Leader." In *Brezhnev Reconsidered,* ed. Edwin Bacon and Mark Sandle, 22–37. New York: Palgrave Macmillan.

Thies, Cameron. 2008. "The Construction of a Latin American Interstate Culture of Rivalry." *International Interactions* 34 (3): 231–57.

Thompson, Alexander. 2009. *Channels of Power: The UN Security Council and US Statecraft in Iraq.* Ithaca: Cornell University Press.

Thompson, William. 2003. *The Soviet Union under Brezhnev.* London: Pearson Longman.

Thornton, Richard. 1991. *The Carter Years: Toward a New Global Order.* New York: Washington Institute Press.

Tollison, Robert, and Thomas Willett. 1979. "An Economic Theory of Mutually Advantageous Issue Linkages in International Negotiations." *International Organization* 33 (4): 425–29.

Tonelson, Alan. 1979. "Nitze's World." *Foreign Policy* (35): 74–90.

Tsebelis, George. 2002. *Veto Players: How Political Institutions Work.* Princeton: Princeton University Press.

Turner, Jonathan. 2002. *Face to Face: Toward a Sociological Theory of Interpersonal Behavior.* Stanford: Stanford University Press.

Van Atta, Dale. 2008. *With Honor: Melvin Laid in War, Peace, and Politics.* Madison: University of Wisconsin Press.

Vance, Cyrus. 1983. *Hard Choices: Critical Years in America's Foreign Policy.* New York: Simon and Schuster.

Van Evera, Stephen. 1999. *Causes of War: Power and the Roots of Conflict.* Ithaca: Cornell University Press.

Volten, Peter. 1982. *Brezhnev's Peace Program: A Study of Soviet Domestic Political Process and Power.* Boulder, CO: Westview.

Von Neumann, John, and Oskar Morgenstern. 1944. *Theory of Games and Economic Behavior.* New York: John Wiley and Sons.

Waever, Ole. 1998. "Insecurity, Security, and Asecurity in the West European Non-War Community." In *Security Communities,* ed. Emanuel Adler and Michael Barnett, 69–118. Cambridge: Cambridge University Press.

Waltz, Kenneth. 1979. *Theory of International Politics.* Boston: McGraw-Hill.

Warner, Geoffrey. 1972. "The United States and Vietnam 1945–96. Part 1, 1945–54." *International Affairs* 48 (3): 379–94.

Weber, Steve. 1991. *Cooperation and Discord in US-Soviet Arms Control.* Princeton: Princeton University Press.

Weingast, Barry. 1995. "A Rational Choice Perspective on the Role of Ideas: Shared Belief Systems and State Sovereignty in International Cooperation." *Politics and Society* 23 (4): 449–64.

——. 1996. "Off-the-Path Behavior: A Game-Theoretic Approach to Counterfactuals and Its Implications for Political and Historical Analysis." In *Counterfactual Thought Experiments in World Politics: Logical, Methodological, and Psychological Perspectives,* ed. Philip Tetlock and Aaron Belkin, 230–46. Princeton: Princeton University Press.

Wendt, Alexander. 1987. "The Agent-Structure Problem in International Relations Theory." *International Organization* 41 (3): 335–70.

——. 1995. "Constructing International Politics." *International Security* 20 (1): 71–81.

——. 1999. *Social Theory of International Politics.* Cambridge: Cambridge University Press.

——. 2003. "Why a World State Is Inevitable." *European Journal of International Relations* 9 (4): 491–542.

——. 2004. "The State as Person in IR Theory." *Review of International Studies* 30 (2): 289–316.

——. 2006. "Social Theory as Cartesian Science: An Auto-Critique from a Quantum Perspective." In *Constructivism and International Relations: Alexander Wendt and His Critics,* ed. Stefano Guzzini and Anna Leander, 181–219. New York: Routledge.

Wendt, Alexander, and Michael Barnett. 1993. "Dependent State Formation and Third World Militarization." *Review of International Studies* 19 (4): 321–47.

Westad, Odd Arne. 1996/7a. "Moscow and the Angolan Crisis, 1974–1976: A New Pattern of Intervention." *Cold War International History Project Bulletin* (8/9): 21–32.

———. 1996/7b. "Concerning the Situation in 'A': New Russian Evidence on the Soviet Intervention in Afghanistan." *Cold War International History Project Bulletin* (8/9): 128–32.

———. 1997. "The Fall of Détente and the Turning Tides of History." In *The Fall of Détente: Soviet American Relations during the Carter Years*, ed. Odd Arne Westad, 3–34. Oslo: Scandinavian University Press.

———. 2007. *The Global Cold War: Third World Intervention and the Making of Our Times.* Cambridge University Press.

Wheeler, Nicholas, and Timothy Dunne. 1996. "Hedley Bull's Pluralism of the Intellect and Solidarism of the Will." *International Affairs* 72 (1): 91–107.

Widmaier, Wesley. 2003. "Keynesianism as a Constructivist Theory of International Political Economy." *Millennium* 32 (1): 87–108.

———. 2004. "The Social Construction of the 'Impossible Trinity,' " *International Studies Quarterly* 48 (2): 433–53.

Winkel, Jorg, and Gabrielle Winkel. 1987. "US Conservatives on a Dangerous Course." *International Affairs* 33(11): 140–41.

Wohlforth, William. 1993. *The Elusive Balance: Power and Perceptions during the Cold War.* Ithaca: Cornell University Press.

———.1994/5. "Realism and the End of the Cold War." *International Security* 19 (3): 91–129.

Wohlstetter, Albert. 1974. "Is There a Strategic Arms Race?"*Foreign Policy* (15): 3–20.

———. 1975. "Optimal Ways to Confuse Ourselves." *Foreign Policy* (20): 170–98.

———. 1980. "Half Wars and Half Policies in the Persian Gulf." In *National Security in the 1980s: From Weakness to Strength*, ed. W. Schott Thompson, 123–71. New Brunswick, NJ: Transaction Books.

Woodward, Bob. 2002. *Bush at War.* New York: Simon and Schuster.

Zagare, Frank. 1987. *The Dynamics of Deterrence.* Chicago: University of Chicago Press.

Zahavi, Dan. 2001. "Beyond Empathy: Phenomenological Approaches to Intersubjectivity." *Journal of Consciousness Studies* 6 (5): 151–67.

Zubok, Vladislav. 2007. *A Failed Empire: The Soviet Union in the Cold War from Stalin to Gorbachev.* Chapel Hill: University of North Carolina Press.

INDEX

Page numbers followed by letters *f* and *t* refer to figures and tables, respectively.